The Peak Performing Professor

The Peak Performing Professor

A Practical Guide to Productivity
and Happiness

Susan Robison

JOSSEY-BASS™
A Wiley Brand

Published by Jossey-Bass
A Wiley Brand
One Montgomery Street, Suite 1200, San Francisco, CA 94104-4594—www.josseybass.com

Jossey-Bass books and products are available through most bookstores. To contact Jossey-Bass directly call our Customer Care Department within the U.S. at 800-956-7739, outside the U.S. at 317-572-3986, or fax 317-572-4002.

Wiley publishes in a variety of print and electronic formats and by print-on-demand. Some material included with standard print versions of this book may not be included in e-books or in print-on-demand. If this book refers to media such as a CD or DVD that is not included in the version you purchased, you may download this material at http://booksupport.wiley.com. For more information about Wiley products, visit www.wiley.com.

Library of Congress Cataloging-in-Publication Data

Robison, Susan, 1945–
    The peak performing professor : a practical guide to productivity and happiness / Susan Robison. — First edition.
        pages cm
    Includes bibliographical references and index.
    ISBN 978-1-118-10514-6 (pbk.)
    ISBN 978-1-118-41886-4 (ebk.)
    ISBN 978-1-118-41621-1 (ebk)
        1. College teaching.   2. College teachers.   I. Title.
    LB2331.R54   2013
    378.1′2—dc23
                                                                                                            2013022220

Printed in the United States of America
FIRST EDITION
PB Printing   10 9 8 7 6 5 4 3 2 1

Contents

About the Author

Susan Robison, Ph.D., is a psychologist, author, coach, counselor, and consultant. A former academic department chair and professor of psychology at the Notre Dame of Maryland University (NDMU), Susan is the author of two leadership books (*Discovering Our Gifts* and *Sharing Our Gifts* published by the National Council of Catholic Women) which formed the basis of a leadership development series for a national women's organization held at various sites throughout the U.S. and Europe for twelve years, training over 3,000 participants for leadership positions.

Susan was part of the consortium team that coauthored a faculty development book (*Thinking and Writing in College* published by the National Council of Teachers of English) with Barbara Walvoord and Lucille McCarthy which led to numerous articles on research and to invitations to conduct faculty development workshops in writing-across-the-curriculum pedagogy at colleges around the country.

Susan received a B.S. in psychology in the natural sciences from Loyola University (Chicago), and a M.S. and Ph. D. in general experimental psychology from Ohio University. At her first teaching job at a branch campus of Ohio University in Lancaster (OU-L), she was the only psychology professor on the faculty and in her second job at NDMU, she taught all of the undergraduate psychology curriculum except for abnormal and psychometrics. Susan has been particularly known for her curriculum innovation. While at OU-L, she designed what might have been the first psychology of women course in the country and at NDMU designed the first human sexuality course in an undergraduate institution in the Baltimore-Washington area. In her later teaching days, Susan taught graduate leadership courses in the graduate program in nonprofit leadership and development at NDMU and consulted to national nonprofit leadership teams. She has been honored to work with a number of National Science Foundation Advance programs at various universities, a privilege to give back to the agency from which she received funding both during graduate school through an NSF traineeship and as a young faculty member through a NSF Research Grant.

After achieving tenure and the rank of full-professor, Susan broadened her education in the scientific part of psychology by training in counseling through a one-year post-doc in cognitive-behavior therapy sponsored by the Maryland Psychological Educational Foundation followed by several years of individual counseling supervision. She and her husband opened a counseling private practice where Susan still works part-time today. She is a well-known community speaker to church, civic, and business groups in the Baltimore area on diverse topics such as marriage, parenting, and time and stress management. Her consulting work with women executives and business owners led to her receiving a prestigious business woman's award, the Mandy Goetze Award in 2004 and being selected in 2007 as one of the top 100 minority and women owned businesses in Maryland, Virginia, and the District of Columbia.

Currently, Susan divides her time between her local counseling practice and her faculty development consultation business, providing faculty development workshops and consultations on college campuses and at higher education conferences to professors who want to work productively and live happily.

Acknowledgments

Many people have contributed to the creation of this work. I am grateful for the:

Urging and encouragement to even think about doing a book: Barbara Walvoord.

Empowerment, encouragement, and empathy: David Brightman (Executive Editor, Higher and Adult Education, Jossey-Bass).

Professional, supportive production management: Cathy Mallon (Production Manager, Jossey-Bass).

Gentle, wise copy editing from Cathy Cambron (Jossey-Bass copy editing).

Insights, challenges, and feedback from faculty coaching clients and workshop attendees.

Feedback and good cheer from friendly readers: Dorothe Bach, William Day, Christine Gray, Tracey Manning, Barry McCarthy, Phil Robison, Kathryn Lord, and Barbara Walvoord.

Spiritual support: Dot Keczmerski, Tracey Manning, Ellen McDaniel, and Donna Townsend.

Expert, helpful pre-submission editorial assistance: Phil Robison, Christine Gray, and Tracey Manning.

Supportive, daily live-in therapy, dancing and other healthy distractions: Phil Robison.

Dedicated to my daughter, Christine Robison Gray, and her generation of professors that they might have productive careers and happy lives.

Introduction

PACE Yourself for Productivity and Happiness

Purpose and laughter are the twins that must not separate.
Each is empty without the other.

—Robert K. Greenleaf

TO OUTSIDE OBSERVERS, a career in the professoriate may look like a pretty cushy job. People think all you have to do is show up for class 15 hours a week, give some tests, do a little grading, maybe write some stuff. You get a long winter holiday to spend with your kids, and you have summers off. What could be stressful about a job like that?

What isn't obvious to outside observers is the set of performance demands imposed by the tripartite job of the professor. Like a triple-threat actor, who sings, dances, and acts, many professors also perform three very different professional activities—teaching, writing, and serving—each of which could itself be a full-time occupation. You have to do all three jobs—and well. No wonder you can feel distracted and pulled in many directions.

Peak Performing Professors

The professoriate has never been an easy career, and it is not getting any easier. Part of the challenge is historical: the vocation was designed for celibate male monks in the Middle Ages. If this history seems new to you, ask yourself what you wore to the last graduation ceremony you attended. Our cap-and-gown dress is reminiscent of the monk robes worn by those early professors, even though the professoriate gradually evolved into also being a calling for celibate men who were not monks, then for married men, and then for single women. Only recently have married women, dual-career professors, and two-professor couples aspired to combine the demands of the professoriate with the demands of family life. It is no wonder that attempting to have a personal life while at the same time working at a career designed as penance for celibate monks presents a near-impossible challenge (Pannapacker, 2012).

In addition to that legacy, changes in definitions of faculty work that are related to national economic trends are adding to current faculty stress (Gappa, Austin, & Trice, 2007) and are contributing to what Lee, Bach, and Muthiah (2012) call "the malaise of the academy" (p. 69). Increased workloads result from both changing student enrollments and fewer teachers teaching more courses. Major institutions are experiencing a downturn in enrollment at the same time as many urban and community colleges are experiencing an increased enrollment of adult students. The trends listed here illustrate the stressors affecting the professoriate today.

- *More online or blended courses:* Mastering the technology to manage these courses can entail a considerable learning curve for faculty while increasing demands for staff support time from overloaded technology support services.

- *MOOCs (Massive Open Online Courses):* These free online courses sold to universities as a substitute for courses taught by local faculty are scaring faculty, deans, provosts, and university boards alike worried about the quality of degrees and the future of brick-and-mortar higher education.

- *Budget cuts affecting pay, benefits, programming, equipment, and staffing:* Faculty experiencing e-mail and website breakdowns may find fewer technology wizards on campus to rush to their rescue.

- *Loss of perceived job security* through decline or elimination of tenured and full-time positions on many campuses.

- *Increased expectations* from accrediting agencies that the outcomes of higher education be quantified.

- *Increased pressures for faculty scholarship funding,* coupled with increased competition for limited grant money, which makes those pressures unrealistic.

- *Demanding students* and their helicopter parents.

These trends repeat the theme of doing more with less and underscore the toll that career demands take on faculty, their health, and their social networks (Astin, Astin, & Lindholm, 2011).

If you are challenged by the tripartite job description and the increased pressures listed here, you are not alone. Only 22% of professors report that they are simultaneously performing all three professorial roles well (Fairweather, 2002). That statistic means that at any one time, 78% of professors are struggling with one or more of their roles or with the demanding combination of all three. Add to those demands the fact that graduate education usually emphasizes the preparation of future scholars with little if any preparation for students' future teaching and service roles.

Professors who do not hold the tripartite job description but have mainly teaching or research positions experience proportionally increased job demands in the roles that they do occupy. For example, the job description of a community college professor often requires teaching six courses a semester with many service obligations such as advising large groups of students. Similarly, professors with primarily research positions are under constant pressure to submit successful grant proposals to support equipment, graduate students, and their own salaries.

Although changes in higher education have increased pressures on faculty, studies have long found that the biggest stressors for faculty may come from within themselves (Gmelch, Lovrich, & Wilke, 1984). A more recent study by the Chronicle of Higher Education in 2009 confirmed that conclusion. The three biggest stressors faculty reported—namely, self-imposed high expectations, lack of personal time, and difficulty managing household responsibilities—are self-inflicted (Chronicle of Higher Education, 2009). These stressors are caused either by professors' unrealistic perceptions or by their limited ability to set and carry out goals. To paraphrase the words of Walt Kelly's cartoon character Pogo, "We have met the enemy, and it is us." When faculty project their frustration onto their institutions, the downside is that the process causes independent faculty to relinquish control for their stress. A more hopeful mind-set for autonomous faculty is to approach stress reduction by increasing skills in self-regulation. Readers will not need to implement all of the practices found in this book to do so. Even small changes can make big differences.

When I do workshops on work-life balance and time management at higher education conferences and on college and university campuses, I hear three kinds of concerns.

Time management and work-life balance

- How do I balance all the responsibilities of teaching, writing, and serving?

- How do I streamline my class preparation and grading time and still promote significant student learning?

- How do I get unstuck on my research projects so that I can respond to editorial comments on articles to "rewrite and resubmit" and so that I can direct projects from concept to completion in a more timely fashion?

Work habits

- How do I set priorities and keep track of all of my tasks so that I don't forget deadlines and details for my tasks, whether they are urgent, short term, or long term and whether they are driven by my own agenda or other people's?

- How can I cut down on distractions and get to work?

- How do I stay focused on work or personal goals and prevent stress crossover, in which I worry about home at work and work at home?

- How do I stop myself from falling further and further behind?

- How can I manage my productivity so that I can feel good about my workdays?

Requests and demands

- Can I achieve what I want and what my institution wants of me and still have a life?

- How do I decide about requests for my time? How do I say "No" without upsetting people?

- How can I work well with colleagues toward mutually beneficial goals so as to not waste their or my time?

- What can I say to people who want to gossip, complain, and interrupt me with their social trivia?

With so much to do and so little time to do it, the professor's job seems at times to consist of an unending series of performances badly done, half-done, or left undone. Even when done well, those performances sometimes don't seem to be appreciated either for the effort involved or for the results obtained.

As I visit campuses around the United States, what professors tell me is that they want to live well while they do the good they do in their jobs, caring about students, knowledge, and their institutions. However, concerns about unfair workloads, mistreatment by "them" (students and administrators), poor pay, underprepared students, vague tenure requirements, and overloaded e-mail in-boxes can so preoccupy professors that they engage in less-than-healthy coping strategies, such as meeting in the lunchroom to engage in that favorite faculty diversion, the "ain't it awful" complaint session. These faculty sufferers seem to agree with Saint Alphonsa Muttathupandathu, a mystic of the early 20th century, who said, "A day without suffering is a day lost."

If you are searching for a more optimistic mind-set but wonder whether you are deluded in the hope that you might ever experience work-life balance, please be reassured that it is possible to combine a well-done job as a professor with a satisfying personal life. The purpose of this book is not to solve the institutional problems touched on here; that would be the goal of a different book, one that I hope colleagues with institutional experience and perspectives will write. The purpose of this book is to give readers the tools to increase their own productivity and satisfaction in areas over which they have control—namely, how they manage the challenges of their professional and personal lives.

One activity that won't help you work better or live more happily is participating in those gripe sessions with fellow faculty-lounge sufferers, even though sharing such complaints might give you a bit of short-term validation about how tough life is. The need for you as a professor to approach your job with intention and skill has grown more urgent. To ignore that need is to risk being swept away by the job's demands into an unhappy and dysfunctional state at a time when you are increasingly held accountable for your time and tasks.

What will help is taking action to better your life by working more intentionally, streamlining your work habits, improving your relationships, and taking good care of yourself. The key difficulty we as faculty face in using these strategies is the battle within ourselves. We approach our careers like children at a well-supplied buffet, so hungry that we heap too much on our plates and then are unable to eat it all. We worry about how to get it all done. We want to produce scholarly work, but class time looms on the clock and we must prepare. Just as we get moving on some writing, it is time to stop and visit Mom. The internal conflicts of all our goals present the biggest challenge to our ability to self-regulate. Because our careers are so rich in possibilities, we will always be challenged by having too many goals, a condition that can paralyze a person so much that few goals are accomplished (Baumeister & Tierney, 2011).

The antidote to rumination and paralysis is a system for selecting key, high-yield goals and focusing on them in the moment. The ability to select key goals is called willpower: deciding what is worthy of your time and attention. The ability to focus on these goals is way power: the know-how to get specific tasks done quickly and effectively. The early parts of this book (Parts 1 and 2) will lay out the practices of peak performing professors who exhibit good habits of willpower and way power. As you will see later in this book, both willpower and way power need support—the support of helpful others and the support of your own wellness and well-being practices to be successful (Parts 3 and 4). These practices can be summarized by the acronym *PACE*, which will help you remember key practices of all peak performers:

- **P**ower your work and life through purpose.
- **A**lign all of your activities with that purpose.
- **C**onnect with people who support your purpose.
- **E**nergize yourself to thrive in this interesting and engaging career.

The last part of the book will apply the practices outlined here to the specific professional and personal roles and responsibilities of the professoriate (Part 5).

Who Are the Peak Performers?

While stressed-out faculty loungers are depressing themselves over reheated mac and cheese, other faculty are working productively and enjoying life. These peak performing professors are not an elite group of Nobel Prize winners. They have the same degrees, disciplines, and teaching loads as their colleagues who are struggling to meet the job's endless deadlines. Peak performing professors, however, are characterized by two qualities: their long-term happiness about their work and lives and the quality of their performances in each of their professional roles. This combination results in teaching that leads to learning while using a minimum of focused preparation, scholarship that earns the respect of their colleagues and builds a body of work instead of merely a series of publications, and service that infuses their institutions with wisdom and leadership. In short, peak performance is about what professors do and how they feel.

These professors aim to do competent, even creative work, year after year, while at the same time creating satisfying lives. Their careers and lives demonstrate that those goals are not mutually exclusive. I am intrigued whenever I meet these professors at conferences and campuses, marveling at how these faculty manage all that they do while many of their colleagues struggle so painfully with the demands of the profession.

It may seem paradoxical and even unfair that the professors who work at having a life in addition to working on their careers often do better with both. These professors get awards for teaching and research, receive promotions on the first try, and are honored for their service to their institution and their professions. They are not professors with a solitary focus, for while they achieve at work they also seem to have time for other pursuits. They play oboe in the community orchestra. Their kids are eating quiche in the dining room instead of gobbling pizza in front of the TV. They and their spouses are reading the Great Books aloud to each other in front of the fireplace while many of their colleagues can't seem to find time to check in with their mates about car pool schedules.

These peak performing professors are not perfect people. They have their bad days and semesters just like all of us. However, peak performing professors spend the majority of their time and energy in interesting work and enjoyable personal time. Rest assured, you can join those productive, happy faculty by adopting similar practices of working intentionally from a sense of meaning and purpose. Like many of my readers, I too struggled as a young professor to do a good job at work while balancing the rest of my life. A few years into my second academic job, I hit a wall of frustration. I was shocked because on paper, I had everything I needed and wanted: a job at a nice college compatible with my values, a great husband, a house in the suburbs, and a wonderful baby. Why wasn't I happy? Was I ever going to feel less overwhelmed?

As a psychologist trained in research I looked for answers in the psychological literature. There weren't any. The psychological research literature presented nothing at that time that could help an overwhelmed assistant professor become happier and more productive. I did find some helpful information in business books on time management (Bliss, 1978; Lakein, 1973). Although I wasn't entirely satisfied with the results, those *first-generation* ("Generation I," or "Gen I") time management programs helped me piece together a way of working and living that would prove to be more satisfying and productive than what I had been doing. I learned to ask myself periodically during the day, "Is this activity the best use of my time right now?" (Lakein, 1973), and "Am I spending my time on important activities such as preparing for class or merely on urgent ones that are less important such as visits from textbook sales reps?" (Bliss, 1978).

Then a chance occurrence prompted me to experience a paradigm shift toward a new way of thinking about time management. One steamy Baltimore July afternoon, I decided to keep cool by cleaning out my basement. While going through some childhood mementos, I discovered a little notebook from the first retreat I attended back in seventh grade. It contained notes about my purpose in life that, although written in childish and overly flowery language, reminded me that even at that age I already knew that my life purpose involved education and service.

As I challenged myself to write a more current purpose statement, I realized that I didn't have to do everything right to be successful as a professor. What I needed to learn was what you will learn in this book: how to use a purpose statement to figure out the right things to do, how to do those things quickly with sufficient quality, how to connect to the right social support for my work and life, and how to energize myself with adequate self-care practices to continue to do these things for many years without burning out.

With a simple criterion for evaluating how to spend my time, anything I did that fit the purpose statement was a good use of my time, and anything that didn't probably was a waste of my time. Those insights helped me reorder my relationship with time. We became good friends and have remained so ever since. I shifted from the advice of the Gen I time management books and workshops to a different understanding of time management, what I am calling second-generation time mangement, "Gen II": the understanding that managing one's time is really about managing one's life by connecting all one's activities to a sense of purpose. I learned that the same units of time could produce frustration or rewards, depending on whether my activities were related to my purpose. Since that time in the mid-1970s, other consultant-writers have also created systems based on living from purpose (Covey, 2004; Warren, 2012).

In a sense, this present work found me. When my Gen II practices helped me earn rank and tenure and opened scholarly and service opportunities that added to the quality of my work life, other faculty observed that I seemed to "have it all together" and asked for my advice. The truth was that I didn't have it entirely together, and you don't have to have it all together either; but I did find that the practices that had helped me become more productive and happy were also useful for other professors.

I have continued to develop the peak performing professor model by listening to faculty concerns and questions and by incorporating research on peak performance from seemingly disparate fields into a model that is simple, easy to understand, and doable. Here is a sample of some of the lessons developed in the last ten years in this seemingly unconnected literature.

- *Business productivity research*: Peak performance work habits for time and project management predict employee engagement (Harter, Schmidt, & Keyes, 2002). Peak performers successfully set goals and sustain energy (Goldsmith, 2009; Gollwitzer & Oettingen, 2011; Halvorson, 2011; Hays & Brown, 2004; Loehr & Schwartz, 2004).

- *Happiness, well-being, wellness, and positive psychology research*: Peak performers live longer and better and work more easily (Csikszentmihalyi, 2008; Frederickson, 2009; Lyubomirsky, 2008; Seligman, 2002).

- *Sports psychology research*: Peak performers in seemingly different fields such as sports, music, the military, and the martial arts produce consistent achievement without burnout by focusing on deliberate practice and mastery (Brown, 2011; Ericsson, 2009; Garfield & Bennett, 1984; Leonard, 1992; Loehr, 1991, 1997; Loehr & Evert, 1995).

- *Neuroscience and social intelligence research*: Peak performers make the most of brain processes for fast, effective thinking and for effective connections with helpful colleagues (Amen, 2006; Arden, 2009; Davidson & Begley, 2012; Goleman, 2006; Medina, 2008).

- *Faculty development research*: There are predictable best practices for aspects of the tripartite faculty roles in teaching (Bain, 2004; Fink, 2013; Walvoord, 2008; Walvoord & Anderson, 2010), research and writing (Boice, 1990, 2000; Gray, 2010), and serving in the academy (Kouzes & Posner, 2003).

Running through these bodies of knowledge is a consistent thread about how people feel when they are at their best. Call it flow or optimal experience (Csikszentmihalyi, 2008), personal best (Kouzes & Posner, 2012), ideal performance state (Loehr, 1991), full engagement living (Loehr & Schwartz, 2004), expert and exceptional performance (Ericsson & Smith, 1991), or "the zone" (Lardon & Leadbetter, 2008; Young & Pain, 1999), there is a state that when experienced brings out the best in people. That state seems to be created when purpose and skills combine with challenge to produce the magic of the *peak performance zone*, that place where one's labor is rewarding, engaging, and productive.

I knew this switch from time management to life management was bearing fruit when a doctor at a workshop for medical school faculty came up to me during the break, grabbed my hand, and with tears in her eyes said, "This workshop is exactly what I needed. None of the half dozen time management workshops I have attended have spoken to my specific needs as a faculty member. What is different in your model is that it goes beyond time management to help me integrate my sense of meaning and purpose into my work and my life as a professor. I hope you will put these practices into a workbook for other faculty."

The result of that conversation is this volume, a faculty development book that goes beyond presenting a set of tips on time management to helping readers create a life management system to weave their professional and personal roles into a seamless garment of productivity and satisfaction. To be a peak performing professor, you don't have to be a star who wins awards; you just need to perform at a level closer to your own individual peak performance zone by clarifying your goals and implementing them. Applying the practices of this book will move you beyond the immediate concerns of what to do during the next workday to high-yield activities that lead to both long-term success and to a legacy of work well done and a life well lived.

Who Will Benefit from This Book

This book is for the professors whom I have met at my workshops, who want great work and a great life. Although some of them are feeling overwhelmed, disorganized, and unproductive, others are doing fairly well but want to produce more for their efforts. Some, including faculty development directors, directors of teaching and learning centers, and deans and vice provosts or presidents of faculty, have even discovered and applied many of their own best practices during their careers and are now interested in helping their students and colleagues live better lives. These academics recognize that faculty with low engagement cost their institutions both directly, through lower productivity and increased health care expense for stress-related disorders, and indirectly, through hiring costs entailed when faculty leave after failing to meet tenure requirements.

How to Get the Most from This Book

While this book has a scholarly basis, it is primarily a workbook with short didactic lessons on the practices of the peak performing professor. Instead of presenting a whole new technology for you to master, this book codifies and improves on activities that you already do, such as designing courses, preparing for classes, and making to-do lists. With better practices in place, you are likely to perceive that you have more time, both because you have more joy in your workdays and because you are working more effectively, leaving you with more discretionary time to use as you wish.

This journey to a better life is individualized and does require that you expend a bit of time and effort to develop and maintain important habits; however, let me reassure readers who are worried that the practices in this book will make them feel guilty about yet another list of "shoulds." I know that most readers are not starting from scratch. As a professor you already know some key lessons about learning that can reassure you that it is a process, not a state.

- Learning takes place when the brain changes (Zull, 2002). Those changes are not instantaneous but rather happen in stages (Ambrose, Bridges, Lovett, DiPietro, & Norman, 2010; Duhigg, 2012; Ericsson, 2009; Robison, 2010). When it comes to brain neurons, what fires together, wires together (Hanson & Mendius, 2009). True mastery of a complex skill may take as much as 10,000 hours of practice (Ericsson, 2009).

- Active learning leads to more change than mere reading does (Bonwell & Eison, 1991).

- A growth mind-set (a belief that with instruction, feedback, and practice, knowledge and new habits can be acquired) trumps a fixed mind-set (the presumption that people are born about as smart as they are ever going to be and are limited in how much they can change [Dweck, 2008]).

The steps for learning practices that can help you replicate your personal best consistently and that result in continual improvement include the following:

1. Use assessment tools to assess your best and worst performances.

2. Experiment with a new way of working.

3. Seek and apply feedback on your performance from students, colleagues, and coaches.

4. Improve your performance through practicing the lessons learned.

5. Repeat steps 1–4.

Since I don't know where you are in the process of learning good professorial work habits, I will lay out the life management system from the beginning. Most readers will benefit from reading and doing the assessment in Chapter 1 and the exercises contained in Parts 1 and 2, which are foundational to setting up your system. With that foundation in place, you can individualize your tool kit with the practices in Parts 3 through 5 that address your current, most pressing needs, such as improving collegial relationships, engaging in better self-care, and applying these practices to professorial roles and responsibilities at work and at home.

You may already have systems that work well for you and just need to tweak them to perform at your peak more of the time, or you may be struggling to figure out how to live the life of a professor. Either way, this book can help you *tesser* quickly to a new experience of productivity and happiness. In case you missed reading Madeleine L'Engle's best-selling children's science fiction novel, *A Wrinkle in Time*, to tesser is to travel through a portal in the time-space continuum, like a space warp or wormhole. Imagine that a car is traveling down a road when suddenly the road surface folds, as though a giant is folding a map, and the car continues seamlessly along the road, skipping all of the mileage in the middle of the trip. With tessering, someone can travel instantly from one place to another without traversing the real-time pathway of the trip. I hope that the techniques in this book will allow you to tesser to your peak performance zone, skipping some of the mileage and mistakes that I went through in my journey from being a stressed-out young professor. What you have in your hands is the book that I wish I had had back then.

Robison's Rule
PACE yourself for a productive career and a happy life.

The Peak Performing Professor

Chapter 1

Practices of Peak Performing Professors

If you want to change the world, whom do you begin with,
yourself or others? I believe if we begin with ourselves and do
the things that we need to do and become the best person we
can be, we have a much better chance of changing the world
for the better.

—Aleksandr Solzhehnitsyn

"BOY, DO I need you," said the slightly disheveled, out-of-breath woman as she flopped into one of the last remaining seats near the front of the hotel ballroom where my workshop on peak performing professors was about to begin. Her lopsided name tag identified her as Mary, and she looked as if both her alarm clock and her hairbrush had failed her this morning. She continued, talking more to the air than to me: "I'm a mess. I can't seem to figure out what to do, when to do it, and for whom to do it." As if the "for whom" didn't give her away as a professor of English, my guess was confirmed when she took the Peak Performance Assessment Tool (see the exercise later in this chapter) and distracted herself by correcting my word choice and punctuation.

Later that afternoon, during the coaching session that the conference organizers had arranged, I met with Mary, who expressed concerns similar to those of other faculty discussed in the Introduction to this book. After her download, she exclaimed, "Wow, I'm even more of a mess than I thought! I really need your help in managing my time better." I reassured her, as I am reassuring you, that things might not be as bad as they seem. Many faculty are just a few tweaks away from living their ideal lives. Because these professors are so close to their own situations, however, they just can't see what those key changes are—or they would have already made those tweaks. What many professors think they need to resolve their confusion is better time management. As it turns out, they are misguided in their quest.

Why You Don't Need Time Management

The effort to manage time so that you can get more done is misguided for three reasons. First, time can't be tamed. We can't actually manage, save, or borrow time. The ideas that we can "find time," "make time," "save time," and "lose time" are not helpful concepts because time exists only as a mental construct, one that varies independently of anything you do to control it. Humans confuse their devices, such as calendars and clocks invented to measure the movement of the moon, sun, stars, planets, and seasonal changes, with the grandiose notion that we actually manage those celestial occurrences.

Instead, every Sunday night at midnight the magic reset button is pushed, and you get a new supply of 168 hours for the new week. You don't control getting those 10,080 brand new minutes, but you can use them any way you wish. While you are thinking about this precious gift, one minute has passed and you have only 10,079 minutes left in the week. The key question is what to do with all that time that is given to you free of charge each week. Each decade Americans gain more "free time" but perceive they have less (Robinson & Godbey, 1997), because they fail to make conscious choices about how to best use that time. No wonder we panic and think time is running out (Pillemer, 2011).

Second, the goal of trying to manage time is likely to leave us feeling discouraged and inadequate. The reason is that while we are fooling ourselves that we can control time, we are not focusing on what we can control, namely, our actions—actions that can lead to high-impact work and great lives.

Third, Gen I time management techniques were developed to help office workers sitting at desks manage pieces of paper—not to help professors. Tips such as "handle each piece of paper only once" probably work well for office workers at desks. Such techniques, however, don't help you manage the many responsibilities of your tripartite job description, a job that takes place in the classroom, lab, clinic, and meeting room as well as at your desk and that requires you to handle ideas and relationships in addition to pieces of paper.

Faculty want more time to get all of that work done. While it is logical to look to time management to help with that quest, the key to your "getting more time" into each day, week, and year is to change your perceptions about time by bringing your choices about how you use time under more conscious control. What we need instead of time management is life management, a set of practices that help us manage the entirety of our lives and especially the precious resources of our energy, attention, and relationships.

What You Need Instead: Life Management

Life management requires you to answer some important questions. You want more time—but time for what? What do you want to accomplish in your work and in your life? How do you wish to live? Your answers form the foundation of a system that will connect all your activities and goals to a deep sense of purpose and that will lead to what most professors long for, a more authentic sense of vital work and a vital life (Lee, Bach, & Muthiah, 2012). As a natural result of being connected with your purpose, you will find it easier to connect your countless tasks with the time available to do them.

Every day you make hundreds of decisions about how to spend your time and what tasks to do:

- Should I start writing this article or finish the other one?

- How long should I prepare for class? How will I know when I'm done?

- Should I chair that committee I've been asked to chair?

- What do I want to do on my next sabbatical?

- When should I leave work?

- What work shall I do tonight after dinner?

Even though we autonomy-loving professors want to feel free and in control of our destiny, making hundreds of decisions a day about how to use our time can wear us down. Research on the effect of choices on satisfaction highlights an interesting paradox: too many choices, beyond eight options at a time, can paralyze us from making a decision (Iyengar, 2010; Schwartz, 2004). Furthermore, making many different decisions a day about what to do, when, and how can lead to what Roy Baumeister and his associates have called "ego depletion," the experience of fatigue and overwhelm caused by using the brain to make those micro decisions all day (Baumeister & Tierney, 2011).

Ego depletion is caused by a chemical phenomenon in the brain. Doing things by sheer willpower and effort can deplete the glucose supply to the brain, causing the fatigue of ego depletion, in which people can no longer push themselves to act disciplined even if they value such actions. Baumeister and Tierney (2011) suggest that this factor can lead to less ability to match our decisions to our true values and therefore to poorer performance on our jobs. You know this effect when you get paralyzed about what to do in the 15 minutes between the end of class and the start of your next meeting. You also know it when you have controlled your diet all day only to succumb to the temptation of a cookie binge after dinner.

The key to working your brain at its peak all day, every day, is to underwhelm it. I'm not advocating that you make laziness and sloth your new lifestyle. Instead, this book will help you PACE yourself to front-load your decisions about your activities, by making a few value-based decisions on the front end of a month, week, or day and then working from your plan instead of straining your brain with hundreds of micro choices a day. Baumeister and Tierney (2011) promise this benefit of doing so: "Ultimately, self-control lets you relax because it removes stress and enables you to conserve willpower for the important challenges" (p. 17).

First, get clear about why you are engaged in this career and what specific goals you want to work on (the *P* or *Power* of PACE). Second, divide the steps toward those goals across time and monitor your progress so that you stay on target toward completion of those goals (the *A* or *Align*) without having to make micro decisions about what to do next all day long. Third, enlist the help of mutually supportive others in your professional and personal lives (the *C* or *Connect*). Fourth, maximize the energy available to do all that you want to do without burnout (the *E* or *Energize*). By applying the magic of precommitment to your plans, you will remove the overthinking that leads to ego depletion, because you make a few key decisions at the front end that can unfold almost automatically at the back end (Baumeister & Tierney, 2011). For example, writers who write at the same time each day get more writing done than those who hope to get some writing done sometime during the day only to find out that they lack the "willpower" to do so (Boice, 1989).

The participants in my workshops call the paradigm shift from Gen I time management to Gen II life management "life changing" because it puts time management in proper perspective, as a set of tools to support a life based on a sense of meaning and purpose, rather than as a goal in itself (Seligman, 2002; Sinek, 2009). (For a detailed summary of the differences between the Gen I and Gen II approaches see the appendix to this book.) The benefits of this shift are well worth the effort to learn how to create great work and a great life.

Great Work, Great Life

If you are like most faculty, you entered the academy motivated by the concept of doing great work—work that is meaningful, impactful, challenging, and successful (Stanier, 2010). You also want to have a great life, one that you find satisfying and meaningful because it represents your most authentic self. In other words, you hope to be a peak performer who does good while feeling good. Exercise 1.1 invites you to define what having great work and a great life mean for you at this time in your career and life. Doing so will help you establish a baseline so that you can measure how close you are to your ideal.

In case you had trouble defining "great work" in this exercise, let me offer a definition relevant to this book: effectively doing high-impact work in a timely fashion. Living a "great life" means different things to different people, but just in case that question stumped you, I will again offer my description: experiencing a moderate level of happiness, well-being, or life satisfaction frequently in the short term and a steady, moderate level of satisfaction over the long term of your life.

Whatever concerns you have written down in this exercise have been voiced by your peers who have attended my workshops. For the past seven years, I have collected their pre-workshop concerns and post-implementation comments during workshop follow-up interviews. These professors, perhaps like you, had unanswered e-mail, desks piled with papers, and never-ending to-do lists. These professors, perhaps like you, were letting obstacles keep them from their maximum productivity and satisfaction. While most of those professors came to my workshops hoping to learn a Gen I system for managing time, what they got instead was a Gen II system that goes beyond managing time to managing life. In the complementary coaching sessions after the workshops, these professors reported that implementing just a few tools or techniques from a workshop helped them to tame their paper tigers, say "No" more frequently and gracefully, and improve their self-care. In short, these professors learned how to find and stay in their peak performance zone.

Your Peak Performances

You might not have thought of yourself as a performer, but, like the jobs of actors, athletes, teachers, writers, and leaders, the job of a professor is one of performance, with much in common with the jobs of other performers because you produce observable products for audiences who score or measure your performances. As you learn to better manage yourself and your tasks, you will achieve and stay in your peak performance zone consistently and get back into it readily when things go off course.

Your personal peak performance zone is that sweet spot where the challenge of your tasks meets the ability of your skills in the right environment. This right environment is both external, when you are performing for the right audience in the right venue and format, and internal, when

EXERCISE 1.1

Self-Assessment on Great Work and Great Life

What is your definition of great work for yourself? What does "great work" mean to you at the present time? The more specific you are about what great work means for you, the clearer your focus will be for your current and future work activities.

How close are you to that ideal? You can use a percentage from 0 to 100% or a more descriptive statement. What are the discrepancies between your definition of great work and the current reality of your work? What interferes with you doing more great work?

The next question asks you to reflect on your subjective sense of life satisfaction. Defining your great life might include spending time with children, vacationing with your spouse, having a clean and organized home, pursuing one of your hobbies, feeling less pressured while you work, exercising regularly, and other activities that contribute to your quality of life. Research from the field of positive psychology tells us two things about happiness: that happiness and well-being can be measured and that people have an intuitive sense of their own happiness (Seligman, 2002). Once again, the more specific your definition of life satisfaction is, the easier it will be to attain.

What does living a great life mean for you?

Using a percentage or a description, how close or how far are you from your ideal life? What are the discrepancies between your ideal vision and the current reality? What interferes with the ideal life you are called to live?

Take a moment to put words to your biggest concern about what interferes with your ability to have great work (productivity) and a great life (happiness)—in other words, your ability to do good while living well. List several concerns if you wish, especially emphasizing things over which you have control.

your brain is well rested, well fed, and in the right mind-set. When you are in the peak performance zone, you know it and your audience knows it. This response from your audience may be obvious when you are teaching and can receive immediate feedback from students, but audience response is also a factor in your scholarly work, even though the delay between submission and feedback is so lengthy that you may have forgotten you even wrote the piece that just got accepted. Your service work also involves production—of decisions, reports, and facilitations. Lest you think this book recommends that you approach your work like a robot, rest assured that the book aims at helping you experience satisfaction in your work and your life. With your life management system in place, you will be at your peak much of the time as you perform those responsibilities, while maintaining better work-life balance. In case this sounds like a promise that can't be kept, the truth is that you have already had some experiences in which you were performing at your peak.

Exercise 1.2 asks you to study the elements of one or more of your own peak performance experiences so that you can extract their similar lessons and apply them to your current situation. Maybe you have experienced this peak performance zone while teaching, writing, or chairing a meeting. Perhaps you had such a moment back in graduate school while writing your dissertation or in your youth when you were in a school play or competing in sport.

If you study several experiences when things went well and when you did not feel you performed at your best, you are likely to see that the elements of the second category contrast sharply with those of the first. Peak performance is working at your personal best as you define it, not in competition with anyone else. As researchers have studied peak performance experiences, however, several similar elements emerge as people describe those experiences, including focus, timelessness, ease in moving through the work, feeling at one with the task, clear goals and feedback. People also describe nonpeak experiences in similar terms, reporting distraction, a feeling of being overwhelmed or confused, a sense of time-dragging tedium, and a feeling at being at odds with the task (Csikszentmihalyi, 2008; Ericsson, 2009).

The peak performance zone is not merely a momentary feel-good experience, such as a good time on vacation. The zone also produces results. The product or outcome might be a well-prepared class, a well-run meeting, or a well-written article. The goal of peak performing professors is to find the sweet spot in which their efforts consistently produce good outcomes. This book is a workbook of practices that can move you closer to your

EXERCISE 1.2

Explore Your Peak Performances

Think of a time when things went very well. You were working on something interesting that you were able to do. The pieces fell into place almost magically. You felt you were born to do this work. Describe that experience:

This next question might be difficult but it will also give you some very important information. Imagine a time when you were working and you did not feel at your best. Perhaps you were bored or overwhelmed by what you are working on or distracted by other things. Perhaps you just didn't know how to do the things you were doing. Describe what that experience was like:

peak performing zone and, if you already are performing well, increase the chances that you can stay consistently in that zone. These practices also will help you increase your satisfaction level with all areas of your life. But don't just trust me on these promises; do your own assessments, before and after you put these practices into action.

How Productive and Happy Are You?

The words *assessment*, *evaluation*, and *measurement* strike fear in the hearts of academics, who conjure up images of student evaluations, promotion and tenure committees, and regional reevaluation teams. Professors scare themselves needlessly, because assessment can be extremely useful. Centuries ago Plato taught that "the unexamined life is not worth living." I would add: "That which is not measured cannot be improved." Whether you measure your effectiveness with qualitative data such as journal entries and descriptors or with quantitative data such as scores on assessment tools or numbers of articles published, data can assess both your starting point and then your progress toward your goals.

For the peak performing professor, assessment is helpful on both a micro level and a macro level. On the macro level, your institution may require objective methods to assess faculty productivity, usually most strongly emphasizing the scholarly aspect of the tripartite job description (Middaugh, 2011). Your teaching may also be evaluated on the basis of student evaluations, a practice that recently has been called into question as researchers delineate the difference between measuring student perceptions of good teaching and measuring student learning resulting from the teaching (Nilson, 2010). Furthermore, very few institutions evaluate the quality of service, although some institutions I have visited are starting to use 360-degree leadership measures, such as the Leadership Practices Inventory, to evaluate administrators (Kouzes & Posner, 2003).

There are several problems with the use of the term *productivity*. It evokes for many an industrial-age image of widgets rolling off a conveyor belt while an efficiency expert with a clipboard stands by making notes. Academic productivity is often measured by number of scholarly publications, a macro measure that is too narrow since it fails to take into account any measure of teaching and service. Assessment on the basis of publication measures outcomes over which faculty have only marginal control, since journal editors determine whether articles are published or rejected. Using publication as a measure of productivity means that faculty's effective efforts are separated from measurable results by such long periods of time as to make the assessment meaningless to the daily life of the faculty. Although life as a scholar might be measured by publications, it is lived from one writing session to the next. The peak performance literature across fields such as sports and neuroscience emphasize that peak performers improve their overall performance by improving their micro-level performance, setting small achievable goals for practice sessions, measuring those results, and taking a gradual approach to building helpful lifelong habits (Ericsson, 2009; Gollwitzer, Fujita, & Oettingen, 2004; Halvorson, 2011).

Higher education assessment experts define and study helpful institutional productivity measures, but this book will ask you to develop your own definition of productivity by dreaming globally and acting locally. In the academy, faculty have bosses with reasonable performance expectations about the faculty tripartite job description. You should know what those expectations are and incorporate them into your long-term planning. The reality, however, is that your academic bosses do not manage your days and goals; you do. And that's a good thing, because research on employee autonomy has shown that employees with greater choice regarding how to do their own work had greater job satisfaction, which contributed to better performance (Spreitzer, Kizilos, & Nason, 1997). Given that level of autonomy, faculty are more like self-employed entrepreneurs than employees. This book will take the controversial position that if faculty define productivity and happiness for themselves with a view to their own long-range success, they will achieve goals that serve both themselves and their institutions and will stay engaged for the potential long haul of those partnerships. Your bosses may not see the everyday ways that you are working, but they will notice the results. The real boost to productivity, even on institutional measures, will occur when you first define productivity in ways that fit your values, including the value of success in academe, and then manage your productivity on a micro level. This book aims to show how to do both these things.

We will begin with several global measures of your self-rated productivity and happiness, and then we will use a specific survey measure to assess how PACE practices might bring you closer to becoming a peak performing professor. Using these subjective measures will increase both your motivation and your focus as you target the areas across your job description that you want to improve.

On a practical level, your own definition of great work must eventually intersect with that of your workplace or you will be an iconoclast working in isolation with no support from your institution—or, worse yet, you might even become unemployed. So in addition to practices that will improve your work habits and increase your satisfaction, this book also includes practices that guide you to negotiate with like-minded colleagues and bosses so that your great work is part of a larger whole—an institution that provides high-quality education for students and a supportive environment for scholarship (see Part 3 of this book).

Global Measures

These two scales will give you a subjective, baseline measure of your productivity and satisfaction.

Use the numbers on the first scale to indicate your intuitive sense of productivity on your most recent workday, from 1 (not very productive) to 6 (very productive).

1	2	3	4	5	6
(Not very productive)					(Very productive)

Use the next scale to indicate how satisfied and happy you felt on your most recent workday. You have two other options as well: you can rate your professional and personal lives separately, and you can also rate a day on which you did not work such as a weekend or vacation day.

1	2	3	4	5	6
(Not very satisfied)					(Very satisfied)

If you use these global assessments only once, they will be not very representative of your actual work and life quality. For example, completing them on a sunny day rather than a rainy day may produce better scores. However, if you repeat the assessments daily for a couple of weeks, the assessments would begin to yield an average score for your work and your life (Kahneman, Krueger, Schkade, Schwartz, & Stone, 2004).

Specific Assessments

This book divides the practices into four peak performance areas (Power, Align, Connect, and Energize) and then applies those practices to typical faculty roles and responsibilities at work and at home. If you grew up reading the "Choose Your Own Adventure" books or playing computer games, you know that your choice of options constructs the course and outcome of the adventure or game.

The assessment tool in Exercise 1.3 can give you an overall sense of whether you are thriving or struggling in your career as well as in what areas your practices are supporting your success or need improvement. Your scores on the PACE-R subscales will direct your adventure to the specific chapters of this book where you will find the clues that will lead you to your peak performance zone. Four of the scales ask you to rate yourself on the four practices, PACE, that characterize all peak performers (Parts 1 through 4 of this book), whereas the fifth factor, R, measures peak performance in your professorial and personal roles (Part 5). Using your scores on the items in the five subscales to diagnose how you are doing with each practice and application area, you can choose your own adventure by identifying what you may want to do to incorporate peak performing practices into your work and life.

The following sections contain an expanded description of the five subscales or practices (PACE-R) that characterize peak performing professors. Looking at your subscales will suggest which practices will be most helpful for you to integrate into your work habits. You may be closer to your ideal life than you think.

Power Subscale

The Power subscale measures how you power or motivate yourself—specifically, how your motivation connects to your sense of meaning and purpose. A high score on this subscale indicates that you are a peak performer who energizes your work and your life by having a clear idea of what it means to do good work and to live well. Lower scores indicate that you have not yet figured out how your work and your life fit together into a system that connects your strengths with your sense of meaning and purpose. Without that connection, you probably have problems staying motivated and on task. You might find yourself procrastinating about things you want to do and then later feeling guilty and frustrated.

Part 1 of this book will help you set up a Gen II life management system using the Pyramid of Power, in which you anchor all you do to your sense of meaning and purpose.

Align Subscale

The Align subscale measures how well you align your activities, projects, and tasks with your power and purpose. A high score indicates that you are able to focus on the most important tasks related to your purpose and mission, manage all of your projects, and know which goals you are working on in the short and long term. A low score indicates that you may be wandering from task to task, becoming overwhelmed by all that it seems you should

EXERCISE 1.3

Peak Performing Professor Assessment Tool

To see how close you may be to your peak performance as a professor, use this scale to answer the following questions.

1	2	3	4	5	6	7	8	9	10
(None of the time)								(All of the time)	

_____ 1.   I usually manage my time pretty well.

_____ 2.   My life is rich, full, and satisfying.

_____ 3.   My life has a good rhythm, balancing productive work with activities that relax and refresh me.

_____ 4.   I have protocols for class preparation, which include making use of previous experiences along with folding in new information.

_____ 5.   I receive consistently good feedback about how I relate to others.

_____ 6.   I am proactive about my career, looking for opportunities that will build productivity.

_____ 7.   I have arranged my environment to support my work.

_____ 8.   I have a vision for how my work and personal life might fit together over the long haul, and I review and revise my vision from time to time.

_____ 9.   I feel a part of a community in my institution and my personal affiliations.

_____ 10. I meet most of my personal responsibilities well.

_____ 11. I am able to choose, from among the many service opportunities on campus and beyond, those that are consistent with my vision.

_____ 12. I can take the big picture of a goal and break it down into smaller steps.

_____ 13. I have the social skills to work collaboratively with colleagues even when there are conflicts or differences of opinion.

_____ 14. I have protocols for writing, which include ways to generate ideas and capture them in rough drafts.

_____ 15. I design courses with clear goals and clear grading procedures, so that students know how to budget their time to achieve a good course grade.

_____ 16. I keep track of all my current projects and know what needs to be done next.

_____ 17. I have at least one intimate relationship (with a mate or a best friend) in which I can be myself.

_____ 18. I am known for my consistent contributions to committee, advising, and leadership roles.

_____ 19. I have a pretty good match between my skills and my work tasks.

_____ 20. I have a method for choosing the opportunities to say "Yes" to.

_____ 21. I maintain healthy boundaries between my professional and personal lives.

_____ 22. I am able to separate the composing function of writing from the revising and editing functions.

_____ 23. I check in with helpful others who support my goals on how I'm doing, including my mate, coach, mentor, friends, or learning community.

_____ 24. I manage stress and emotions pretty well most of the time.

_____ 25. I revise my writing by getting feedback from others.

_____ 26. I have streamlined recurring tasks at home so that they can be done with a minimum of effort and thought.

_____ 27. I maintain good energy through good health habits.

_____ 28. I have protocols for classroom assessment and grading based on sound pedagogical methods that benefit students while keeping my job from becoming all-consuming.

_____ 29. I feel productive most workdays.

_____ 30. I weave together my professional roles by looking at the potential return on investment of my energy to my career development.

_____ Total Score

Scales

Your total score gives you an indication of whether you are thriving, striving, or struggling in your career as a professor whereas the individual scale score gives you an indication of how you are doing in each area. On the scales that follow, the first numbers represent the range of overall scores in each assessment category. The second number (in parentheses) is the average item score for that range.

270–300 on overall measure (average item score 9 and above): You are definitely _thriving_ in this career. You could have coauthored this book and saved me some time. Consider mentoring other faculty who are open to learning from you.

250–269 (average item score 8): You are _thriving_ but could reach even higher levels of productivity and satisfaction by implementing a few of the techniques in the areas of your lower scores.

225–249 (average item score 7.5): You are _striving_ at a moderate level of functioning. You probably experience dips and highs in your day-to-day life. You can function at the _thriving_ level by implementing techniques that relate to the PACE-R areas in which your scores were lower.

205–224 (average item score 7): You are _striving_ and probably experience a combination of some success and a lot of frustration in your daily life. You can get closer to your peak performance zone by setting up and maintaining a peak performing professor life management system.

185–204 (average item score 6): You are between _striving_ and _struggling_. You do a fairly good job at work and home, but you are working way too hard for the results. You can improve your productivity and ease by implementing practices in this book and possibly setting up accountability with a mentor, coach, buddy, or faculty support group as you build new habits.

165–184 (average item score 5): You are definitely _struggling_ but are probably making this job way harder than it needs to be. You will enjoy your work and life much more if you take the time to design and implement a good life management system. Also consider keeping on track by following ongoing guidance from one or more of the accountability sources listed above.

145 and below (average item score below 5): You are *struggling* and limping along in this career (or this area) either because you don't have the skills to manage it yet or perhaps because it is not a good enough match for your talents and interests. Before you consider a career change, however, implement some of the suggestions in this book with the help of a support system to keep you on track. If you implement those suggestions and still are not as productive and happy as you would like to be, consider getting career coaching to explore a career change.

Scale Scoring

Insert the score you gave yourself for each numbered question in the following chart.

				Roles and Responsibilities				
Power	**Align**	**Connect**	**Energize**	**Professor**	**Writing**	**Service**	**Life**	**Teaching**
2. ___	1. ___	5. ___	3. ___	6. ___	14. ___	11. ___	10. ___	4. ___
8. ___	7. ___	9. ___	24. ___	30. ___	22. ___	18. ___	21. ___	15. ___
19. ___	12. ___	13. ___	27. ___		25. ___		26. ___	28. ___
23. ___	16. ___	17. ___						
29. ___	20. ___							
								Grand
Total								Total

Now that you have completed this assessment tool, the picture may look bleaker than it really is. Remember, just before a soufflé is finished, it is still mushy eggs, flour, and milk; then, with a little more heat, voilà—the soufflé rises and turns golden brown. Like other faculty members who moved from scores in the struggling range to scores in the thriving range, you may just need to turn up the heat on the soufflé of your ideal life.

be doing. Many of the concerns listed in the Introduction to this book arise when faculty fail to align their life purpose with their projects and activities.

In Part 2 of this book you will learn how to align your resources of time, people, energy, space, and attention with your purpose so that your life management system practically runs itself, freeing you for your most creative work. The time management tips in that section are ones designed specifically for professors. These tips will make sense once you have put a life management system into place.

Connect Subscale

The Connect subscale measures how well you are connecting with helpful colleagues, friends, and family for mutual support and benefit. A high score on this subscale indicates that you using your social intelligence to accomplish goals through mutually supportive relationships. A low score indicates either that you have not yet developed the specific relationship skills needed for the work of a well-connected professor or that you have chosen to remain more isolated in your approach to your work. In all professions, the most successful are those who build and sustain relationships in their circles of influence. In Part 3 of this book, you will learn how to build and sustain relationships that can advance your career goals and support you in work and in life.

Energize Subscale

The Energize subscale measures the extent to which you are actively sustaining yourself to handle the demands and stress for the long haul of your career and life with grace and mastery. A high score on this subscale indicates that you stay resilient, energized, and motivated for an interesting and lengthy career by regular self-care through wellness and well-being practices. If you have a low score on this subscale, it is likely that you frequently feel as if you are behind the eight ball, about to be hit with the next crisis or deadline. You may tire or get sick easily and probably don't feel good about the productivity of your workdays. You may be at risk of eventually burning out and becoming disengaged.

In Part 4 of this book, you will learn practices for diet, exercise, and stress and emotional management that will help you stay engaged, healthy, and balanced so that you are operating at your peak without exhausting your resources. Rather than delaying self-care until everything else is done, peak performers build their days around a minimum and effective amount of self-care, so that they can work in their peak performance zone while saving time, improving concentration, and increasing productivity.

Roles and Responsibilities

The Roles and Responsibilities subscale measures how well you are doing in the three major roles of the typical academic career—namely, teaching, writing, and serving—and in several personal roles common among faculty members. A high score means that you have established good work habits that produce results in your tripartite job description. A low score means that you may be working too hard and too ineffectually in some or all of your roles and that you could benefit from the research-based practices described in Part 5 of this book to make your activities in those roles more structured and productive. Part 5 will present tips for balancing your professional roles and responsibilities with several typical personal roles.

Now that you have assessed yourself on the peak performing professor survey, you are ready to move to the first step toward better work and life: powering yourself through a sense of meaning and purpose.

Robison's Rule
Less is more. Picking only one or two things to work on at a time results in quicker improvement than overwhelming yourself with more "shoulds."

Part One

Power Your Work and Your Life with Purpose

Efforts and courage are not enough without purpose and direction.

—John F. Kennedy

DOES YOUR OFFICE ever look like mine did back when I was a young professor—little scraps of paper with research ideas, messages, phone numbers, and to-do lists scattered all over the desk, file cabinets, and credenza? Do you wish you had some way of getting and staying organized that still makes room for your creativity?

My excuse was that there was no easy way to affix little scraps of paper to each other all in one place. However, ever since 3M's genius Art Fry invented the Post-it note, using a low-tack adhesive that allows a piece of paper to be affixed somewhere, then removed and re-affixed somewhere else, none of us can use that excuse. In Part 1 you will take advantage of the fabulous invention of movable sticky notes to increase your productivity by organizing all of those disparate thoughts and scraps of paper in one place. As a result you will design a life management system that will capture and store all of your exciting new ideas in one place while you decide what to do and when and how to do it. So bike, jog, or drive down to your office supply store, get yourself a pack of 800 small sticky notes and a small pack of the next size up, and be prepared to be amazed at how effortlessly you can become organized and stay that way.

You will begin the design of your life management system by creating your Pyramid of Power, the foundation that will provide a philosophical and practical prism through which you can evaluate opportunities, set priorities, and make decisions about resources.

Sometimes faculty balk at building this foundation, which seems to be an irrelevant detour from their goal of learning how to manage time better. However, in this Gen II life management program, time management tips are deferred until Part 2, after you have constructed the Pyramid of Power which you will use as a basis for aligning your power with your resources of time, energy, people, and space. Professors who push themselves to create and use their Pyramids reap huge benefits for their tolerance of this seeming detour. My best testimonial came from a professor at the end of a workshop, who said, "I'm really glad you forced me to do this philosophical work which I didn't want to do. Now I see how all of my work connects to who I am"—a great observation from a professor of philosophy!

How Part 1 Will Help You Become a Peak Performing Professor

This part of the book will show you how to do the following:

1. Set up a life management system to manage your life—not just your time—using the Pyramid of Power and Dream Book, two tools that provide a visual and verbal reminder of how all of your activities, professional and personal, flow together seamlessly.

2. Articulate your purpose and use it to motivate yourself to work on tasks, big and small, knowing that they are all connected to the big picture of your ideal life.

3. Clarify your mission about how you use your strengths and your values to serve the people who need you so that you can work and live at your peak.

4. Create a vision by specifying the outcomes for your goals.

5. Collect and manage all of your goals, personal and professional, in one Dream Book so that they are readily available when you are ready to act on them, without your having to hold them in your memory.

6. Work your system by regularly reviewing and updating your Pyramid of Power and Dream Book.

Chapter 2
Your Ideal Life

EVEN THOUGH THE definition of faculty careers is changing rapidly (Gappa, Austin, & Trice, 2007), the professoriate is one of the few remaining careers, along with ministry and medicine, that engages people for their entire work life. Your teaching, scholarship, and service can make a difference in the lives of many people, contribute to the world's body of knowledge, and provide you with a satisfying life of fulfillment and intellectual stimulation—that is, as long as things are going well. Once professors lose their bearings, however, they are prone to burnout from dealing with the dark side of the academy: the conflicting role expectations, vague job descriptions, campus politics, and lack of appreciation from the students. Burnout threatens the quality of their work, their health, and their commitment to education (Astin et al., 2011).

Articulate Your Internal Agenda

In order to become motivated and stay motivated you need to power your life by articulating an internal agenda for yourself and your job. Articulating that agenda provides you with the willpower to guide your day-to-day time management decisions and your negotiations with the leadership of your institution about how to best serve. This chapter will help you to articulate that agenda. Later chapters will help you develop the way power for your goals by managing goals, relationships, and energy. Exercise 2.1 will help you explore your motivations for entering and staying in this career while Exercise 2.2 will help you articulate a specific agenda to continue doing good while living well.

If you are like most professors, you want to become a peak performer, doing good while living well. You want to teach well, contribute to your research field, and serve your institution. At the same time, you would like to experience the benefits of that hard work: job satisfaction, opportunities, recognition, and a salary commensurate with your training and experience.

EXERCISE 2.1

Exploring Your Work Motivation

Begin this articulation by reflecting on why you were initially attracted to this career.

I entered the career of college teaching and research because I wanted to:

If you have been in the professoriate more than a couple of years, your motivations for keeping this life-style may be different from the motivations you had at the beginning of your career.

I now want to stay in the career of college teaching and research because I want to:

EXERCISE 2.2

Definitions of Key Concepts

In your answers to the questions that follow, clarify your personal definitions of doing good while living well. These questions will get you started on a general definition of what doing good and living well mean for you.

What specifically does "doing good" mean for you?

If you were someday to receive a lifetime achievement award for your accomplishments, what would those accomplishments be? Consider areas of your life such as teaching, scholarly work, and service, both on and off campus. For example, doing good might include creating and sharing knowledge with students and colleagues.

What specifically does "living well" mean for you?

If you were given an award for a well-lived life, what would you have done to deserve it? Consider both professional areas, such as accomplishments, income, and collegial relationships, and personal areas, such as friendships, family life, marriage or partnership, hobbies, home, and travel. For example, living well might mean creating a nourishing and loving family life with your spouse and children.

Envision Your Ideal Life

Now that you have articulated your image of living well while doing good, let's get more specific about designing your ideal life.

About 20 years ago, Wendy's fast-food restaurants had a series of television commercials in which "people on the street" were asked to pick what kind of hamburger they would prefer to eat, the shriveled-up, dry burger from the leading competitor or the "hot and juicy" one, which we all knew was the Wendy's burger. One woman with a frumpy, pin-curl hairstyle and clutching her purse on her lap chose the dried-up burger. The announcer asked her if she wouldn't reconsider her choice, "Wouldn't you like a hot and juicy burger instead?" She answered, "Well, I would like that hamburger, but I'm not used to getting what I want. I asked for a glamorous hairstyle and I don't think I got it. What do you think?"

Are you getting what you want out of life, or are you settling for a stale and shriveled-up life when, with a little tweaking, your life could feel more hot and juicy? Even a previously satisfying life can become less than ideal when there is no longer a fit between what you want and what you get.

When I ask workshop participants what stands in the way of their living their ideal life, people most often list money, time, and other people. People never guess that the real obstacle that stands in the way of getting the hamburger, the hairstyle, or the life that they really want is the vagueness of their self-definition. By the end of this chapter that obstacle will no longer stand in your way to a hot and juicy life.

Now that you have developed general definitions of great work, a great life, doing good, and living well, you are ready to get more specific about what living a more balanced life means to you. Use your imagination to picture your ideal life. What would be happening in the major areas that are important to you? Don't limit yourself by these suggested areas. Add or subtract as you see fit. You might consider assessing how well you feel you are managing each area of your life using a scale of 1 (poor) to 10 (excellent).

- *Work:* Are you doing work that is satisfying and that meets your economic needs?

- *Relationships:* Are you giving and receiving the support and love that you want from friends and family?

- *Environment:* Are you living and working in environments that support you and your goals?

- *Financial:* Are you earning what you should for your training and experience? Are you managing your finances in ways consistent with your values?

- *Community:* Do you have connection and involvement in your community consistent with your stage of life? (For example, your school-aged children may often need your support with school volunteer activities, Scouts, or sports.)

- *Spirituality/inner life:* Do you take time to reflect on how your life is going? Do you have practices of worship, prayer, meditation, or communing with nature that are meaningful to you and that anchor you to what you value?

- *Intimacy:* Do you have an intimate partnership? Do you have a few intimate friends? How are these relationships going? How could they be even better? What do you need to do differently?

- *Health:* Are your health habits supporting your present life and helping to promote your long term well-being? What might need improvement?

- *Recreation:* Do you have hobbies that refresh you? Do you spend regular time pursuing them?

- What other aspects of your life, not listed here, are important to you?

Anchor Your Ideal Life to Your Pyramid of Power

Next we will anchor that image of your ideal life with a visual tool called the Pyramid of Power. A pyramid is the most stable of all building structures because of its wide base and narrow top. The Pyramid of Power provides both the stability and the power to fuel your activities. Just as cars, computers, and cell phones need energy sources to run properly, your life needs power to keep you energized, engaged, and committed.

Setting up your Pyramid of Power will help you protect your ideal life by allowing you to become crystal clear about how your work and life choices tie into the real you. This authenticity is the key to handling those difficult moments when distraction and lack of confidence attack. When you connect your activities to your power source, you will no longer feel frustrated, as Professor Mary did in Chapter 1 of this book, that the day's activities are random and unconnected to one another.

Articulate the Elements of the Pyramid of Power

The source of many professors' confusion about what to work on next is their huge set of goals floating in the air without any grounding. By contrast, as you work through the exercises in this book, your goals will be anchored to your sense of meaning through your Pyramid of Power. As Figure 2.1 shows, there are four levels to this pyramid, like the floors of a

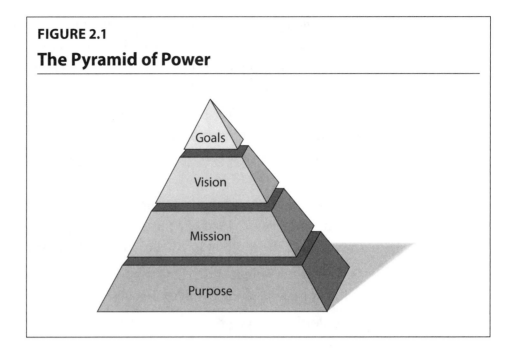

FIGURE 2.1

The Pyramid of Power

four-story house: from the bottom up, these levels are purpose, mission, vision, and goals.

The construction of the Pyramid of Power begins when you develop its wide base by articulating your Purpose. Layered over that solid foundation are the other floors of your motivational house, which represent your mission, your vision, and, at the pinnacle, your goals. Once you create your Pyramid of Power, it can act as a prism, allowing you to evaluate which activities suit who you are and why you are here on this earth. The following are the four elements of your Pyramid.

Purpose expresses the reason you are here on earth, or why you do what you do. Purpose answers the question, "Why am I here on this earth?" Well-written purpose statements usually sound abstract, philosophical, and general, but they express you and your life in one sound bite. A well-articulated purpose statement will probably be true of you for your lifetime and will provide a continuity of motivation no matter what your specific jobs or life stages are.

Mission articulates how you are living that purpose. It answers the question, "Given my purpose in life, how shall I be acting?" Your mission is more specific and behavioral than your purpose and will probably be revised as often as every three to five years. Your mission is the engine that keeps the machinery of your life running. Mission links your unique package of strengths and talents and your most cherished values with the people to whom you offer those talents and values.

Expressed in a statement that directs your choice of activities, mission provides the criteria to answer that old Gen I time management question, "What is the best use of my time right now?"

Vision describes the six to eight outcomes that you hope will result from doing your mission. Vision answers the question, "If I live out my purpose by doing my mission, what will be happening to me and the world around me?" The "me" part may include the elements of your work, such as where you live and work, how much money you earn, and what satisfactions you gain from your work. The "world around you" can include your immediate environment, both physical and social, as well as the larger world on which you may have an impact. Vision answers the question, "What am I aiming at with these activities?"

Goals are the actual activities, projects, and tasks that you work on to make your vision outcomes happen. Your goals answer the question, "What shall I work on now to fulfill my purpose, live my mission, and reach my vision." In the goal attainment research cited in this book, the term *goal* is sometimes used in a general way to describe anything a person wants and is sometimes used in a specific way to refer to something a person *does* to get what they want. By the first definition, purpose, mission, and vision are also goals. By the second definition, goals would only include the action steps toward your purpose, mission, and vision. In the exercises in this book, I will use the second definition unless otherwise stated.

Once you have created your pyramid, your power or motivation will build upward from purpose to goals following the path shown in Figure 2.2.

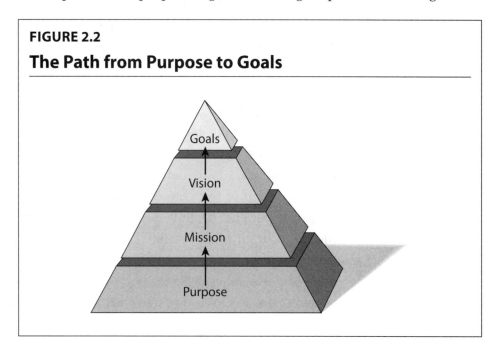

FIGURE 2.2

The Path from Purpose to Goals

Meaning and motivation follow naturally when your goals are tied to the other elements of the pyramid rather than floating in the air unconnected to one another or to anything else of importance to you. Once you have made these connections, you may still have many of the same goals as you do now but they will feel different—more integrated to the larger picture of your work and your life and therefore easier to manage.

Work from Purpose

Your brain is bombarded by millions of bits of information daily. With so many opportunities and distractions in an academic's life, how do you decide in what direction to focus your senses and brain? Some bits of information grab your attention because of immediate survival needs—for example, when you swerve to miss a car stopped in your lane. Other bits correspond to maintenance needs, such as managing thirst, hunger, and loneliness.

Beyond the information related to those basic needs, the bits you attend to are determined by where you direct your senses and brain. In a now-classic experiment (Chabris & Simons, 2010), a group of students were filmed passing a basketball around a circle. Half of the students were wearing white T-shirts, half were wearing black T-shirts. Study participants were instructed to watch the video (which you can view at http://www .theinvisiblegorilla.com/videos.html) and count the number of passes made by the students in the white T-shirts. Most subjects were fairly accurate in their count of the passes by students in white T-shirts. But when subjects were asked about the number of passes made by the students in black T-shirts, the counts were not even close to accurate. Now for the interesting part—spoiler alert!—very few of the observers ever noticed the gorilla.

What gorilla, you ask? In the video, a guy in a gorilla suit wandered out in the middle of the game and crossed back and forth among the students. Subjects primed to watch the passes by students in white T-shirts never saw the gorilla. Now that I've told you about the gorilla, you would be able to see him in the video and still count the ball passes. However, you might experience slightly lowered accuracy and increased fatigue, because your brain must use more energy to concentrate on both those tasks simultaneously.

The demands of the gorilla study are like those of your typical workday. Your brain offers an interesting trade-off. Attend to all of the gorillas—that is, distractions—and you will lose accuracy and speed on your main task. Concentrate on just one thing at a time, and you will be more accurate and speedy. However, you might miss a few interesting gorillas.

Faculty often blame their distractibility on a lack of discipline or will-power. What they really lack is the clear sense of purpose that fuels willpower. Our brains are cognitive misers that can't split our attention without costing us accuracy and speed (Fiske & Taylor, 1984). Whenever you multitask, your brain shifts back and forth rapidly between tasks like a toggle switch being repeatedly flipped. If you check for e-mail while writing a scholarly article, your speed and performance quality on both tasks drop off drastically. Success in work and life as a peak performer depends on a combination of intentionally attending to purpose and working on specific actions that advance it, while at the same time decreasing attention to distractions (Loehr & Schwartz, 2004).

In Gen II life management you can work at your peak a good amount of the time without exhaustion by deciding for what end in the big picture of your life you are managing time, attention, energy, and other resources and then by focusing on activities that are anchored to what is most important to you. To maintain speed and productivity, attend to only one of these important tasks at a time. When you practice intentional attention, you decide on your goals for the day, then pause regularly—every 90 minutes or so—to reassess where you are in completing those goals and to notice any interesting gorillas that may be more important than your original agenda. If you set up practices such as writing at the same time each day and checking messages only three specific times a day, many of your daily tasks will run on automatic pilot, thus freeing your higher cognitive centers for creative work.

In the next chapter, you will craft the elements of your pyramid, the foundation of your life management system.

Robison's Rule
You don't need time management; you do *need life management.*

Chapter 3

Your Purpose

PURPOSE IS THE foundation of your Pyramid of Power (Figure 3.1) because your purpose expresses the reason you are here in this life. The purpose statement is a short phrase, comprehensive enough to encompass all that you do and inspiring enough to motivate you to keep doing it. The purpose statement taps "that deepest dimension within us—our central core or essence—where we have a profound sense of who we are, where we come from, and where we're going" (Leider, 1997, p. 1). As the basis of your ideal life, purpose gives you direction and establishes significance in all that you do. For many people, purpose connects with the spiritual element in their lives in whatever way they define that element, whether as a divine being, an inner energy, or a connection to something larger than self.

The most compelling source of purpose is spiritual, the energy derived from connecting to deeply held values and a purpose beyond one's self-interest. Purpose creates a destination as it drives full engagement by prompting our desire to invest focused energy in a particular activity or goal (Loehr & Schwartz, 2004, p. 131).

FIGURE 3.1

The Pyramid of Power: Purpose

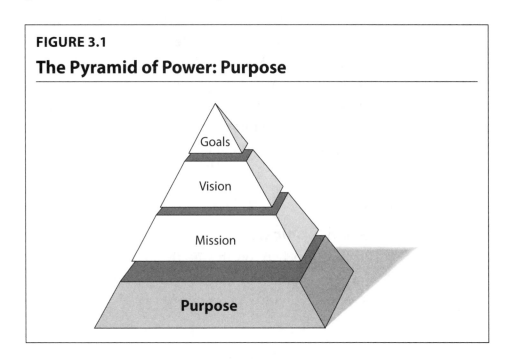

Articulate your life purpose. Warning: this is not as easy as it looks. My purpose in life is:

Faculty panic when trying to think about their purpose, because shrinking their entire life down to one simple statement sounds intimidating and impossible. That panic usually comes from holding one of these myths about purpose:

- My purpose has to be new, creative, and startling. Reality: your purpose might be something you are already living.

- My purpose has to be world-changing, such as finding a cure for cancer. Reality: everyone is called to change the world of their influence. As a teacher you are influencing students. As a parent you are shaping your children.

- If I articulate my purpose, I'll be locked in and stuck. Reality: you are the author of your purpose; you can write it in pencil and use a big fat eraser as often as you want until you have a statement that works for you.

- I'm too complex to boil my life down to a single statement. Reality: yes, you are complex, but your statement of purpose represents your complexity in an overarching summary of why you exist.

- Writing my purpose is too hard. Reality: it might pop out at you during one of the other exercises that follow in this chapter.

If you have easily written your purpose statement, skip to writing your mission statement (see Chapter 4). If you feel stuck writing your purpose statement, you might try one or more of the paths listed in the sections that follow to discover your purpose. If those paths don't bring clarification, move on to writing your mission statement anyway. Sometimes getting specific with other levels of the pyramid is an indirect route back to articulating a good purpose statement.

Paths to Purpose

Philosophical Path

"Why am I here on this earth?" is an easy question to answer if you have thought about it in a retreat or life planning workshop. If you feel stumped about what your purpose is, answering these questions might help:

- Why do I do what I do?

- What good do I do in this world, my life, and my work?

In case you are tempted to write two purpose statements, a generic life purpose statement and a specific career purpose statement, I urge you to articulate one comprehensive purpose statement encompassing your whole life. For example, one professor wrote: "My life purpose is to make the world a better place." Then she wrote, "My career purpose is to make the world a better place by increasing knowledge." Later she merged these statements into a comprehensive one: "My purpose is to make the world a better place in both my personal and academic world through acquiring knowledge and applying wisdom." You will see an opportunity to separate the areas of your life later as you write your mission and vision statements.

Because your purpose statement is usually tied in with your deeply held values, it changes very little across your lifetime. Your purpose statement may change in language but not in concept; the statement is usually as true about you at age 12 as it is at age 82.

Here are some examples of purpose statements from the philosophical path.

- "I have a dream."(Martin Luther King)

- "I came so that they might have life and have it more abundantly." (Jesus Christ)

- "Be the change you wish to see in the world." (Mahatma Gandhi)

Uniqueness Path

What are you about? What is it that only you can do in this world in your unique way?

Marketing experts, when devising a plan to promote a business, look for the business's unique selling proposition (USP) or unique selling advantage (USA) as a way to find some unique quality that distinguishes the business from competitors that offer similar products or services. For example, there are a lot of coffee shops, so what is the USP of Starbucks? Many people who answer that Starbucks is a superior coffee can't pick it out from other comparable strong-tasting coffee in a blind taste test. Starbucks is the most popular place to pick up that morning cup of java, however, because Starbucks is cool. Their business is selling not just coffee but atmosphere; Starbucks is a cool place to take your laptop or a cool place to meet a friend. The baristas treat you as though you are very cool. It is very cool to walk into a department meeting with your cool white-and-green Starbucks cup.

Don't conclude that you have no USP because you are only one of many English or history professors; you are still unique in some way. What is it that only you can do? What are some things that you do that are unique in your little corner of the world or that are even unique in this great big world? Here are some examples:

- The only professor in the department who helps women graduate students build their confidence for job interviews.

- The only one with a certain line of scholarly inquiry.

- The mother of Taylor, age 6.

Activity Path

Although it seems abstract, a good purpose statement usually sums up the practical activities of the writer. For example, author Donna Schaper pastors a church in New York City where she also does community outreach. She states her purpose as "I am made for Spiritual Nurture and for Public Capacity" (Schaper, 2007).

What activities do you carry out every day? Examples might include loving, teaching, or facilitating. What is a generic summary of these activities? For example:

- "I love my family and try to be thoughtful to each person's needs."

- "I teach developmental English to students who are challenged by writing at the college level."

- "I facilitate committee discussions so that people listen to one another."

Larger-than-Self Path

Often, purpose statements show a connection to something larger than oneself such as a higher power or a community. The larger-than-self path connects you to deep values and spiritual matters and answers the questions, "How am I connected to the universe? Who am I when I am the best I can be?" You might write, for example, "I am here to learn and develop as a human being," or "I am here to serve others," or "I am here to serve Allah/God/The Source/The Feminine Divine." Here are some examples that my workshop participants have shared with me:

- "I am a bridge connecting ideas and people for the greater good." (faculty member whose responsibilities were 50% teaching and 50% community liaison)

- "I am here to manifest God's love." (psychology professor)

- "I add joy and peace to the world." (political science professor)
- "I bring order and beauty to an ugly and chaotic world." (art professor and working artist)
- "I am here to share my wonder about creation, especially about the human body." (physiology professor with a joint appointment in the biology department and the medical school at a large private university)
- "I am here to love knowledge and people." (sociology professor)

Do you have a connection to someone or something larger than yourself? What does believing in that being or energy require of you?

Passion Path

Do you have a passion for your field and for your place in it? *Passio* is a Latin word meaning "to suffer." What are you willing to suffer for? When do you feel most alive professionally or personally? What actions are you doing when you feel that way? What new projects get you excited and motivated?

The opposite feeling of working from purpose is feeling drained. Studying the moments when you feel drained will give you clues about what activities to decrease or eliminate from your purpose. For example, if meeting with your graduate students in your lab energizes you but meeting with your colleagues on a committee drains you, your purpose might be more about teaching and mentoring than about leading and organizing.

Dream Path

What is the essence of your dreams? If you could be or do anything, what would that be? For example, many people like to write but have different dreams about why that writing is important. One writer might like to "challenge minds," while another likes to think of himself as "calling people to action."

If a law were passed that prevented you from working as a college professor, what alternative career would you pick? This question does not imply that you should leave college teaching for that other career. The question merely gets at unfulfilled dreams that might be folded into your current career path.

While you play with this question, don't put any restrictions of time, money, talent, or training on yourself. Dream big and see what you want to do with the results. Then ask yourself if you would like to incorporate any aspects of that mythical job into your present job. Alternatively, the fruit of exploring this path might suggest avocational activities rather than vocational ones.

Role Model Path

If you had to be anybody other than yourself, who you would like to be? The Dalai Lama, Taylor Swift, the president of the United States? What characteristics of that alter ego do you most admire? Is the person kind, gutsy, powerful, wise? How are you most like your alter ego? How could you be more like him or her?

Ideal Workday Path

What constitutes a really great workday for you? What are you doing? With whom? With what? Why? What is happening as a result?

If you find that you can't narrow your ideal workday down to just one but instead imagine several different great days—in the classroom, clinic, or lab—your purpose should reflect your multiple roles. For example, one cardiology professor stated her purpose as "promoting a healing heart." The play on words expressed her desire to discover, teach, and apply research on heart health while bringing her caring to her clinical work.

If you have difficulty conjuring any great workdays, don't panic and decide that you have to change careers. Your difficulty might merely mean that your imagination is stuck. To prompt your imagination, ask yourself what it would take to get closer to better days. Would better class preparation or regular scholarly time help? What purpose would be fulfilled by those changes if they did produce better workdays?

Legacy Path

How did you answer the legacy questions in Chapter 2 of this book about receiving a lifetime achievement award for your body of work and your well-lived life? What would those awards represent? If you could change the world, what would it be for? If you died today, what would be the greatest thing you would leave behind? What would you most want to be known for? What would you be most pleased about in your life?

Life Talent and Dream Path

Looking at the skills you possess can help you develop your purpose statement. This exploration also lays the foundation for your mission statement, the next level of the Pyramid of Power.

1. What do you do well? Teaching, writing, collaborating, leading, something else? For scientific approaches to finding out your strengths, see the assessments listed in Chapter 4 (Virtues in Action, Gallup Strengths Finder, and Realise 2).

2. Review your answers to the questions in Chapter 2 (the exercise about exploring your work motivation) about your motivations to enter and stay in college teaching. Ask yourself these questions about your career:

Was this field a good match for my interests, passions, and talents?

Is it still a good match?

What talents of mine need further development? What untapped talents are not used by my career? How could they be?

Do I feel passionate about this field and my place in it?

3. What interests, strengths and dreams did you exhibit in childhood? How do those connect to your field? For example, if you loved reading mystery stories as a kid, it doesn't mean that you should spend your life writing mysteries, majoring in literature, or working as a crime solver. It might be that your interest in solving mysteries gets expressed in solving problems in math or science—or in helping your students discover their satisfying career paths.

My college teaching career fulfilled my secret childhood desire to do standup comedy without having to endure the cigarette smoke and late nights. In the latter part of my teaching career, I deepened the connection between teaching and comedy by taking several improv classes at my community college and applying many of those exercises in my classes and workshops. Later I discovered that other academics were also making the connection between teaching and improv by borrowing games such as warm-ups, introductions, and listening exercises from improv and applying them to good classroom teaching (Gesell, 1997; McKnight & Scruggs, 2008).

4. What do people say about you when they are engaged in "good gossip" about your talents? Do they say things like, "You know what she is really good at?" Or maybe, "You know what I like about him?" You may even be fortunate enough to have someone who knows you so well that they tell you directly, "You know what you are all about?" If you can't recall any good gossip, ask yourself what are the major points that you want people to get about you. What might they say about you at your retirement party or funeral? What would you rather they say?

Third Ear Path

You might find that you are just too close to your own story to find the clues to your purpose statement but that someone else listening to your story can hear those clues. Consider asking a friend or a professional coach to listen to your answers to the questions in this section to see whether that "third ear" can hear something you have not heard. You might even do a "listening exchange" with a friend, helping each other draft purpose statements by listening to each other's stories.

Review your answers from all of these different paths to purpose, and look for themes from your answers. Can you distill them into one statement that answers the following?

My life purpose is

I am here on this earth to

Evaluate Your Purpose Statement

The following criteria will help you know whether you have found your purpose.

1. Purpose uses your gifts. Your purpose describes your identity at its best and does not require you to become someone else. The best purpose statement usually requires no retraining or career changes, although your statement might require you to engage in some form of continuing learning if you wish to keep moving toward mastery in your field.

2. Purpose simplifies and organizes your life. As the foundation of your life management system, purpose ties your values to concrete intentions and gives you external direction and a priority system in which your time management, your files, your money, and your calendar all flow together.

3. Purpose energizes your life. Purpose defines the person you aspire to be, connects you with your deepest values and spiritual qualities, and guides how you behave in the world. When you are living your purpose, you will not feel like you have to drag yourself through life, making yourself do disagreeable tasks that you hate. When you work from purpose, you will spend most of your time working on things that put you into your peak performance zone.

The wisdom literature of the world emphasizes the success that comes from working from authentic purpose (Schwartz, 2010). The Buddhist tradition refers to purpose as "right livelihood." The Christian tradition refers to purpose as "calling." In the words of poet William Stafford, "Ask me whether what I have done is my life. . . Our deepest calling is to grow into our own authentic selfhood, whether or not it conforms to some image of who we *ought* to be" (Palmer, 2000, p. 16).

4. Purpose lowers stress and brings success. Working from purpose prevents you from getting overwhelmed and provides meaning in the complexity of your life. Working from purpose will help you to be more effective in your job and more relaxed in your personal time. You will no longer worry about what to do next or whether you are really doing what you are "supposed" to do.

Once you align your tasks with your purpose, engaging in even the most mundane tasks such as filing will energize you because these tasks serve as a means to living your bigger purpose. Lowering stress through living from purpose may lead to living longer (Buettner, 2010).

5. Purpose has an impact on other people. Your deepest purpose connects you with something other than yourself and engages you with the larger world of your job, family, college, and community. Your purpose has an impact on others, directly through the actions you take to teach or inspire and also indirectly through the sense of community you create for yourself and others. Stated simply, when your life has meaning, not only are you happier but others in your life experience the emotional contagion of your better mood (Hamilton, 2011; Hatfield, Cacioppo, & Rapson, 1994). In addition, individual happiness can build collective cultural happiness for others, rippling out as far as a whole nation (Buettner, 2010).

6. Purpose is the foundation for good time, task, and life management. Purpose connects you to more than just the moment by giving you the long view of your life, in which past, present, and future are all connected. You make progress toward a legacy while at the same time enjoying each moment, because everything important to you is in place and running in the background. Purpose defines the boundary between opportunity and distraction. When you are clear about your purpose, other people understand who you are, what you need, and how they can be resources for your goals.

Robison's Rule
Simplify your work by working from purpose.

Chapter 4

Your Mission

ONCE YOU HAVE articulated your life purpose, you are ready to build the next level of your Pyramid of Power (see Figure 4.1) by defining a mission statement. A mission statement answers the question, "How do I live out my life purpose?" Richard Bolles, author of the world's leading career book, *What Color Is Your Parachute?* (2013), wrote, "Your mission is where the world's deepest hunger and your heart's greatest gladness intersect."

Unlike your purpose statement, which will usually be true your entire life, a mission statement usually serves as guidance for about three to five years, although, in periods of rapid change, your mission statement may change even more frequently. It gives you direction until either it is achieved or it starts to seem outdated, at which point you will rewrite it, given your new opportunities and interests.

FIGURE 4.1

The Pyramid of Power: Mission

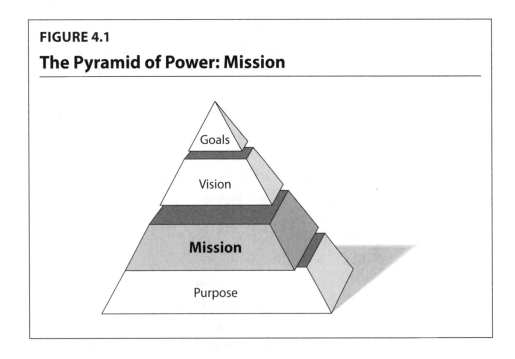

Here is the simplest form of the mission question:

If_____ is my purpose, then what shall I do to live out that purpose?

According to consultant and author Laurie Beth Jones, your mission represents a match between who you are and what you are doing. Longer and more concrete than a purpose statement, your mission statement will be written through a process, adapted from Jones's book, *The Path* (1998), that will guide you to explore your values, strengths, and the current and potential recipients of your actions. A good mission statement does three things: it uses your strengths, to serve people, in ways that you value.

Start with Strengths

In developing your mission statement, focus on your strengths; don't worry about your talents. Talents usually emphasize the part of a strength that is a given, an inborn ability; strengths are behaviors that you are naturally able to do, that you have developed further through education and practice, and that you engage in frequently enough to have mastered. Working from strength has been shown to bring happiness (Fredrickson, 2009) and lead to less stress and greater self-esteem, vitality, and positive affect (Wood, Linley, Maltby, Kashdan, & Hurling, 2011). In contrast, overrating talent can bring unhappiness (Colvin, 2008), because talent without its development does nothing for you or your world.

To understand the relationship between talent and strength, imagine your undeveloped talent as a precious stone—a diamond in the rough. Your strength is a diamond that has been cut and polished—a shiny miracle reflecting light off its facets. Although the presence of natural talent allows you to move through the learning process faster, just about anyone can learn a skill if they start early enough and practice extensively with the right feedback. In your discipline you have already developed many strengths through your education and accomplishments.

As in the joke about the tourists driving through Cambridge, Massachusetts, who asked how to get to Harvard and were told, "Study, study, study," a less talented person with more study and practice will exceed the accomplishments of a naturally talented person who never develops his or her talents. Peak performers achieve their best by combining natural talents with passion, study, and practice (Dweck, 2008; Ericsson, 2009). Your mission statement recognizes that sweet spot where your passion and your strengths meet.

List three strengths stated as action words that most describe you. Fill in each blank with a verb expressing some activity that you do well:

I_____ well.

I_____ well.

I_____ well.

Paths to Strengths

You have many more than three strengths, but for the sake of simplicity, aim at listing just three. In case your three greatest strengths didn't jump out at you, here are some ways to find them.

Formal Assessments

These are suggestions for three well-researched assessment tools that measure strengths.

1. The Virtues in Action: Chris Peterson developed this instrument (known as the VIA; see http:www.authentichappiness.com) by examining the virtues or strengths of all the major world religions, cultures, and philosophical systems and then distilling the results in a measure of 24 key strengths (Peterson & Seligman, 2004). The VIA compares your questionnaire answers to a worldwide sample and gives you feedback on both your top five self-rated strengths (out of a possible 24) and how your strengths compare to the people in the sample with demographic characteristics similar to yours.

The strengths revealed in the survey's feedback should feel like you. Here are some questions to test their authenticity.

Does this sound like me?

Would people who know me well say, "Yes, that is you"?

Does this strength come so naturally to me that I presume others are good at it too?

In my free time do I often use this strength during hobby and leisure activities?

Have there been times in my life when this strength, when overused, has gotten me into trouble? (For example, a person with the strength of humor might have gotten into trouble at school as a child for clowning instead of studying.)

2. The Gallup Strengths Finder: This instrument, developed by the Gallup Institute, compares your answers on a questionnaire to well-researched norms. Your top five strengths out of 34 are identified. Unlike the VIA, which is free online, the Gallup, with a hefty price tag of more than a thousand dollars per employee, is usually purchased by corporations. Individuals can take a shorter form of the instrument by purchasing the book *Now Discover Your Strengths* (Buckingham & Clifton, 2001) and using the included code to log in to the testing website. An alternative is to read the descriptions of the strengths described in *Strengths Finder 2.0* (Rath, 2007) and intuit which ones seem most like you.

3. The Realise 2: This instrument, developed by British psychologist Alex Linley measures sixty strengths. It is similar to the first two assessments listed here and has led to research on the relationship between strength development and increased potential for happiness and success (Linley, 2008; Linley, Willars, & Biswas-Diener, 2010).

Intuitive Methods

These non-instrument methods can help you discover your strengths.

1. Self-assessment: Think about skills you have. Some of the precursors for these strengths go back to your childhood activities that you did well in school, games, sports, hobbies, or family activities.

Ask several people closest to you what you do best. Interviews with work and personal friends might reveal different aspects of your personality but the overlap of the answers will provide clues to your strengths.

2. Interview assessment: A skilled coach can work with you to discover your strengths by asking questions similar to those listed earlier in the chapter. Adding the follow-up questions listed here will give you a more fine-tuned description of your strengths.

What do you love doing?

What parts of your current (or past) jobs have been so much fun, you can't believe you have been paid to do these things?

What do you do at work that makes you lose track of time—for example, teach, write, work in the lab, treat patients?

Allowing for some vocabulary differences, all the instruments and assessments discussed here should yield consistency in describing your strengths.

Try again to write your top strengths. Fill in each blank with a verb expressing some activity that you do well:

I_____ well.

I_____ well.

I_____ well.

Like your purpose statement, your strengths won't be totally unique since others are also good at those skills but it is the combination of your skill set that begins to shape what you do easily and well.

Explore Your Values

Your mission statement needs to be connected to your deepest values and to relate to your spiritual purpose—not in the sense of religious beliefs, although if you have such beliefs they may inform your discovery, but more in the sense of your responsibility to the greater community. Spiritual writer Matthew Fox referred to this kind of interconnected spirituality when he wrote, "both life and livelihood are about living in depth, living with meaning, purpose, joy, and a sense of contributing to the greater community" (Leider, 1997, p. 74).

To explore your relationship with the greater community, ask:

- How am I connected to the community?

- Who am I when I am the best I can be?

Values are abstractions that you care about and want to see more of in the world. Examples include truth, justice, beauty, love, faith, and success. You can probably write down many values that are important to you, but for this exercise narrow your list down to your top three to eight values. You are aiming at values that your authentically cherish, not just words on a page that sound good.

Another good way to discover your values is to explore what frustrates, annoys, or infuriates you, which suggests that you value the converse. For example, the fact that it bothers you to be lied to might suggest that you value honesty.

Faculty development expert and author Parker Palmer (2000) noted that his understanding of how his values informed his sense of purpose changed across his lifetime. While in his youth, he tried to "conjure up the highest values I could imagine and then try to conform my life to them whether they were mine or not." Later on, his understanding of vocation meant a calling he could hear: "Before I can tell my life what I want to do with it, I must listen to my life telling me who I am. I must listen for the truths and values at the heart of my own identity" (pp. 4–5).

To find out how you are living your values, observe how you spend your time and money. For example, if you buy convenience foods, then you probably value convenience. If you buy fresh ingredients and cook them yourself, then you probably value eating well over convenience.

Completing a twenty-four-hour time log for seven days will also reveal a lot about your values. After doing this assignment, one faculty client came to her next coaching session with this insight: "I must really value cleanliness, because I spend a lot of my time cleaning and straightening my house."

When your values conflict, decide how to honor those values in ways that show who you authentically are. Professor Clean decided to limit her cleaning time so that she could honor the values she held about her scholar role. When she enlisted the help of her husband and children in straightening up for 10 minutes at the end of each day, she felt that each morning brought a fresh start. The decision to reexamine her cleaning time led to her publishing more scholarly articles and brought the family closer as a community.

My values are the following:

Select the top eight values for your mission statement.

Identify Your Audience

Did you ever wonder why sometimes your teaching, writing, and professional presentations seem to go better than at other times? Most likely, things go well when you experience alignment among your purpose, strengths, values, and the needs of your audience. Specifying the ideal recipients for your professional activities will increase the chances that you perform at your peak while you are teaching, writing, or presenting for that audience.

List three groups of people for whom you use your strengths. Examples could include students, family, colleagues, synagogue members, or hiking club members.

Write Your Mission Statement

Using the raw data that you've compiled by identifying your strengths, values, and audience, fill in the blanks in this formula (Jones, 1998).

My mission is to_____,_____,_____ (action words)
for/ to/ with_____,_____,_____ (people or group),
who want_____,_____,_____ (your key value(s)).

You may want to write two mission statements, one for your professional life and one for your personal life.

My professional mission is to_____,_____,_____
(action words) for/ to/ with_____,_____,_____
(people or group), who want_____,_____,_____ (your key
value(s)).

My personal mission is to_____,_____,_____ (action
words) for/ to/ with_____,_____,_____ (people
or group), who want_____,_____,_____ (your key value(s)).

Your personal and professional statements will likely be similar and overlapping but may draw on different strengths and values or may be directed at different groups, such as students and colleagues at work and friends and family at home. One professor in a comparative anatomy department of a large medical school included "animals" in his professional mission because his job was to provide veterinary care to the research lab animals in the other departments at the medical school.

Here are some examples of faculty mission statements:

- "My mission is to research, promulgate, and teach the wonder of creation to and with my colleagues, students, and family who want fun, honesty, compassion, discovery, and wisdom." (biology professor at a mid-sized liberal arts college)

- "I teach, empower, and inspire students, family, and friends who want knowledge, wisdom, and perspective." (sociology professor at a small, private, religiously affiliated university)

Frequently Asked Questions

This section presents answers to questions that often came up in my workshops as participants developed their mission statements.

How do I know when I have a good mission statement?

A good mission statement does all of the following:

- It sounds like you.

- It inspires you.

- It includes specific actions you do.

- It provides a framework for other people to refer opportunities that will energize you.

What are the benefits to having a mission statement?

A mission statement gives you focus for your activities. However, your mission statement will be more concrete, behavioral, and action-oriented than your purpose statement. Your mission statement spells out what strengths you are choosing to develop at this stage of your life, what people you are choosing to serve with your activities, and what values you are emphasizing.

Do the people I serve really want my values?

Sometimes yes, and sometimes no. When you are living your mission, your audience of students and others get the real you with all your values and strengths, even if you never mention these things. Sometimes your audience is looking for those values, finds them in you, and appreciates their expression in your work. Other times, people in your audience might not even know, at the time, that they need those values but eventually might come to appreciate the way you lived those values.

A few years ago, I was doing this exercise with the audience at a higher education conference when one woman jumped up and declared, "Now I know why some of the students I work with tire me and others energize me. I have been spending more time with the group that does not appreciate my values when I should be spending more time with those that do."

How long will my mission statement be relevant?

While purpose statements are usually broad enough to describe a person from age 12 to age 82, mission statements change more frequently, often in cycles of three to five years. Since you have many talents in your talent gift package, your current mission will be specific to the current strengths, populations, and values that you are drawing on, whereas a future mission might draw on other strengths, populations, and values that are also authentic to who you are. For example, a professor early in her career might emphasize her teaching, writing, and research, with students as her prime target audience. That same professor in late career might teach fewer classes but focus more on mentoring younger associates in her lab and in her discipline.

After coaching many professors, I have developed a rough gauge for how long mission statements remain relevant during the stages of academic careers. Although there is a tendency for faculty early in their careers to base their choices on what others suggest as professional activities and for late-career faculty to be more self-determined, there are wide individual differences in applying these norms.

Junior faculty (year 1–6/7): every 1–3 years

Midcareer faculty (year 7–15): every 3–5 years

Senior faculty (year 16+): every 4–6 years

How do I know when I am doing my mission?

When you are choosing activities that you value, your to-do lists flow from your mission (more on this in Part 2 of this book). Even the boring or tedious tasks necessary to a job well done will go better when they are tied, at least indirectly, to your mission.

What if what I am working on is not on my mission statement?

This mismatch might happen because your mission statement has become obsolete and does not describe what is important to you at this time in your life and career or because you are not staying on task by matching your activities to your mission. If your mission statement is outdated, rewrite it so that your current activities align with it. If you are not staying on task but still value your mission, you may wish to make yourself accountable to others, such as a mastermind group (a group of colleagues who meet regularly to support one another and to hold one another accountable), a buddy coach, or a professional coach to keep you on task with activities consistent with your mission. Such accountability agents can also help you decide whether your mission statement still feels current and when to rewrite it if it is no longer current.

How do I deal with a transition when my mission needs to change?

First repeat the exercises in this chapter to review your strengths, values, and the list of people you work for and with. Then reshape your activities to match your new mission. Manuel, a philosophy teacher at a large, research-intensive university, began to experience his teaching assignments as mismatched to his newer scholarly interests in world peace issues. As his interest in teaching and researching peace studies deepened, he decided to create a small peace studies track for philosophy majors. Later, other departments with similarly interested faculty collaborated on a new interdisciplinary peace studies major and selected Manuel as director of the new program.

With your new mission articulated, you will see more clearly what activities to say "No" to that formerly were interesting and what new things to say "Yes" to. This transition will require some attention on your part and the use of your social intelligence skills (see Part 3 of this book) to gently handle the push-back you may receive from colleagues or friends who have locked in on the old you. In times of such change, seek social support for your new ventures.

Robison's Rule
Mission makes for strong yeses and easy nos.

Chapter 5

Your Vision and Goals

YOU HAVE ARTICULATED your purpose to describe why you are here on this earth. Then you stated your mission to describe what you will do when you live that purpose. Now it is time to develop a vision of the outcomes that will result from living your mission (completing your Pyramid of Power; see Figure 5.1). As you write your vision you will also write your goals, the action steps that lead to the accomplishment of your vision.

A vision translates your purpose and mission into the language of day-to-day choices and actions. Your vision gives clarity to your mission and purpose because vision compels you forward to the outcomes you hope will result if you live your ideal life. Leadership expert Peter Block (1993, 1996) called vision "the deepest expression of what we want." For professors, writing your vision means envisioning outcomes for your tripartite job description, such as improving your teaching by planning class assessments based on your pedagogical goals, building a body of work by publishing scholarly articles that connect to one another, and influencing your institution's development through service opportunities that match your strengths and interests. Vision answers the question "What will happen if I live my mission?"

FIGURE 5.1

The Pyramid of Power: Vision and Goals

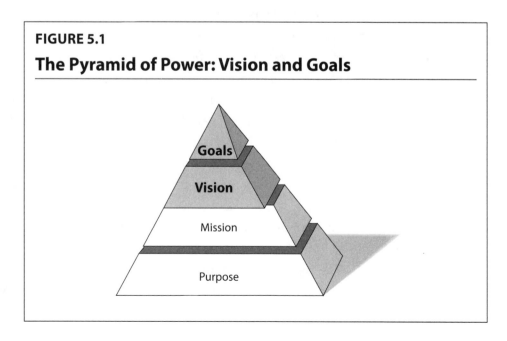

Here are some key terms I will be using throughout this chapter.

Vision: Vision describes the overall ideal life that you want. Your vision follows from your mission and purpose and is made up of six to eight vision statements that represent the areas of your life, such as family, home, work, and travel, that you consider to be most important. The vision statements act as structures to organize your goals. For example, if you have a vision statement about health, your vision statement might read, "I maintain my health so that I am vibrant and energetic for my work and my life." Nested under the health vision statement are goals related to health such as "to exercise regularly and to eat healthy." A vision statement about your scholarship might read, "My research is carefully done, creative, and contributes to my field." A scholarship goal under that vision statement might be "to write for thirty minutes a day."

Goal: A goal is anything you want to do or are already doing. Although the other elements of your pyramid could be considered goals in a general sense, in this chapter, the term will usually refer to the specific action steps that make the abstract philosophical pieces of your pyramid come alive and become real, answering the question "What will I do to live my mission so I can attain my vision?" Vision consists of an ongoing outcome or outcomes attained through the completion of goals.

To write the vision statements and goals, you will begin by imagining an overall vision. Later, you will develop the categories that serve as organizing structures for your goals, writing a vision statement as an umbrella summary of each category to describe the outcome experienced if you successfully reach the goals within the category. All your goals, personal and professional, will be nested inside of your six to eight vision statements. Your goals will answer the question "What are the actions I will do to reach my outcomes?"

Ron, an assistant professor of American history, has a vision about his research that states that he "contributes to my field through scholarly work." Under that vision he groups together one set of goals about how to stay current with relevant literature in the research field and another set about collegial collaboration. Both of those sets of goals help him attain the vision of contributing to his field. In the first set, he would include what he would read and what conferences he would attend to stay current in his field. In the second, he would include goals about his collaborations such as "collaborate with Sandra for the conference presentation," "brainstorm ideas," and "submit proposal."

The next sections will show you how to write your vision and your goals, a process that not only will yield the six to eight vision categories that give an organized structure to the many goals that you already have but also will allow for new goals and will connect all your goals to your purpose and mission.

How to Write Your Vision and Goals

Overall Vision

Experiment with writing an overall vision statement in response to this question about outcomes:

If I am doing my mission, what would be happening in me, the people close to me, my organization, and my community, both locally and globally?

The "me" part can include where you live and work, how much money you earn, what you gain from your work, and the like. The "world around you" part can include your immediate environment, both physical and social, as well as the larger world that you and your work might impact. Your vision represents all the results or outcomes, both proximal and distal, of your mission.

Magic Phone Call Question

This is another prompt for articulating an overall vision, in which you imagine the phone ringing in five years with someone on the other end asking you to do something you really want to do and have been training all your life to do. Who is it and what do they want you to do?

In building your Pyramid of Power, you will connect the answers to these questions by imagining future outcomes in your career and life that result from living your purpose and doing your mission in the present moment. Linking your goals with your vision completes the creation of your life management system, in which all that you do is connected to the results that you care about. Creating your pyramid will align your goals with your purpose so that you will feel less scattered, stressed, and overwhelmed.

Writing Vision Statements

Whereas your purpose and mission statements were short expressions of your purposefulness and intentionality, your vision statements will be the longest, most interesting, and most practical of the elements of your Pyramid of Power (see Figure 5.2) that we have covered so far.

There are two ways to approach writing these vision statements, the inductive method and the deductive method. If you use the inductive method, you will generate goals, including those you are already doing and those you might want to do, and then sort the goals into vision categories such as teaching, writing, health, and so on. If you use the deductive method, you will first define the vision categories of your life and then generate goals inside each category. Both methods are described in more detail later in this chapter. Although most professors prefer the inductive method, some prefer the deductive, so experiment with both methods to see which is more helpful to articulate your vision statements.

After using one or both methods, you will eventually have the same result: categories of vision areas with goals inside of them. At that time you will learn a specific method for writing the actual vision statements to describe how the goals in each category relate to an outcome for that category. The vision statements will be more descriptive than the short

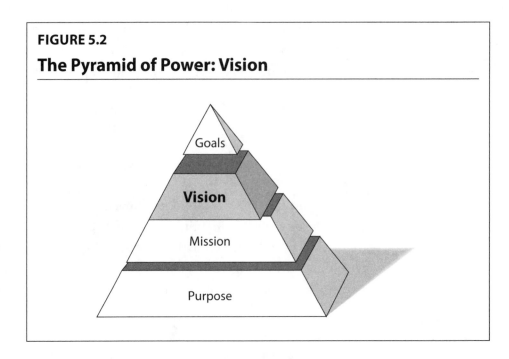

FIGURE 5.2
The Pyramid of Power: Vision

title of the category. For example, you might have a vision category about your teaching with a vision statement that reads, "I teach well using innovative teaching and assessment methods and creating stimulating learning environments." Inside that teaching vision would be many goals about revising courses, trying new pedagogical methods, connecting well with the students, and assessing the results.

Writing Goals

You already have many goals—more than you can complete in a lifetime. You probably make New Year's resolutions, set goals for what you want to accomplish in a semester or a summer, establish goals for house and garden maintenance on the weekend, and articulate long-range research, teaching, and other professional goals.

The key to creating the life you want is to have a system for organizing your goals so that you work on them in a timely fashion. As shown in Figure 5.3, your goals represent the final level of your Pyramid of Power and are always anchored to the rest of the pyramid. Studies show that you don't have to think about all your goals constantly to accomplish them. In fact, you don't want to use your brain's limited working memory to hold more goals than you are working on in the moment. You need a system to park and organize most of your goals so they run in the background while you work on a select few at a time (Baumeister & Tierney, 2011; Locke & Latham, 2006). During this step of developing your life management system, feel free to use the more general definition of goals to collect all of your goals, big and little, present and future, committed and not committed, outcome and action step—getting them out of your head and onto

FIGURE 5.3
The Pyramid of Power: Goals

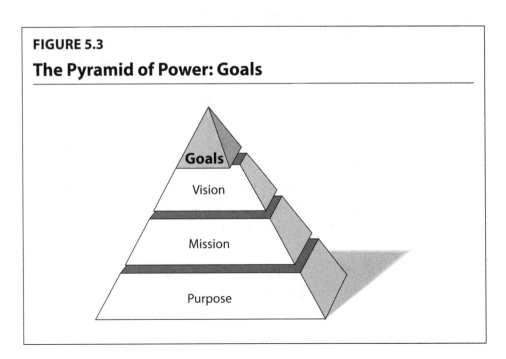

paper, so you can work on them in a timely fashion and free your prefrontal lobe areas to create, solve problems, and plan rather than trying to hold your goals in your awareness.

These specific terms will help you sort through all of the different kinds of goals you may be generating in the exercises that follow.

Goals: These are action steps toward an outcome inside a vision. Goals represent actions you really want to do as well as actions that you might not like to do but that are needed as a means to complete another goal. For example, you might not like filing your class notes, but you do like being able to find those notes later. Eventually, in Part 2 of this book, you will break down your goals into smaller units until you get them into *to-do's*, very small goals usually taking just fifteen to thirty minutes that can be put on a to-do list. A synonym for *to-do* is *task*. Example: "In order to write the Revolutionary War article, I am going to review and edit the first half of the article's literature review."

Fantasy goals: These are things that you want someone else to do but over which you have little or no control. Fantasy goals should be reconceptualized as goals over which you do have control. For example, a fantasy that your son will clean his room every Saturday is a fantasy because only he can choose to clean his room. To change that fantasy into a goal, set a goal of approaching your son with a proposal that if he cleans his room he can use the family car on Saturday night.

Dreams: These are results that you may want but to which you are not committed at this time. You may have varying degrees of control over these goals. What I call "dreams" resemble what Collins and Porras (2002) referred to as "BHAGs" (Big Hairy Audacious Goals)—goals that can be so outlandish they seem almost like fantasies, except that there just might be a way to achieve them. For example, "winning a Nobel prize" is a fantasy because you do not have control over being picked by the Nobel committee. You do have control over two related goals, however—namely, doing the kind of work for which the committee often awards prizes and networking with world-famous people in your field so that your name comes up when nominations are made. You don't have to figure out exactly how to make your dreams reality as you write them. For purposes of this goal-writing exercise, just get your dreams down on paper. When the time is right, you can get practical about how you will turn your dreams into goals.

Vision statements: These are the six to eight statements that describe aspects of your ideal life with an emphasis on outcomes. These statements act as categories that collect all of your goals so they will be less overwhelming. Later in this chapter you will write the actual vision statements, but first you will generate goals, using either the inductive method, in which you write goals and then sort them into categories, or the deductive method, in which you establish categories and then generate goals inside the categories.

Inductive Method: From Goals to Vision

When you use the inductive method, you will first write your goals and then sort them into vision categories. For this exercise, keep an open mind about goals in the general way discussed earlier—that is, include outcomes, dreams, and actions. This method follows these steps: (1) you first write your goals, then (2) you sort them into categories, and finally (3) you write vision statements summarizing each category.

Although you will eventually categorize your goals into six to eight vision categories, for the present moment just generate goals. Write your goals on small sticky notes (usually 2 inches by 3 inches)—one goal to each sticky. Using sticky notes allows you to move, park, and organize your goals in ways that are hard to do with written or electronic lists. Write as quickly as possible without editing or censoring yourself.

Eventually all of your goals must relate to your purpose, mission, and vision—in other words, the big picture of why you are here in this world, what you are doing while you are here, and what results you hope will result from your actions. For now, don't worry about how that will happen or whether some of your goals will compete with one another for resources. Trust the process; you will sort out the practicality of your goals later.

Here are some additional tips for writing goals:

- The goals you write do not have to be future oriented. It is important that you write goals for things you are already working on as well as for maintenance activities.

- Think about goals with varied time frames, from tomorrow to next week, next year, and 40 years from now. Goals can be as big and long-term ("I would like to retire at age 70 to do missionary work in Borneo") or mundane and short-term ("I want to take the dog for his checkup next week").

- Do not let money or other practical matters censor you. For the moment, suspend all your disbelief. At this point, you do not need to figure out whether that Victorian house you dream about is in San Francisco or on a farm in Iowa, or how you will get there from your present apartment in New York City.

- Use the "overall vision" and "magic phone call" questions discussed earlier in this chapter to ask yourself to imagine an outcome in the future that might result from your current activities. Then ask what you need to be doing now to increase the likelihood that you will reach that outcome.

These additional questions might be helpful prompts to generate goals:

- If I were living my purpose what would I be doing?
- What specific ideas come from my definitions of great work and great life?
- What are the most important things I want to accomplish professionally and personally in my life?
- What tasks are relevant to my mission and vision of my ideal life?
- How would I spend a typical day in my ideal life?

> The difference between a goal and a dream is the written word.
> —Gene Donohue

You might also use the "bucket list" method. In the movie *The Bucket List*, two men meet in a cancer ward and decide during a period of remission to do everything they want to do before they "kick the bucket." What is on your bucket list of professional projects you would like to complete before retirement? What is on your bucket list of life goals?

- What professional accomplishments would you like to complete?
- What fellow professionals would you like to collaborate with?
- What famous people do you want to meet?
- What awards would you like to win?
- What would you most want to be known for?
- What hobbies would you like to explore?
- Where would you like to visit?
- Do you want to have a/another child?
- What daring or exciting things would you like to try? E.g. parachute out of an airplane? Live in an exotic land? Play a flute in a quartet?

Don't be afraid of using too many sticky notes or making a mess. At this stage, you are just brainstorming goals without committing to any of them. We will organize the mess shortly.

Include broad goals like "write some books," "have children," "renovate a Victorian house," and "save for retirement" as well as specific goals like "continue working out at the gym three times a week for 20 minutes," "write for 15 minutes a day," and "redesign the lab procedure on sensation and perception for Intro Psych." It might take you several days with bursts of goal writing before you wind down. Even then, push yourself to come up with a few more. The more sticky notes you create, the better. Aim to produce hundreds of goals written on sticky notes. The object of this exercise is to get all of your goals and dreams out of your head. Later you will corral them into a Dream Book. Your life management system will hold the goals so that your brain has space in your working memory to focus on a few goals at a time.

The process described here allows your goals to be:

- parked until relevant

- completed in a timely fashion when relevant

- eliminated when no longer relevant

- created as new opportunities present themselves

Writing every goal, present and future, helps your brain in three ways:

1. Writing your goals prevents cognitive overload. Your memory has a limited capacity, although it is probably not rigidly restricted to seven items, plus or minus two, as urban legend would have it. Memory capacity depends on content, chunking bits of information with like items, individual differences, and other complex variables (Miller, 1956, 2003). No matter what your individual memory capacity, it would be presumptuous of you to think that you could hold hundreds of goals in your memory without writing them down.

2. Writing your goals opens a spaciousness in your brain that makes you smarter and more creative as new ideas find their way in. This process helps you avoid the "Dead Sea" phenomenon, in which new ideas cannot flow into your brain because nothing ever flows out.

3. Writing helps you create goals that will be real, compelling, and inspiring (Klauser, 2001). Writing down goals activates your reticular activating system (RAS), the section of your brain that acts like a telephone switchboard, sending messages to higher centers about what to attend to. In its default mode, the RAS is usually too busy looking for danger and novelty to notice your life goals, but the process of writing and reviewing your goals primes your RAS to notice ways to make the dreams come true. Your ideas will seem to connect more easily and, almost as if by magic, opportunities and supportive people will come into your life—people and opportunities that would never have appeared as long as your goals remained only in your mind and not on paper. What people might call "luck" is actually the result of this priming.

When you have written down all your goals, you are ready to connect the dots of your vision by grouping similar goals. Temporarily, park your goals on your dining room table, rug, wall, a poster board, or different colored sheets of 8½-by-11-inch pieces of paper. Collect similar goals into categories representing areas of your life. Although the exact categories will vary from person to person, keep to only six to eight categories so that you can manage them later. The categories will act as containers for catching and holding new dreams and goals. There is no one perfect way to categorize. You can keep reorganizing as you go. Once you have categorized your goals, you can skip down to the section on how to write your vision statements, or you can read the next section on how to experiment with the deductive method for generating goals.

Deductive Method: From Vision to Goals

The deductive method asks you to describe the overarching vision of your life, broken down into six to eight categories with goals nested inside those categories. Then you will write a vision statement as an umbrella over each category, summarizing the desired outcome if the goals in that category are accomplished. This method follows these steps: develop life categories, then write goals inside the categories, and finally write vision statements summarizing each category.

1. Start with an overarching vision of your life. This vision is the answer to the question "What will my life be like if I live my mission?" You might review your answers to the questions listed at the beginning of Part 1 of this book. In case you are stumped, here are some common inspirations for vision:

- Famous people who have accomplished things you admire

- Societal change such as opportunities for women or the arrival of the Internet

- Historical events such as the terrorist attacks of September 11, 2001

- Inspirational literature, such as sacred scripture or a groundbreaking book in your discipline

- Perceptions of social problems such as poverty

- The deepest desires of your heart

2. Break your big life vision into smaller areas of vision. Each vision area is the answer to the question, "What do I want out of life in this area?" Use the categories of your ideal life as you described them in Chapter 2 including categories such as health, teaching, work, and others.

3. Generate goals under each vision area that would make this area of your life satisfying. Write these goals on small sticky notes. For example, if one of your areas is teaching, you might write goals about learning the new course website program and about experimenting with a new assessment method.

These questions might help you generate goals in each vision area:

- What would be happening in this area of my life if I were living my purpose by doing my mission?

- For this area of my life to go well, what would I have to do?

- If order for my vision to come true, what goals would I need to work on?

- What goals am I already doing that support this area?

Packages of small sticky notes contain 800 notes; write as many goals as possible in each category. Writing a goal does not constitute committing to it. The beauty of using sticky notes is that you can toss the irrelevant ones later without having cross-outs staring at you from a written list.

After generating goals inside your vision areas, you are ready to write vision statements.

Guidelines for Writing Vision Statements

Whether you used the inductive method, by writing your goals and then dividing them into vision categories, or the deductive method, by creating vision categories and then writing the goals, you are now ready to write *vision statements*.

1. Look at the six to eight categories in which you have placed the sticky notes. Aim to work with categories that give you a "good enough" system to get started for where you are with your life. Like your mission, your vision will change as you and your life change.

2. Write a vision statement for each category on medium-size sticky notes, describing the outcome of what will happen for you and the world around you if you live your mission and complete the goals inside that vision category.

3. Write the vision statements in the present tense even if those statements are not currently true. While common sense would suggest that a vision statement should be written in the future tense because the vision concerns the future, vision statements written in the present tense creates immediacy by priming your brain's reticular activating system to scan the

environment for people to call, things to do, and places to go. This state will propel one's brain forward to resolve the discrepancy between the status quo and the dream by setting into motion actions or goals.

4. Experiment with writing big vision statements, or Big Hairy Audacious Goals (BHAGs; Collins & Porras, 2002)—goals so big that they seem unachievable even though they can be articulated concisely. An example of an organizational BHAG is President Kennedy's 1961 exhortation to "put a man on the moon by the end of the decade." A personal example might be "to retire to Maui in ten years."

Carla, a biology teacher who valued the wonder of the human body, wrote this vision statement about caring for herself: "I am a good steward of my health in body, mind, and spirit." Although her ideal practices for eating well, exercising regularly, and getting plenty of sleep were not yet consistent when she wrote the vision statement, the discrepancy between her vision statement written in the present tense and her present state propelled her to set small goals that would eventually make the statement true.

5. Write the vision statements as vividly as possible. Use sensory images to see, hear, and feel what is happening as a result of living your mission. You might choose to bring vividness into your vision with poems, songs, drawings, or collages of pictures representing aspects of the vision.

About her teaching, Carla wrote, "My teaching is like pebbles I drop into a very large lake to create far-reaching ripples as my students apply the information from my well-prepared classes to live more intelligently in the world."

And here are examples of nonprofessional vision statements that other professors have written:

> "I learn, practice, and perform music with my flute in order to stay relaxed and refreshed for my work."

> "My home is clean, organized, and aesthetically pleasing and supports me, my spirit, and my work."

> "I am saving 5% of each paycheck for the future to be able to travel with my husband and family."

6. Double-check to see whether all the goal sticky notes that you like fit somewhere under the overarching vision statements. If some of the sticky notes don't seem to fit anywhere, park them in a location labeled "miscellaneous" or "later." Keep refining your vision statements until they describe six to eight main themes that can encompass all the sticky notes, allowing you to eliminate the "miscellaneous" category.

7. Review and revise your vision statements as needed without becoming perfectionistic. You may never arrive at a "perfect" set of vision statements, since vision statements can change quite often, sometimes in less than five years. You may have several successive visions developed from one mission statement, or you may create new visions to coordinate with new mission statements. Sometimes, some of the same vision statements remain viable, even when you find it necessary to rewrite your mission, because those statements are still desired outcomes of your new mission.

8. Continue writing goals as you think of them. Carry a pack of sticky notes with you. Have them on your desk, in the kitchen, where you read, and next to the chair where you watch TV. Every time you have a thought about something you want to do (for example, "we should get that chair reupholstered"), write the thought down on a sticky note. Capture research ideas, book ideas, grocery lists, home improvement projects, and gift ideas.

9. Once you have been writing down your goals for a while, you might notice information related to your goals coming into your life. For example, if you have a goal of building an addition to your house, you will notice when a friend mentions a building contractor who is remodeling his home. This synergy results from priming your reticular activating system to scan the environment for resources.

By now you have quite a mess of sticky notes on your dining room table, grouped into categories, with vision statements written for each category. It is time to organize that creative mess into a wonderful tool that will house your vision, sub-visions, projects, and to-do's, both professional and personal, in one place where you can review and revise them as you choose.

Robison's Rule
You will always have more goals than you can achieve. A life management system will help you achieve the ones that really matter.

Chapter 6

The Dream Book

NOW THAT YOU have created your Pyramid of Power, you are ready to use the Dream Book as the second key to productive and effective life management. The Dream Book functions as your guidebook to the life you want to live.

Dream Globally, Live Locally

A two-fold tool that helps you manage your life, the Dream Book allows your creative brain to generate many ideas—to dream globally. The Dream Book also provides a place for your discerning brain to decide which goals to invest in—in other words, to live locally.

Once you reassure yourself that an abundance of goals is a good thing, you will get in the habit of noticing ideas as they bubble up. Transferring goals into the Dream Book will help you feel less overwhelmed because you don't have to take up brain space to remember your goals. While it is possible to attempt to work on too many goals simultaneously, you can never have too many stored goals, as long as they stay stored until you are ready for them. The Dream Book gives you one place to create, park, and organize all of your goals, personal and professional, until you are ready to work on them or discard them. To paraphrase the Paul Masson wine slogan, "No goal before its time." For example, if you want to learn to play a flute someday, write goals about buying a flute and taking flute lessons. Park them in the Dream Book under your vision statement about hobbies or artistic expression until you are ready. Later you can make practical tasks for the goal, such as "research flute stores." The Dream Book can also provide a tool to track and manage long-range goals and large projects, such as writing a book, as you work on them across months or years until completion.

All of these instructions for developing your Dream Book can be translated into a Dream Wall or into electronic systems. Whichever you choose depends on how your brain likes to work. In my workshops, about one out of six participants prefer a Dream Wall on which they park all their sticky notes, where they can be managed daily; the other five out of six participants prefer a book or electronic file because they don't like the visual clutter of a Dream Wall. You may find that using a wall or another method that suits you better but for shorthand purposes I will just refer to the Dream Book. Caution: don't get too fancy with commercially available project management software; you can get bogged down in managing the software instead of managing your life.

Constructing Your Dream Book

To put together your Dream Book you will need the following:

- An 8½" × 11" three-ring notebook
- Three sheets of plain white paper
- Several sheets each of six to eight colors of 8½" × 11" copy paper
- Notebook dividers
- Plastic presentation sleeves

You will place the three pieces of plain white paper in the beginning of your notebook followed by the dividers and colored paper. First, punch holes in the papers and line them up in this order:

- *Page 1:* Your purpose statement, printed in a large font—this is like a dedication of your Dream Book.

- *Page 2:* Your mission statement—this is like a preface that tells the reader why this book is written. If you have written both a personal and a professional mission statement, include both on this page.

- *Page 3:* A table of contents, designating your vision statements as chapter headings.

- *Page 4 and after:* Vision chapters, formed by using a notebook divider or tab for each vision. Follow each divider with paper in a different color for each category of your vision, such as green pages for your household goals, blue for teaching, yellow for research and writing, and so on. Paste the appropriate sticky notes, for goals related to each vision statement, onto the colored paper in the chapter for that vision statement.

Some people like to get artistic with their Dream Books by color-coding the titles of their vision statements on the table of contents page in the same color as the colored pages in that section and having extra tabbed pages for subvisions or projects (ongoing large goals or time-limited ones). Keep your Dream Book as simple as possible so that you will actually use it instead of just admiring it.

From Global Dreams to Local Lives

Once you have most of your goals organized into the vision categories, you will probably notice that some of your big global goals have smaller goals nested under them that need to be completed in order to complete the big goals. Some of those big goals, such as "continue to publish my scholarly work," are ongoing parts of your vision and will never be completed until you no longer do scholarly work. You might think of this first type of big goals as *subvisions* of your vision. In contrast, you will also have big goals of a second type: these are time-limited and will be completed. We will refer to these goals as *projects*. An example of a project would be a specific scholarly article that will be completed and published.

Your goals may start to organize themselves into subvisions and projects, but if not, don't be concerned. It is fine to keep many goals in each vision category until it is time to follow the directions in Part 2 of this book for taking big general goals and breaking them down into small, specific, doable goals that can be put on a daily to-do list. In case it makes sense to you to continue the categorizing process here, the breakdown of your vision categories might look like this: (1) vision breaks down into (2) subvisions (ongoing) and projects (time limited), which in turn break down into (3) goals.

> ### *Example: Subvisions and Projects*
> *This example shows how one professor, Carla, used the complexity discussed in this chapter in her Dream Book. If you want a simpler system, just collect all of your goals under your vision until you are ready to work on them.*
>
> *After Carla wrote the vision statement about her teaching vision category, she found she had a number of ideas about how to improve her teaching. She grouped these into ongoing subvisions, with a project grouped under one of her subvisions and goals that will be her action steps grouped under the project.*
>
> - *My students are gaining the professional training they will need for their jobs.*
>
>   *Design and teach a new practicum course*
>
>   > *Study the research about practicum education*
>   >
>   > *Collect syllabi from other practicum courses*
>
> - *My students are developing the critical thinking skills to evaluate information and sort it out with wisdom and discernment.*
>
> - *My students are applying their knowledge to their families and organizations where they work.*

When it is time to work on that project, Carla will develop and track it following the steps outlined in Part 2 of this book. Carla could also add project ideas to the other two subvisions as well or just park them for later when she chooses to work on those areas.

There are two options for organizing the pages of each vision chapter.

1. Option One is to post related goals on a separate piece of colored paper perhaps grouped into subvisions or projects.

Example 1: Health and fitness vision→Exercise goals→Learn Pilates→ Sign up for a Pilates class at the community center
Example 2: Work vision→Teaching goals→Improve course design→ Take workshop on course design at Teaching and Learning Center

2. Option Two is to organize the categories within the vision chapters by time frames. Under each vision statement, different pages are devoted to different time frames, as follows:

First page—immediate goals, further organized into projects or left alone

Second page—midrange goals, further organized into projects or left alone

Third page—long-range goals, further organized into projects or left alone

You can mix the two organizational options as you create your Dream Book or invent your own organizational plan. What you are aiming for is a system that makes sense to you. Any system that doesn't work for you is a waste of your time and effort, which could be better spent working on your goals.

You can set up your vision pages with a portrait orientation or with a landscape orientation (so that you turn your Dream Book sideways, with the notebook rings and binding at the top). Leave the backs of the pages in your Dream Book free, so that you can move completed goals there for easy reference when it is time to do an annual report or rewrite your resume.

Table 6.1 gives you a template for the order of the pages of the vision section of the Dream Book, followed by an example in the right-hand column of how the template could be used by our exemplary professor, Carla. The vision chapters of your Dream Book provide the place to park random goals and develop projects under each vision. This is a typical arrangement that other professors have used, but whatever arrangement you use, make it flexible for your needs. Limit the number of your vision statements to six

TABLE 6.1

Vision Chapters: Sample Organization with Examples

Sample	Example
Vision 1	Home: My home is clean, organized and aesthetically pleasing and supports me, my spirit, and my work.
Subvision 1	Aesthetically pleasing
Project 1	Remodel the bathroom
Goals	Look through bath design books
	Collect referrals for bath people
	Go to booths at home show
Project 2	Refurnish the living room
Goals	Visit furniture stores
Vision 2	Scholarly work: I develop and complete creative ideas for research that contribute to the field.
Project 1	Submit three articles for peer reviewed journals a year
Project 2	Conduct four conference presentations a year with my students

to eight. You can have as many vision categories, projects, and goals as you like as long as you don't expect to work on them simultaneously.

Example: Developing Projects

Carla continued to use the template in Table 6.1 to develop all of her vision statements and all of the components nested under them. Practice writing a title for one of Carla's teaching projects represented by the following goals:

- *Give students ungraded "before" and "after" tests on key course concepts before the course starts and after it ends.*

- *Analyze the differences in the concepts before and after.*

- *Outline an article to be submitted to an academic journal.*

Title of project:

Carla used the title "Teaching—Scholarship," because she wanted to study student learning in preparation for publishing research on her teaching effectiveness. Since these goals are part of Carla's research plans, the goals could also be moved to her research pages. The Dream Book is a flexible system; there is no one perfect way to use it except as it works for you. In Table 6.1, you will notice that Carla keeps her goals for her personal visions (house remodeling) and her professional ones (scholarship and teaching) in the same Dream Book.

Use the Dream Book for Any Project

Use your Dream Book as a planning tool for developing a project. Store articles, photos, business cards, sticky notes of tasks, and any other auxiliary materials related to a project inside the pages of the relevant vision chapter, using plastic sleeves for loose items. If you prefer filing articles in manila folders or storing them on a research site in the cloud, place a sticky note in your Dream Book in the appropriate vision chapter to remind you where the files are located.

Sometimes a project will outgrow your main Dream Book and need its own dedicated Dream Book. Some examples of large projects needing separate Dream Books are the following:

- *Research article:* A goal about an article you want to write might start out with a single sticky note on a page in a vision chapter, grow into a project with several pages of its own, and then expand into its own Dream Book containing sections like "literature review" or "equipment design ideas." You might house photocopied articles abstracts inside plastic sleeves (or in the cloud) within the sections, along with any notes, outlines, lists, and sticky notes. By the time you sit down to work on the article, most of your background reading will be collected.

- *House remodeling project:* An extensive house project may begin with a few brochures on kitchen cabinets and granite selections dropped into a plastic sleeve in your "Home" vision chapter. When your project expands to its own Dream Book, the project will have many goals in subcategories for "cabinets" "paint colors," and "granite types."

- *Special events:* You might use a separate Dream Book for a personal event such as a wedding or for a professional event or conference, gathering business cards for various vendors of programs and invitations, videographers and sound technicians, hotel or event spaces to rent, and food services, and corralling them inside plastic sleeves in the relevant sections. Eventually, you would keep the signed contracts in the Dream Book and toss the other information. Then you would bring the Event Dream Book along to the event just in case there were any contract glitches with the vendors.

Work Your System: Some Reminders

Your work on your Pyramid of Power and Dream Book is futile unless you make your Dream Book a living document that you use. The following practices will make it a long term motivator:

- Keep small packs of sticky notes and little golf pencils in your coat pocket, in your briefcase, by the side of your bed, on the bathroom vanity, in the car, on the kitchen windowsill, and so on. Then any time you get a thought about something you hope to accomplish in your career or something fun that you want to do, write it on a sticky note and park it in the relevant chapter.

- About once a month or so, have a planning session in which you generate and gather goals. Park them in the vision chapters in the Dream Book, on the Dream Wall, or in an electronic device. Park those goals that don't fit anywhere in a location designated "miscellaneous" or "later."

- Whenever you find yourself unable to categorize a large number of miscellaneous goals, revise your vision or mission statements to ones that most currently represent your work and your life.

- Review the Dream Book periodically (monthly or quarterly, and annually) to pull out goals that you want to work on.

- When the goals are completed, store them in the Dream Book on the back side of the relevant chapter pages.

- Following the practices outlined in Part 2 of this book, take dreams, decide whether or not to do them, and turn them into actionable goals with smaller subgoals or to-do items as steps.

Alignment Anxiety

Your life management system is created. You have articulated your dreams about your ideal life. So the rest should be easy, right?

It isn't. And you shouldn't expect it to be.

If you are feeling a bit anxious as you complete the exercises in this part of the book, you are normal. Anxiety is a natural reaction that goal-oriented professionals experience as they recognize the gap between their dreams and their current reality. Workshops and books like this one raise your expectations about wanting something better for yourself and the world around you. The more passionate you are about your vision and the clearer it is, the more you will want it, and the more you will hurt when what you want seems so far away from where you are.

In the next section, we will set in place a key strategy for lowering this anxiety: the principle of alignment, which supports you in developing habits and practices about your use of time and other resources, practices which will help you to get closer to your ideal life. Instead of getting up each morning and starting on a to-do list wondering why you are doing those things, you will start from the "why" of doing things and proceed to create a to-do list that makes sense to you and that you are excited about. As a result you will feel in charge of those lists instead of controlled by them. Your anxiety will be more manageable as you complete goals in a timely and even enjoyable way, while the vision of your ideal life unfolds with ease, harmony, and balance.

Robison's Rule
Dream big; sticky notes are cheap.

Part Two

Align Your Life with Your Power

I am personally persuaded that the essence of best thinking in the area of time management can be captured in this single phrase: Organize and execute around priorities.

—Stephen R. Covey

ONCE YOU HAVE articulated your philosophy of life in your Pyramid of Power, the classic time management questions of "How do you want to use your time?" and "What are time wasters for you?" become useful, because the pyramid gives you a tool to align your time and activities with your priorities. The danger in creating your pyramid and Dream Book, however, is that you may park your dreams in your Dream Book never to look at them again, so that all you end up creating is an archive of your unlived life. Even those professors who put together dynamite pyramids often fall short in implementing them, not because these professors are lazy or unmotivated but because they suffer from *alignment anxiety*, the discouragement, guilt, and anxiety that people may feel when they contrast their conceptualized ideal lives with their actual lives.

Panic may set in as you ask, "Am I walking my talk?" You may feel that you are not living up to your own ideals. The natural response to that anxiety is to escape or avoid our goals so they don't remind us of our failure to achieve them. While following such a path of least resistance does allow you to stop feeling bad in the short term, in the long term it leads to a maladaptive pattern of avoiding work on the very goals that would narrow the gap and bring your ideal life and your current life into better congruence (Fritz, 1989).

Experiencing alignment anxiety is not such a bad thing. Research shows that when people get too complacent about what they have accomplished *to date* they sometimes lose motivation and end up not completing a project, yet when they look ahead at what they still need *to do*, they become motivated to stay the course (Koo & Fishbach, 2008). The effective antidote to alignment anxiety is not to avoid goals but to approach them by implementing practices that keep you working on your highest-priority goals without becoming overwhelmed by trying to do too much at once. Studies on conflicting goals show they are not good for you because they cause you to increase worrying and get less done; if the conflicts are long term, they can cause your psychological and physical well-being to suffer (Emmons & King, 1988).

Although no one ever closes the alignment gap all the way, the techniques in this part of the book for planning and executing the steps toward your dreams will help you narrow that gap sufficiently to lower the anxiety or at least make it tolerable, to stop the avoidance that occurs whenever you think about your goals, and to allow you to live closer to your ideal life with balance and grace. These tips will help to prevent discouragement, paralysis, and procrastination about what you still need to do to get closer to your ideal:

- Keep perspective about alignment. You have to both do the right stuff and do stuff right. To do the right stuff, you will learn a discernment exercise to define what the right stuff is—namely, the high-impact tasks that extend your sphere of influence to students, colleagues, family, and friends. To do stuff right, you will learn a set of practical techniques that will help you to complete high-impact work in a timely fashion so you have the free time and energy to create the non-work part of your life.

- Set a proactive agenda for work and life, by creating goals from your vision and establishing your priorities for their completion. Your agenda forms the basis of how you discern whether new opportunities, especially other people's requests, align with your agenda. Professors often take on projects because they "sound interesting" without any regard for how those projects fit with the other things going on at that time. Unlike Gen I time management programs that encourage you to pack more and more into the same time frames, Gen II life management programs emphasize working from alignment so that you do not overwhelm yourself by working on too many things at once.

- Break large goals into smaller ones, so small that you can complete a few of them each work day until their completion cumulates towards the completion of big goals and projects.

To prevent being overwhelmed, continue to park all those wonderful ideas, one idea to each sticky note filed under the appropriate vision statements in your Dream Book, at the same time as you follow the process outlined in this part of the book to translate a finite number of great ideas into action. The long-term cumulative effect of completing those goals will be increased productivity and satisfaction.

How Part 2 Will Help You Become a Peak Performing Professor

This part of the book will guide you through these steps:

1. Review your Dream Book and prioritize the vision statements or projects that seem particularly important or timely to you right now. These will become the focal point of your activities.

2. Pull out all goals relevant to that current vision and organize related goals into projects that you want to work on at this time.

3. Organize projects using the task management tools (backward planning, Tracking Sheets, Daily Tracking Sheets, VAST to-do lists, the Focused 15) described in the chapters that follow to outline the tasks of each project and break those tasks into smaller and smaller subtasks until you have daily to-do lists of small actions that allow you to complete each of the projects without becoming overwhelmed.

4. Organize your resources (time, money, people, and space) to support the completion of each project.

5. Set the standards that you wish to attain and the ways you wish to measure your success.

6. Celebrate that success.

7. Repeat steps 1–6 as needed.

Chapter 7

Establish Priorities

THE FIRST STEP to better alignment between your real life and your ideal one is to use your Pyramid of Power as a prism through which to filter your many opportunities into a few commitments. In Part 1, you wrote all of your goals—big and small, present and future—on sticky notes, categorized them into vision statements, and then used those statements as the organizational structure for chapters in your Dream Book. You may start noticing that some of your goals group themselves readily into subvisions and projects, whereas some goals may not seem to be connected to any others.

Now, you need to figure out which projects, with their accompanying goals, you wish to work on. You will do best to focus on just a few projects or a small number of goals at a time. Limiting the number of projects and goals will actually result in you getting more done over the long haul. Exactly how many you can work on simultaneously depends on many factors, such as how large and ambitious the projects are as well as how they coexist with one another, but I generally recommend no more than three projects at a time. The determination of your workload is an empirical matter: if you are overwhelmed, you are doing too much; if you are bored, either you are not working on enough projects or you are working on the wrong ones.

Organizing goals into a structure will go a long way toward lowering alignment anxiety because it allows you to work on many goals within several projects without overwhelming yourself. Even before you have completed your goals, having a plan to do so will boost your confidence. But first we have to decide what goals to work on.

Let us review the organization structure of your Dream Book that we established in Chapter 6. The simplest structure is to place your goals that are written on sticky notes inside of your vision chapters much the way that little Russian wooden dolls, called *matryoshka*, are nested inside each other. Some of your goals are small enough to stand alone while others will be organized or nested inside your vision chapters under subvisions and projects. Use the level of complexity that matches the complexity of your work and life. Eventually, you will decide to work on goals and will need to break goals down to the smallest action steps possible, steps that take no more than 15–30 minutes each. In this book, those very small action steps are called to-dos because they are so small that they can be put on a to-do list for the day or week. These small to-dos are the only goals listed on a to-do list. No longer will you write a to-do like "design course," which sits there staring at you every day while you procrastinate about it and feel bad. Your big goal of "design course" will be broken into many small to-dos, such as "review textbook # 1" and "write the Big Questions that the course will answer." To summarize the Dream Book structure: (1) each vision chapter is broken down into (2) subvisions or Projects, which in turn are composed of (3) goals, which can be broken down into to-dos.

> ### Example: Setting Goals
> *Atol is a professor, physician, and researcher at a leading medical school who wants to take better care of himself. Here is an outline of how he sets goals toward that vision:*
>
> I. *Vision: stay fit and healthy*
>
>   A. *Subvision (this is an ongoing goal that is never finished): eat healthier*
>   1. *Goal: eat nine fruits and vegetables a day*
>   2. *Goal: eat a substantial breakfast daily*
>   B. *Project (this is a time-limited goal that has an end): plan meals for two weeks*
>   1. *Goal: cook double batches on weekends to have leftovers*
>   a. *To-do: write shopping list*

You will use three elements—passion, vision, and mission—to establish your priorities. The following sections discuss these approaches.

Passion

When your passion and your work come together you will experience the power of full engagement in which your productivity flows easily, and your satisfaction is high (Loehr & Schwartz, 2004). While many career coaches tout working from passion as an ideal, it may be an overrated ideal, because passion ebbs and flows. Sometimes your work might not be intrinsically exciting itself but might be a means to an end necessary to fulfill a larger passion. Other times your passion may be centered in your personal life or in just one area of work but may not be evoked in all areas of your life. You can still do great work even when your passion is not evoked, as long as the work feels somehow connected to your sense of meaning and purpose.

You should also be aware of the dark side of passion, namely, the suffering. The word passion comes from the Greek verb *passio*, which means to suffer. When Joseph Campbell exhorted a generation of workers to "follow your bliss," he might have forgotten to mention that the word *bliss* comes from the French word *blessure*, an injury (Campbell, 1991). When you want something badly and it does not go well, it is as though you have suffered an injury. Sometimes even when what you feel passionate about is going well, you suffer because of the short-term sacrifices you are making for long-term gain. In support of this point, I offer Exhibit A: this book you are reading. I sacrificed a lot of frivolous fun to write this book, and I sure hope the process will have been worthwhile.

Sometimes, though, you will be in a position of loving what you do so much that you feel it is amazing that people pay you to do it. Working like this in your peak performance zone allows you to experience more flow, when you feel so in sync with your tasks that time melts away, the work becomes effortless, and you do your best work (Csikszentmihalyi, 2008). To give yourself the best chance to work in that zone, ask these questions about your passion and the areas that you might be passionate about:

- What interests have been with me since childhood?
- What activities do I do that are so engaging that I achieve that flow state?
- What work do I already do that I would do even if I weren't paid?
- What interests do I have that I pursue when I have time off?
- What are problems in my field that are holding up progress for me and other scholars and that if solved would open up possibilities?
- What issues in the news particularly annoy or engage me, and how does my training within my discipline prepare me to address them?
- What problems in the world would I help fix if only I had the resources and skills to do so?

Your passion can give you focus. While you won't always get to do only your ideal work, when you do align the right tasks, values, and recipients, it is as if the stars and sun and moon all come together. Here are several prompts for projects that could close your alignment gap, decrease alignment anxiety, and excite your passion.

- Courses
- Students
- Research topics

- Service and leadership opportunities
- Contributions to your discipline
- Community involvement

Vision

The second technique for establishing priorities is vision. Go to your Dream Book and glance at each Vision chapter where you have parked your goals and answer these questions:

Timing

- Which of my vision statement(s) is the most important at this time? Why?

- Are there any vision statements that can be parked until later dates? What is my "default future" or consequences if I don't work on these vision statements at this time?

- Is this the best time in my life for this vision or project and all that it would involve?

- Is there a primary vision statement and a secondary one that I can work on at the same time?

- What dreams do I have parked in my Dream Book whose time has finally come?

- Are there any subvisions or projects that are important and timely?

Job Description and Priorities

- Which vision statements are most important to my job description as defined by my institution? What are the top priorities that flow from my job description and the expectations of my institution, and how are they connected to my vision?

- Are there any parts of my job description that I have been ignoring because of lack of motivation that could become more interesting to me if I tied them into my Pyramid of Power?

- How can I negotiate priorities about this vision (or project) with my boss or bosses so as to serve both myself and my institution?

Mission

A third factor useful in establishing priorities is your mission. These questions help you consider how your projects relate to your mission.

Strengths

- What projects am I considering that make the best use of my strengths?

- What use of my strengths would make the world (campus, community) a better place?

- Do my current projects use those strengths?

- Are my current projects directed toward my mission?

- Are my current projects necessary for my mission?

- Is a particular project of mine the shortest, most effective route to my mission or is it redundant to other projects?

- What are the highest standards for these projects, and what is the minimum standard that would accomplish the goals for the project?

People

- Which people represent the best target groups for my strengths?

- Would a particular project have me working with the people whom I feel called to serve or seem to serve best?

- Are there other groups I am neglecting that might be better aligned with my mission?

- What would it take to be better aligned with those people?

Values

- What are my most important values that I want my target groups of people to get from my work?

- How are my values being expressed in my current projects?

- How could my values be expressed in my proposed projects?

Once you have established your priorities, you are ready to learn how to manage the projects and goals that you have decided to work on.

Robison's Rule
Structure brings clarity and freedom.

Chapter 8

Align Projects with Priorities

THIS CHAPTER WILL help you discern which projects to spend your time on and how to decide on priorities. Having clear priorities would keep you focused on what activities will move you toward your most important goals.

Which Projects Further Your Visions?

Once you have decided which vision statement or statements to work on, examine the pages of your Dream Book pertaining to the chosen vision or visions to see whether any projects emerge from the sticky notes parked there. In this context, *project* refers to a single large goal under a vision with many smaller, interconnected subgoals that will move the larger goal toward completion. For example, writing an article is a project. It involves many tasks of researching, outlining, rough drafting, and revising. Similarly, remodeling your kitchen involves collecting ideas, designing, getting estimates from contractors, budgeting, picking appliances and lighting, and so on.

These discernment questions will help you set priorities about which projects from your highest-priority vision statement or statements are worthy of your time. You won't usually need to answer all of these questions to pick an area or two to work on.

Visions to Projects

- What is the prime activity or set of activities I need to do to move this vision along? Your choices might range from the many steps involved in a huge project to one very small step.

- Are there any projects under a vision that would narrow the alignment gap, bringing me closer to my ideal life? Are there any small goals unconnected to any projects that are worthy of my time and effort right now?

- What are my five top priority goals (for example, income, promotion, new job, happier marriage, a scholarly project)?

- What activities will get me closer to my top goals?

- What is the next actionable step on each of those top goals?

Cost-Benefit Analysis

- Which project or projects have the potential for the greatest return on investment (ROI) for the resources expended (time, money, energy)? Which will bring me closer to my goals compared to resources expended? What will be the benefits to me and to others if I work on these goals?

- What is the opportunity cost—the loss of time, money, energy, and attention that taking this opportunity might mean for other opportunities that I am considering? What is the opportunity cost if I do this project and if I don't?

- Are the costs or sacrifices proportional to the gains? (Sometimes it is hard to tell what the costs and gains will be in advance, but think it through as well as possible.)

- What projects, if not done, will bring the most pain? For example, could taking on the department chair role cost you promotion or tenure because of lost research time?

- Will I gain or lose the good will and support of key people if I take or don't take this opportunity?

Planning Perspective

- How does this project fit my long- and short-term goals (Pyramid of Power)?

- What resources and commitment (time, money, energy, people, and attention) do I need to pursue this project?

- How will I get those resources, especially time, to do this project: get rid of other tasks or say "No" to other opportunities?

You won't need to answer all of these questions, but after answering a few of them, you should become clearer on what you need to be working on at this point in your career and what you should reject or defer until later.

While you are working on your most important priorities, new ideas will keep occurring to you about your other vision areas. If it is not the right time to work on those ideas, capture them on sticky notes and park them in your Dream Book so that they will be available if those visions become a higher priority. Sometimes new opportunities seem so urgent, and so right, that they cause you to reorder all of your priorities and possibly to rewrite sections of your Pyramid of Power.

Plan the Goals Within a Project

By now you have selected a project to work on. You may have started with a big idea, then generated the steps towards its completion (inductive process), or you may have collected a set of seemingly random goals that matter to you to see whether they have a connection (deductive process). Timing is important. You can increase the pressure later, but for now don't commit to more than three projects at this time. A big project such as writing a book should probably not be done in the same semester as a major course revision, but if you budget your time appropriately, a big project could be worked on during a semester when you are teaching already well-designed courses.

Here are the steps for working on a project:

- Once you have a project, name it—for example, "article for *Journal of Environmental Science*."

- Use a mind map to outline the scope of a project and capture the beginning thoughts about the project (Buzan & Buzan, 1996). Place the title of the project in the middle of a piece of paper, circle it and then use the circle as a hub of a wheel with spokes radiating out. Print key ideas on each spoke. Print secondary ideas on lines drawn out from the spoke lines. Write the tertiary ideas on lines drawn from the secondary ideas. You can use different-colored pencils or draw pictures as you go. This brainstorming technique will allow your brain to fire ideas at random in no particular order while a loose structure gradually emerges.

- List everything that needs to be done to complete the project. Break down those goals into subgoals and the subgoals into smaller and smaller tasks by writing them on sticky notes. You can either break down all of the subgoals from a branch on the mind map or jump around to different goals—whatever you find works the best for you.

  - Using sticky notes on the mind map gives you the ability to move the items around on a "storyboard" on the wall, desk, or paper until you are satisfied with the steps leading to the completion of the project. Picture a novelist's storyboard or the TV detective's crime board, with sticky notes in radiating lines out from a central theme (the name of the project). This storyboard is sometimes called a concept map.

- Lay out the goals for the project in logical order and use the Tracking Sheet technique described later in Part 2 to track all the tasks of this and your other projects, personal and professional, in one place so that you can see at a glance when their time lines and deadlines intersect. Prevent overloading yourself with too many intense tasks at the same time.

- Park the mind map and Tracking Sheet for the project in your Dream Book so you can refer to them as you complete the small goals on your Tracking Sheet. Archive the completed goals on the back of the relevant pages in your Dream Book. As you pull out more goals from the mind map, move them to the Tracking Sheet.

- When this project is complete, dip into your Dream Book for other projects and repeat the process.

Byron chose to work on two of his vision areas concurrently, family and teaching. His project in the family area was caring for his elderly father. This family project required many subgoals to implement his father's care such as decisions about medical treatments, housing, and staffing for home health nurses to check on his father.

His project in his teaching vision was a new course design. In this project there were also many tasks. Starting with exploring the Big Questions about why the course mattered, he went on to define course goals, study possible textbooks, review sample syllabi from other teachers, design learning activities and assessments, and explore media resources. During this time period, while he committed to these two new projects drawn from his two vision areas, he kept his six other vision areas on a maintenance level. He taught his classes, completed some preliminary writing on an article he was already working on, grocery shopped, and played with his kids. But he didn't commit to any other big projects until his father's care and his new course were at the maintenance level.

Anchor Your Projects with a Time-Focused Theme

Once you have picked some projects from your vision categories, you might create a sense of urgency by fitting the projects into a specific time frame such as a year, semester, or month. Here are several suggestions about how to establish a theme for the year (semester, month).

- Look backward in time to see if you can see a theme for a previous time period (week, month, or year) that lays the foundation of a related theme for the next period. Does any theme summarize your accomplishments of this period? If last year was the "year of the tenure application," this year might the "year to reconnect with my long term research project."

- Establish a central theme for the current time period, e.g. "the year of course revision." You might create one theme around work and another for home. Your teaching theme might be to "get graded papers back within two classes," while your home theme might be to "monitor children's homework while dinner is cooking."

- Ask yourself what you would like to be able to say about the present time period at this time next year.

Once you have established a theme for the time period, ask yourself, "If this is the year or semester of this theme, what should I be working on?" The answer will help you break the theme down into projects, goals, subgoals, and tasks.

Amy, a midcareer professor at a leading medical school, decided on this theme: "the year of recognition." Amid working on her normal job requirements, she spent some time that year applying for and receiving awards that her research deserved but that she had not taken time to pursue. The increased visibility of the awards at her institution resulted in cinching her promotion to full professor and got her several outside grants and consulting jobs that brought money into her school and led to a book contract.

Live Your Double Life—Temporarily

You probably already had many committed projects before you started following these guidelines for picking new projects. As you create your ideal life, there is a stage where you can begin to see a clearing in the woods but still have a long walk through trees to get there. You can't just hop to the new area, ignoring your present commitments. Instead, you might have to live a bit of a double life for a while, completing your present commitments and clearing out the debris from the habit of doing too many things at once.

As you gradually pursue your new life, the key to closing the alignment gap and decreasing its related anxiety is to work from meaning and purpose in your new ventures at the same time as you complete your current projects. Eventually, a clearing in the woods will appear, where you will no longer feel perpetually overwhelmed.

While you are living this double life, these questions will help you integrate the new projects with the old.

- What are the most important projects I have already committed to that I need to complete or maintain while I begin to establish the new priorities of one or two vision areas?

- Do I need to replace or postpone some of my current commitments until I complete some projects from my new vision or theme?

- Which new projects do I need to postpone until I complete the ones that fit my current priorities?

- What new roles, professional as well as personal, are most important to me at this time in the cycle of life?

Allen, an accounting professor, consulted me because of an interesting dilemma over priorities. He had an idea for an accounting textbook based on material he had developed for his workshops at accounting conferences, but he felt conflicted about making such an intense commitment to a book at the same time as taking on a new role of half-time director of a new faculty development center. It seemed obvious that book writing needed to be deferred until he settled into the new job description. However, a publisher was interested in his ideas and Allen was afraid to let the opportunity slip by. Following my suggestions, Allen continued his conversation with the publisher, while he gradually built a file of ideas, exercises, and scholarly support related to the book. Because he was still teaching 50% of the time, he auditioned these new materials as handouts and worksheets in his classes. After a year in his new job, he had developed ample class materials to form the foundation of the book and was ready to write a contract-winning book proposal.

Relate Your Ancillary Goals to Your Top Priorities

While your goal is to spend a good part of each day or week working on your highest-priority projects and goals, not every minute of every workday will be spent in total bliss connecting with your vision and mission. There are many ancillary activities that support a good alignment between your Pyramid of Power and your activities.

Here are the principles for staying close to your priorities as you attend to tasks:

- *Meaning and purpose:* What level of meaning and purpose does this task have for you—direct, indirect, remote? Stay close to tasks that are directly or indirectly connected to your purpose. Be cautious about engaging in tasks that are only remotely connected.

- *Essentialness:* Is this task essential to your projects? If not, reconsider whether to do it.

- *Uniqueness:* Where are you most uniquely needed or indispensable (sitting with your child during a medical procedure or attending a campus-wide faculty meeting)? This question can help resolve conflict between two worthy tasks. (I am presuming you are not the provost running the faculty meeting and that you normally attend such meetings.)

- *Source:* Who is the source of this task? You will sometimes do things that are only remotely connected to your sense of meaning because your boss asks you to, but beware of doing things for everyone no matter who they are.

In a pinch, when time is limited, those principles will help you resolve most conflicts. Only you can determine their relative weight.

Robison's Rule
Put first things first.

Chapter 9

Organize Projects

THE TECHNIQUES THAT follow will be invaluable to you in keeping track of all the tasks involved in completing large projects. Experiment with these techniques to decide which ones fit your personal style.

Project Management: Planning

Planning is a skill peak performers use to lay out projects, timelines, and tasks so that deadlines are met with quality production. For our purposes, planning involves using three skills to create a project management system.

- Start projects with the end in mind (Covey, 2004).

- Track the steps of a project by planning backward from a vision of the completed project into the smaller steps required to reach that vision. (Sher & Gottlieb, 2003).

- Imagine and commit to the details of the project as much as possible (Gollwitzer & Brandstätter, 1997; Gollwitzer & Oettingen, 2011).

Plan the End

How do you imagine the project turning out? What would be the final outcome? What is the completed project to be used for? How does it fit with your overall priorities? Whose help will you need? What obstacles might occur, and what might you do to overcome them? What resources will you need (people, space, money, and so on)?

Plan Backward

While it is not common sense to think backward, it is effective (Sher & Gottlieb, 2003). When we plan forward we are often rushed at the end and are left with two choices: do not complete the project or lower the standards that the project deserves. One faculty member who was still using forward planning to design a new course over the summer reported, "It's the second week of the fall semester, and I almost have my syllabus ready to give to the students enrolled in the course." Starting with the end in mind forces you to

EXERCISE 9.1

Plan a Project Backward

For this exercise limit yourself to planning a project or a phase of a larger project that needs to be completed in one month (four weeks). Your project probably has several goals required for completion.

- Using the format in Table 9.1, describe the final product of one of the goals of the project due at the end of the month. Then list all the tasks for the last week of the month in which you are completing that goal. These subgoals for the last week go in the last cell where row labeled "Goal 1" intersects with the column labeled "Final."

- In the appropriate cells, list the tasks to be completed at the three-quarter mark (one week before the end of the month), the halfway mark (two weeks before the end), and the quarter mark (one week from the start of the month). If you have written these tasks on sticky notes, you can just paste the sticky notes for each phase into the cells. You are allowed to have more than one small goal in each cell as long as you estimate that you can complete all of them during that same week.

- Once you have outlined the tasks for one of the large goals for the project, plan all the other tasks for the same project starting with a description of the final product in the last cell and working backward from there.

- Not all cells will necessarily contain tasks; tasks may start and finish in different time frames for different goals.

TABLE 9.1

Planning Backward

Project	One Quarter	One Half	Three Quarters	Final
Goal 1				
Goal 2				
Goal 3				
Goal 4				

Example: Savannah, a history professor at a small, historically black university, used the backward planning chart in Table 9.2 to plan her course design goals, starting with defining her learning objectives. Her final task will be to post the completed syllabus to the course website. Notice how she divided her project into goals and further subdivided the goals into smaller subgoals and tasks.

TABLE 9.2

Example of Backward Planning

Project	One Quarter	One Half	Three Quarters	Final
Goal 1: Set course goals and polices	Explore "Big Questions" and learning objectives	Write course outcomes	Write policies	Done
Goal 2: Choose readings	Explore possible readings	Select readings		Done
Goal 3: Plan assignments and grading rubrics		Plan assignments and exam dates; coordinate with college event calendar	Create assignments and exams; write grading rubrics	Done
Goal 4: Print and post syllabus			Edit copy	Print copies for each student or post to online class site

distribute all the tasks needed to complete the project backward over increments of time so that you will complete the project on time. Exercise 9.1 will get you started on planning a project backward.

Plan the Details

The work habits of peak performers illustrate an interesting paradox: peak performers accomplish their goals because they focus on the process of attaining those goals, especially on specific details of their subgoals, while at the same time focusing on the project's outcomes. Specifying the details is known as implementation intention (Halvorson, 2011). Research subjects who committed to when and where they would do a task completed the task at a rate double that of subjects who did not specify the details (Gollwitzer & Brandstätter, 1997; Gollwitzer & Oettingen, 2011). Imagining if-then scenarios about obstacles to goals and possible solutions also increases the chances of success (Gollwitzer et al., 2004). As you plan for the completion of tasks, plan your implementation steps, asking yourself when and where you will do a particular task, whom you will tell about your intention, what will remind you, and what reward or penalty you will give yourself for completing or failing to accomplish your goal. These last steps raise your chances of completion from 35% to 80% (Ayres, 2010). Instead of trying to do your best, set specific, difficult goals (Locke & Latham, 1990, 2002, 2006). Specific goals tell you what is expected; difficult but possible goals cause you to increase focus, effort, and commitment to the goal. This method of setting goals also helps you persist longer and make better use of the most effective strategies. It creates what Lantham and his colleagues (Latham, Locke, & Fassina, 2002; Latham & Locke, 2007) call the "high performance cycle," in which setting specific, challenging goals creates a cycle of success and happiness that can repeat itself over and over again.

Project Management: Keep Track of It All

The muscle of a peak performing professor is developed through the practice of aligning tasks with priorities and strengthened by tracking tasks across time. In Chapter 8, you answered a series of discernment questions to set your priorities. Now the tool you will use to track your projects and tasks is the Tracking Sheet, a task management system designed to align subgoals and to-dos with time deadlines. In project management folklore, Walt Disney is credited with using "work charts" to track the complex output of the animators for his first feature-length cartoon, *Snow White*, because he needed to know what each animator was working on and when that phase of drawings would be completed (Boone, 1938).

Your colleagues in the business department call this technique "project management." Software companies are standing by to take your money for elaborate computer programs that allow you to supply information and track your projects. You don't need a computer program. Your Tracking Sheet can be kept in low-tech format, on an 8½" × 11" piece of paper in landscape orientation, or in a higher-tech word-processing, spreadsheet, or smartphone format. Use whichever format makes it easy for you to look at your Tracking Sheet regularly, several times a week. The steps are the same no matter whether you go low or high tech.

Tracking Multiple Projects

Once you have selected projects to work on, you will track your projects in a Tracking Sheet like the one in Table 9.3. It will look like an expanded version of the backward planning table we used in the previous exercise.

- Label the rows of the table with the names of the project you are working on.

- Label the columns with the dates that end each work week. For most people the transition to a new work week will be between Friday and Monday. (You can use any time unit for the columns, days, weeks, months, or even years for long-term projects such as a five-year grant or a department curriculum revision.)

- Fill in the cells of your first project with the tasks that you plan to complete for each week. Remember to plan backward from the last cell under Date 5.

TABLE 9.3

Weekly Tracking Sheet

Directions: Track several projects simultaneously against weekly timelines by writing to-dos in the cells. Include details about where and when.

Goals/Time	Week One (date of Monday or Friday)	Week Two	Week Three	Week Four	Week Five
Project 1					
Project 2					
Project 3					
Project 4					
Project 5					

- Track all your projects, personal and professional, on the same Tracking Sheet within the same time frames. That way you can see the intersection of deadlines on a research article and a house remodeling project on the same Tracking Sheet.

- The vertical column becomes a task list for each week. Some cells might be empty because you do not intend to complete any tasks for that project during that week, and some cells might have several tasks listed that you know you can complete by the end of the week.

- When you complete tasks, highlight with color or put a slash through each cell (brags).

- As each week transitions to the next, review the Tracking Sheet to make sure all the tasks have been completed. The uncompleted tasks (nags) will stand out because they are not highlighted or crossed out.

- Cut and paste any uncompleted nags one cell over unless they are no longer relevant. The Tracking Sheet allows you to tell at a glance where you are on schedule for each project and where you are procrastinating.

- If you have tracked your projects in either a word-processing table or a spreadsheet, strip the completed vertical week off that table and paste it into an archive table, where it will jog your memory about accomplishments later when you write your annual report or revise your curriculum vitae.

- Add a new vertical column at the right-hand side of the table and write in the cells the next set of tasks that you wish to complete for each project.

- When a project is complete, delete its row and archive (also handy for your annual report or c.v.).

- As you decide on additional projects, add them to the rows of the Tracking Sheet.

Using the tracking system allows you to do the following:

- Get the many tasks roaming around in your head on paper (or on screen) where you can look at them. At first you might feel overwhelmed as you strive to be honest with yourself about all that you are doing. The writing of the list doesn't make it overwhelming; your choices do.

- Track all personal and professional projects—designing a syllabus, writing a grant proposal, planning a daughter's wedding—on the same Tracking Sheet so that you can see at a glance what needs to be done next and how the goals intersect or conflict. While a calendar accommodates appointments and due dates, it provides no way to track progress on projects or to see how the smaller subgoals and due dates of one project intersect with those of your other projects. If you do like to use a calendar for appointments, stick to just one calendar—not one for work and a different one for home—because you need to see potential conflicts.

- Lower your stress by always knowing what project is due on what date while being able to see in an instant where you have overscheduled yourself and when you are falling behind your deadlines.

Daily Task Management

If you are like most professors, your to-do lists already seem endless, because you often add tasks faster than you can complete them. It gets depressing, doesn't it? As you get in the habit of using the Weekly Tracking Sheet, you will probably not need a daily to-do list because your focus will shift from Gen I management of a list of to-dos to the Gen II concept of management of your life and its projects and goals. However, many people have trouble giving up their current practice of daily planning in favor of using the Tracking Sheets by themselves, even though research has confirmed the superiority of monthly planning over daily (Kirschenbaum, Humphrey, & Malett, 1981). In case you still want to use a daily to-do list, described in the following sections are two techniques, the Daily Tracking Sheet and the VAST Strive-for-9, for creating effective daily to-do lists that you will actually complete each day. Neither technique is superior. Experiment with both until you find which works better for you. You may only need a daily system temporarily until you develop the habit of consulting your Weekly Tracking Sheet daily or several times a week.

The Focused 15–30

Just as you prepared to use the Tracking Sheet by practicing the skill of backward planning, you will make better daily to-do lists if you practice the preparatory skill of the Focused 15. This skill will help you create powerful to-do lists by breaking down all of your projects and tasks into smaller units that should take only 15–30 minutes each to complete. A small, daily to-do list of items that will get done is far superior to a list of large items, such as "write a book," that can't be done in a day and that just stare at you, reminding you of your inadequacies.

At first you might balk at using the technique of breaking tasks into 15–30 minute subtasks, preferring to fantasize about working from start to finish on your projects during large blocks of uninterrupted time. I use the word *fantasize* because those large blocks of time exist only in your fantasies. In real life you have too many daily roles and responsibilities to ever have large blocks of time appear in your schedule. Instead, you will accomplish a lot in a year by managing projects in small chunks that fit around your daily responsibilities. When Bob Boice studied faculty writers, he found that those who worked daily or almost daily got more done—64 pages—than those who waited for the magical large block of time—17 pages. By the way, faculty writers in that same study who made themselves accountable to someone else wrote the most—157 pages (Boice, 1989).

The exercise on the Focused 15 (see Exercise 9.2) gives you practice in three essential time management skills: breaking bigger goals into smaller, more manageable goals; planning where and when you will complete them (implementation planning); and comparing your prediction of how long each subgoal or task of a project might take with a record of how long the tasks *actually* take.

This short drill will improve your ability to accurately estimate time to completion on your tasks. The practice of accurately predicting time to completion corrects for the "future planning fallacy," that mistake we all make when we overestimate future time available for our use and underestimate the time that tasks will take (Buehler, Griffin, & Ross, 1994; Kahneman & Tversky, 1979) and will provide a "personal correction factor" for future time estimates. For example, if you consistently find that your estimated time is half of your completed time, then in the future when you plan tasks for the day, you know that you need to double your time estimate. This training tool helps you build commitment to your tasks by planning when and where you will do them. You can use the drill alone or as a basis to create realistic daily to-do lists with either of the two techniques described here, the Daily Tracking Sheet or the VAST to-do list. You won't need to repeat the exercise once you have trained yourself to break tasks into 15–30 minute to-dos.

The Daily Tracking Sheet
This technique looks just like the Weekly Tracking Sheet except that instead of the columns being labeled by weeks, they are labeled by the days of the week as in Table 9.4.

Take the tasks of a vertical one-week column from your Weekly Tracking Sheet and use the Focused 15 exercise to break each task down into 15-minute to-dos. Set up a Daily Tracking Sheet with the days of your work week labeling the columns. (You can adjust the 15-minute length of time if you wish, but remember to correct your expectations for number of completed

EXERCISE 9.2

The Focused 15

Take a task in one of the cells of your weekly Tracking Sheet formed by the intersection of project and date, and break the task down into ordered steps. Each step should take no longer than 15–30 minutes. Record when and where you will do them and a time estimate of how long the steps will take. After you have completed the steps, record the actual time they took.

	When	Where	Time est.	Actual time
Step 1				
Step 2				
Step 3				
Step 4				
Step 5				

TABLE 9.4

Daily Tracking Sheet

Directions: Track several projects broken into tasks simultaneously against daily timelines by writing the to-dos of the tasks into the cells of this chart.

Goals/Time	Monday	Tuesday	Wednesday	Thursday	Friday	Saturday	Sunday
Project 1							
Project 2							
Project 3							
Project 4							
Project 5							

tasks per day. For example, if you decide on 30-minute tasks instead of 15-minute ones, you will complete only half the number of tasks in a day.)

Distribute the 15-minute to-dos across the cells of a Daily Tracking Sheet, limiting the number of to-dos in each column to nine per day. I discovered that number after studying time sheets from faculty coaching clients and observed that faculty average about 2½ hours in an 8-hour day in discretionary time, the time in the work day that is left after subtracting obligation time such as class time or meetings. Completing nine 15-minute items takes 2 hours and 15 minutes, leaving 15 minutes for overflow from a task that took longer than you predicted, for a short personal break, or for the task of correcting your predictions about time to completion with your "personal correction factor." Adjust my math to your own schedules and work habits. Stick with only nine 15-minute tasks a day, and you will get them done.

Table 9.5 is an alternative to a simple Daily Tracking Sheet, to use if you prefer to track the goals of each project with a little more detail.

The VAST Daily To-Do List

This technique is an alternative practice to the Daily Tracking Sheet for writing a productive daily to-do list.

- All of the items on the VAST list are to-dos that take 15–30 minutes.

- The items are categorized into three or four categories, described below.

- You still only get to do nine—or as many as you can fit into your discretionary time.

Many of the early Gen I time management programs recommended setting tasks into categories by whether they were A, B, or C priority, but these programs never taught any way of determining which tasks should

---

TABLE 9.5

Daily Tracking Systems with Task Details

Directions: Track several projects broken into tasks simultaneously against daily timelines by writing the to-dos of the tasks into the cells of this chart. Follow guidelines for Table 9.4.

Project/Goals	Day 1	Day 2	Day 3	Day 4	Day 5	Day 6	Day 7
Project 1: Goal 1		To-do		To-do			To-do
Project 1: Goal 2	To-do	To-do	To-do		To-do		
Project 1: Goal 3	To-do	To-do	To-do	To-do	To-do	To-do	To-do
Project 2 (expand as needed)							
Project 3							
Project 4							
Project 5							

go into each category. In contrast, the category system set out in this section is tied to your deepest sense of meaning and purpose because it flows from your Pyramid of Power.

This practice uses four categories (Vision, Avert, Self, and Tomorrow) with three tasks in each. The questions listed here will give you cues about what items to include in your daily to-do lists. They are prioritized by using the acronym *VAST*. (See Table 9.6 for a chart that will help you develop a to-do list using the VAST system.)

V is for three *vision*-related goals or daily to-dos.

- What are tasks that flow from my vision statements, advance my long-term and short-term goals, and if I get them done, will make my day a great day?

- What are things I can do today to advance productivity in my career and satisfaction in my life? For example, write one page of my book

TABLE 9.6

VAST To-do List

Directions: Practice making a VAST list that will create a doable to-do list for tomorrow and then use this practice every day after that.

VAST	Today	Tomorrow
Vision		
1.		
2.		
3.		
Avert		
1.		
2.		
3.		
Self-care		
1.		
2.		
3.		
Tomorrow		
1.		
2.		
3.		

manuscript, write a small section of an article, or contact remodeling contractors to discuss a home improvement project.

A is for three things that will help you *avert* disaster.

- What are things that, if left undone, will have bad results: the day will go sour, my long-term and short-term goals will be delayed, and disaster will lurk around the edges of my life? An example of such a disaster might be failing to stop for gas on the way home, thus running out of gas and wasting the evening hiking to the gas station.

- What are things that, if not done today, will have the result that dire things might happen to sabotage my best goals for future satisfaction and achievement? An example would be the failure to work on my tenure packet, thus assuring that I won't get it in by the deadline.

- What are things that, if not done today, will mean that I will be in trouble with the students, dean, chair, spouse, or other significant people in my life? An example would be failing to return term paper drafts to the students in time to help them rewrite their drafts.

S is for three things you will do for *self-care*.

- What are things that will nurture me personally and professionally? For example, exercise, sleep, and take a self-paced online course in a skill I want to build.

- What are things that I will do to take care of myself, achieve balance, and refresh myself so that I can continue to serve others and feel great? For example eat five fruits and vegetables, take a walk at lunch, and get to bed by 10 pm.

T is for any goal from *tomorrow's* goals that you can move over to today's list if you have finished your nine tasks and have time. (Hint: this will almost never happen.)

- What tasks from tomorrow's list, particularly in the V (vision) or A (avert disaster) categories, can I start on today? For example, write a bit more on an article, or call to make a dentist appointment.

- What tasks might be considered optional for today but essential for tomorrow? For example, finish my annual report due to the chair by the end of the week.

There you go—three things for each category—a set of twelve tasks, nine of which you have deemed absolutely necessary to call the day a great day and three auxiliary ones thrown in just in case it snows and classes are cancelled. You don't have to use every category every day as long as you don't go too many days without using all categories. The three categories ensure that you work on goals that will lead to completion of projects related to your vision, keep disasters at bay, and maintain yourself so you can do your great work.

The T (tomorrow) category is used only if you complete the nine tasks of the other categories, at which point you can pull some tasks from tomorrow's list to be done today. However, there is no pressure to do any tasks from tomorrow's list. That is what tomorrow is for.

You can vary the number of tasks in each category, as long as each VAST list can be completed in one day. For example, you can use one big vision goal for the whole 2½ hours discretionary time or one goal for vision and three each for avert, self, and tomorrow. You can vary the formula each day. What you want is to prevent drifting back into the habit most people have of carrying over items from one to-do list to the next, feeling guilty and stressed about the "undones."

When you finish your scheduled events such as classes and meetings and complete your nine VAST to-dos, your work day will have been a great day, and you can happily transition to personal time knowing that you got everything done that you wanted to do for the day.

Because you are a creative intellectual professional, you will always think up many wonderful things you might do. You can't get them all done. Never—no way! Not if you work harder, not if you read more time management books, not even if you don't sleep or eat or have any kind of a life. In spite of that terrible failure to do everything you can think up, you can still do great work and have a great life, because you will have all the time you need to work on what is most important. So until you discern that those new ideas are important to work on in the present time frame, park them in your Dream Book, and get back to working on your current projects.

Here are some guidelines for what items go on your project management system (Weekly Tracking Sheets, Daily Tracking Sheets, or VAST to-do lists).

- Link each to-do to your mission and vision statements, either directly from your Pyramid of Power, or indirectly in activities that support those statements.

- Avoid as much as possible those activities that don't fit your mission. If you find activities attractive that are not in your mission, it might be a signal to rewrite your mission statement. If they are not attractive, say "No." Be firm, polite, and skip the explanations. If you have a hard time breaking the habit of agreeing to do things that are not central to your values, practice saying, "That is not part of my mission."

- Don't let urgent but unimportant interruptions distract you from your to-do list.

- Use flexibility to make your to-do lists. You can have as few or many as you wish as long as you get them done.

Here is what you can expect as you implement your project management system:

- You will be extremely skeptical that this system will work. Try it anyway. While it seems to add a whole new set of "shoulds," it doesn't. It is a different, more effective way to do what you already do, which is to plan and review your goals. As with any new behavior, you will have a bit of a learning curve until you get more realistic about what you can do in your limited daily allotment of discretionary time.

- You will no longer park ideas on daily to-do lists and carry them over from one day to the next. Instead, you will park ideas in your Dream Book until you are ready either to work on them or to discard them as no longer relevant.

- You will no longer make the mistake of mixing large and small goals together on a to-do list. Instead, your bigger goals will be laid out as rows on your Tracking Sheets, with your smaller goals nested inside the cells. If you choose to use a daily system, those smaller goals get distributed throughout the week onto the daily lists.

- You will no longer misplace discretionary time during the day on random activities, nor hope that you will get some things done "if there is time." Instead, you will take advantage of pockets of discretionary time to complete items on the daily list. If you have no discretionary time on any of your days, you are either very overcommitted or you are a dean.

- You will feel less guilty as you end each workday because you will have successfully completed your self-assigned tasks. Although you may think you are not getting enough done each day, you will be amazed at how much gets done in a month and a year.

- You will feel less stressed about not getting things done in a timely fashion. Professors who adopt these practices report an 85% reduction in their daily stress. While getting something off your list by doing it lowers stress, so does making a written plan about your goals. A written plan stops the churning in your mind that happens when your less conscious brain keeps trying to remind your conscious brain to do something (Baumeister & Tierney, 2011).

- You will still occasionally overplan, in part because of the future planning fallacy, and in part because delicious opportunities that advance the cause of your professional or personal goals will occasionally coincide in the same time frames because of factors outside your control. For example, you might be invited to write an article, contribute a chapter to a book, and make an important conference address, all with deadlines very close together. In your quest for work-life balance, you may at times choose to overcommit, give up sleep or personal time, and work more than usual. Just don't make those choices chronic.

Task Review

Many professors think implementing the practices discussed here will take up so much time that there will be none left to get any work done. You probably already have a practice of reviewing tasks, but if you are used to planning and reviewing in your head, the task review practice presented here will be far more effective. Professors who adopt these practices, reviewing where they are in their projects and to-dos, gain approximately five hours of discretionary time a week because of the focus these professors achieve in their daily work habits. That is an additional five hours to work, rest, or play.

Here are guidelines for task review, based on data provided to me by coaching clients and workshop participants about how much time they spend with these practices. One coaching client, a faculty development director, said, "I was a skeptic, but I found that these practices have made me more effective and more relaxed. Now I am eager to share them with my faculty."

Weekly (10 minutes)

- At the beginning of one week or at the end of the previous, review the Tracking Sheet to cross out or archive the completed tasks of last week.

- Examine those tasks that have not been completed, and either move them over into the next column for the coming week, eliminate them because you no longer find them relevant, or break them down into even smaller to-dos.

- Review the tasks listed in the vertical to-do list (current column on the Tracking Sheet) for the coming week to make sure they are still relevant. Just because you wrote them doesn't mean you have to do them.

- (Optional) Some professors like to rank the tasks within the cells so that they are sure of completing the top priority tasks first each day before the interruptions and distractions take the day spinning out of control.

- (Optional) Distribute the relevant tasks into one of the daily to-do lists (Daily Tracking Sheet or VAST list) using your skills of backward planning and Focused 15.

Daily (3–5 minutes)

- Add or subtract tasks in your project management system that have a higher or lower priority or urgency than you previously thought.

- At the end of each day review your task lists (Weekly Tracking Sheet, Daily Tracking Sheet, or VAST list), crossing off completed items, examining the incomplete items, and reviewing and creating a list for the next day.

Hourly (60 seconds)

- After an hour of desk work, pause to ask yourself if what you have worked on is what you really wanted to work on.

- Cross items off your daily to-do list. Set priorities for the next hour.

Quarterly or monthly (1–3 hours)

- Review your Pyramid of Power and Dream Book to see if your statements of purpose, mission, and vision are still current.

- Review your vision chapters to see whether any new subvisions or projects are calling to you.

- Add ideas, goals, and materials related to future vision projects.

- Move projects and goals whose time has come into your project management system, subdividing them into smaller goals, subgoals, and tasks.

- Discern new opportunities using the questions from Chapter 8.

- If you feel stuck, take the next actionable step—however tiny—on a high-priority project. As a general rule, the more complicated your work and life, the more you need to consult your project management system to keep on top of things. The simpler your work and life, the simpler the tracking.

Robison's Rule
You only have to be organized enough to be successful.

Chapter 10

Align Resources

IN THIS CHAPTER, you will determine how to best organize your resources (time, energy, people, and space) to support the completion of each project.

- What resources and commitment (time, money, energy, and attention) do I need to successfully complete this project?

- How do I get the time and energy to do it: Get rid of other tasks? Say "No" to other opportunities?

- When does this project need to be completed?

- What skills do I need to develop or master to complete the project?

- What kind of help do I need from advisors, experts, or collaborators on this project?

- What tasks can I delegate to others who are good at and like doing those tasks? (Just because your college doesn't hire assistants for you, that doesn't mean you can't hire your own helpers, such as high school or college students to help you in your home office with filing or data entry work. Be careful not to assign them tasks that involve student records, such as recording grades.)

- What kind of reorganization of my work space do I need to work effectively on this project?

You already know how to allocate time against task by using project management practices from Chapter 9. In this chapter, let's look at how to use your other resources.

Align Supportive People with Your Goals

The skills of backward planning, tracking, to-do lists, and time against task build self-accountability. For many professors these are the only techniques needed to stay on track for high productivity, whereas others benefit from increased accountability with helpful others.

Social accountability provides a powerful motivator: the threat of mild social embarrassment. While most professors would never think of showing up for class unprepared because they don't want to be embarrassed in front of the students, those same professors procrastinate on tasks that do not have urgent deadlines until the tenure clock or promotion clock runs out. Committing to a person or group about one's goals increases the likelihood that you will complete those goals just to avoid the embarrassment of not being prepared (McCaul, Hinsz, & McCaul, 1987).

Social accountability can be an important aid when you are developing new habits of working more productively and is especially helpful when you are feeling stuck on what to do next or having trouble meeting your self-imposed deadlines. As one coaching client confided to me, "I always know that my early mental deadlines are not the real deadlines, so I let things slide. But with a coach for accountability, I know I'm going to report in. Even though I know you won't yell at me, I'm motivated by having you cheer me on when I complete my goals."

You can also use social accountability to make you show up for your own goals by yoking your goals to someone else's goals. For example, meeting a partner for exercise will get you up and out to the gym on cold winter mornings until you have established the exercise habit. Likewise, just knowing you are meeting with someone about your writing progress triggers the pride we all have when we accomplish something and want to brag a bit to someone who cares about us and our goals.

You may find that reporting to a buddy or a coach structures your tasks and time frames so that you complete tasks by their deadlines—maybe even earlier. You might also benefit by having another brain or brains help you figure things out. There is evidence that mentoring can increase your productivity (Barry, 2012).

There are at least three ways you can use social accountability:

1. Buddy system: You and a buddy report to each other on the progress of your projects. You can phone, e-mail, or meet in person. You and your buddy can choose to do things such as the following:

- Work on similar projects, such as writing professional articles, or on different projects—for example, you might be working on an article and your buddy might be working on a new course design.

- Get together to work on your projects in each other's presence or merely report in by phone or e-mail.

- Draw on your collective wisdom and experience to coach each other on your projects, sharing ideas and critiques.

- Reward each other for completing commitments by e-mailing high-fives or meeting for lunch or coffee.

2. Mastermind group: This is a group of people who gather in person, on a telephone conference call, or in a cloud meeting space to support one another's goals. Variations include the following:

- Coach or critique one another's work.

- Meet in a physical or electronic space for a "sit and work" session, perhaps compiling tenure materials or writing conference proposals with similar deadlines.

- Set goals for the next phase of work and specify accountability tasks, then report in.

- Work on solving difficulties with projects.

- Review the year or semester to celebrate accomplishments and motivate one another for the next phase.

- Socialize to celebrate successes such as book publications. Possibly include mates and close friends at these parties.

- Subdivide into subgroups or choose partners who might pair up to work between meetings on pieces of one another's projects and then report in to the larger group.

3. Mentor or coach: In this kind of accountability relationship, you are reporting in to a person of authority or expertise. The difference between coaches and mentors is that mentors are experts in your field, whereas coaches are experts in helping people reach their goals.

- Mentors help you out of the generosity of their hearts for the satisfaction of helping someone who is less experienced. Sometimes they exchange their help for coauthorship credit on scholarly work. Be sure to clarify expectations of mutuality at the front end of the relationship.

- Coaches may or may not be experts in your field, but they are experts in coaching techniques and charge fees for their professional services comparable to those for counseling or business consultations. Coaches support you, hold you accountable, and sometimes teach you techniques that help you complete your projects. You might be able to contract with a professional coach through the faculty development center or employee assistance program at your college. If you wish to hire your own coach, you might find one through referrals from colleagues or friends or through coaches' no-cost or low-cost presentations in the community or online. Coaches usually offer a complimentary consultation to allow you to try out the experience of coaching with them.

In both kinds of helping relationships, the regularity and format of meetings will be determined by the two people in the mentoring or coaching relationship.

Align Your Energy with Your Goals

Staying vital for your whole career requires you to manage your energy, one of your most precious resources. A good flow of energy keeps you productive and leads to a great feeling of satisfaction about your job and life. In Part 4 of this book, which discusses energizing yourself, you will learn specific ways of creating and maintaining good energy from the point of view of wellness and well-being, but here are some practices relevant to alignment.

1. **Create and maintain your energy** while taking care of yourself. Plenty of sleep, good nutrition, and regular exercise combined with good work habits will keep the machinery of you working well for the long haul.

- Make a simple work-life balance plan and stick with it. An example would be to "strive for nine": nine servings of fresh fruits and vegetables a day, eight to nine hours of sleep, nine repetitions of exercises, and nine minutes spent catching up with your mate or best friend at the end of the day.

2. **Work from power**, matching your energy with your priorities.

- Match the use of your strengths and talents with your activities. This matching will lead to a greater sense of meaning and purpose and increase your happiness (Seligman, 2002).

- Spend most of your time in high-yield activities derived from your Pyramid of Power priorities, ones that give you a good return on your investment (ROI) of time by having a big impact on your roles of teaching, researching, and serving. Screen every task you do for its ROI. For example, regarding publications, ask, "Which is the best journal to send this article to?" Regarding teaching ask, "How do I use my instructional time for the best pedagogical goals?" Keep other tasks on the back burner until their time comes.

- Put your best energy into vision goals by using the skills of backward planning and tracking to reassure yourself that your day was well spent.

3. **Match your energy with your tasks**.

- Be clear about your motivation every day. Reviewing the alignment between your activities and the meaning behind them will lower stress and build resilience (Halvorson, 2011).

- Pace your activities to your daily biorhythms. Instead of checking e-mail first thing in the morning as most professors do, leaving high-demand tasks such as scholarly work to the end of the day when energy is low, reverse that order, matching your high demand tasks to peak energy times. If you are in the 10% of the population whose energy peaks late in the day, reverse this advice.

- Complete your high-yield activities at the start of your day before other people's agendas encroach on your own (Boice, 1990, 2000; Gray, 2010).

- Decide on starting and ending times for each day and each work period and stick to that schedule. There will always be more work to do because you are a creative knowledge professional, but only you can set and stick to your personal workday boundaries.

4. **Avoid energy drainers**.

- Limit stress since it is the biggest energy drainer (see Part 4 of this book). Set aside 5–10 minutes a day to produce the opposite of stress, the relaxation response, through yoga, meditation, journaling, listening to music, or other activities that really relax you.

- Limit activities that are too far removed from your Pyramid of Power and its support. If you can't limit those activities, hire a coach to help you problem-solve about what to do to limit, delegate, or avoid energy-draining activities or make them easier and less draining.

- Limit energy-draining people by using the social intelligence skills discussed in Part 3 of this book to set limits on your tolerance for the drama kings and queens in your life. If you are married to one, consider couples' counseling.

- Check your own emotional distractions. What wakes you up in the middle of the night? What makes your mind wander when you are at your desk? Problem-solve about those distractions or get help from your accountability people.

5. **Renew and re-create your energy** regularly following the suggestions in Part 4 on wellness and well-being.

Align Your Attention with Your Goals

Attention is a precious resource, perhaps the most limited of all. Most people can focus on only one main activity at a time, with a few minor ones running in the background. Beyond that, we can easily overload our brains. The practices that follow will keep you focused on moving those important long-term projects along.

- Let your systems—sticky notes, Dream Book, Tracking Sheets, and daily to-do lists—handle your task flow, while you actually work on your goals without having to use mental energy to remember what you are working on or will work on next (Emmons & King, 1988).

- Review your project management systems at the beginning and end of each day and periodically during the day to see whether you are actually attending to what you intended to attend to.

- Continue to write your goals on sticky notes so they can be moved from your Dream Book to your bathroom mirror, calendar, or computer screen and back again when you finish a goal. Similarly, manage goals using electronic media such as computers, smartphones, and tablets.

- Free up your brain to work at its peak by doing routine tasks routinely, such as writing at the same time every day.

- Carry the equipment for a few of your 15-minute tasks from your daily to-do list to work on during idle times in between classes, while waiting for the dentist, or while watching the pasta boil. When our daughter ran cross country she was visible only at the start and the finish of the race, so I used the time she was running through the countryside to knock out several small 15-minute tasks I had brought along with me.

Handling Multitasking, Interruptions, and Distractions

One of the biggest challenges to maintaining attention on high priority tasks is the problem of distractions and interruptions (Jett & George, 2003).

Distractions are any stimuli, internal or external, that threaten to intrude into the flow experience of your current activity; interruptions are any distractions that actually do stop that flow. Distractions have the power to interrupt you or not, depending on the circumstances. A distraction can flit through your field of attention without interrupting you as long as you stay focused on the task at hand.

External distractions can be either environmental, such as when media (phones, timers, e-mail) threaten to call your attention away from a task, or interpersonal, such as when a student or colleague shows up at your office. Distractions can also be internal, such as when you remember a task you forgot to write down or have an emotional reaction to a memory, thought, or the task at hand that suddenly takes over your brain's working memory.

Neither interruptions nor distractions are intrinsically bad. They can be helpful when they call attention to information about the task at hand or orient you to another, more important task than the one you are doing. There are also many times when you need to be able to interrupt one task to move to another; for example, you may need to end a paper grading session to leave for class. However, when distractions or interruptions take you away from a task you deem the most important during that time period, they need to be controlled or limited; once interrupted, most people take some time to recover, ranging from one minute to never, depending on how long or how intense the interruption.

One of the biggest threats to productivity is the attempt to multitask, even though many faculty think that attempting to get more done by multitasking is a bragging point. In spite of your attempts to multitask, your brain has a limited capacity to attend to tasks; you can work productively on only one higher cognitive task at a time. For example, you can write or you can advise a student in your office, but working on both simultaneously will result in more than a 50% decrement in performance for both tasks (Amen, 2002; Hallowell & Ratey, 2011; Medina, 2008). This is the brain-based reason that driving while texting is so dangerous (Robison, 2007; Watson, Terry, & Doolittle, 2012). You can complete two lower-level cognitive tasks or two highly practiced, automatic responses at the same time, such as cooking a familiar recipe while you watch the TV news (Dux et al., 2009). However, trying a new recipe would probably require your full attention.

A better concept to increase your effectiveness than multitasking is "toggle switching," in which you focus on one task at a time until you interrupt that task in a planned way to work on another. A toggle switch moves back and forth between two positions: in this case, your two tasks. Instead of writing at your computer with an e-mail alert turned on so that you will be distracted from your writing to attend to incoming e-mail, protect your writing productivity for half an hour by turning off the alert. After you finish your writing task, you can toggle switch over to the e-mail.

In sum, distractions can be helpful when they add quality and information to your task or raise your awareness to attend to a task more important than the one you have been working on. Distractions are harmful when they cause unnecessary interruptions from your intended work flow.

Preventing External Interruptions

■ Expect that distractions and interruptions will occur and plan in advance for how you wish to prevent and handle them, with the former action usually being superior to the latter (Halvorson, 2011). What are your most likely interferences and distractions?

■ Keep a time log to collect data about your interruptions, including who, when, for what, and for how long.

■ Decide in advance who or what you might allow to interrupt you. If someone else (spouse, student assistant, administrative assistant) screens your interruptions, have a short list of who and what is important enough to be allowed to interrupt your flow.

■ Plan breaks. Your ability to attend to intellectual tasks actually improves when you refresh yourself by proactively choosing to temporarily disengage from the task. Planned positive interruptions result in emotional well-being, job satisfaction, and high work performance in the long run (Loehr & Schwartz, 2004). Plan to stop a work session when it gets stale and your productivity falls off. It is important to pace the break with the work session. Too long a break disrupts momentum. Here are recommendations:

- Breaks of 5–10 minutes every 90 minutes;

- An evening off after eight hours of work, since productivity falls off after that (Robinson, 2005).

- A day or half a day off every six to seven days;

- A few days or a week off every season (after three months or at the end of the semester).

■ Before a break or the end of a work session, leave "cracker crumbs" so you can instantly find your way back through the woods. Jot notes about where you stopped and the next steps to be taken.

■ Block uninterrupted time into your schedule and control the possibility of unwanted distraction:

- Turn off phones and e-mail alerts. Take moments each day with no electronic gadgets nearby. Once a week, take a longer electronic holiday, such as one evening or a Sunday afternoon off from phones, e-mail, and TV.

- Signal others politely whether or not you are available by closing your office door or posting a sign on the door saying when you are next available for interruptions. It won't seem rude if you make it light, perhaps a Peanuts' "Lucy" sign saying "The doctor will be back at_____."

- Work in nondistracting environments.

Preventing Internal Distractions

■ Write down distracting thoughts. Brain researchers suggest that your working memory can get easily overloaded, although probably not to exactly the limit of five to nine items as was suggested in earlier research (Miller, 1956). Keep a stack of sticky notes or a piece of doodle paper on your desk or a blank computer document for notes to yourself. Take a brief moment to log a distracting thought and get back into the flow.

■ Increase your memory capacity by blocking things into categories to improve memory. For example, if your memory capacity is only 5–9 items, you can expand it by nesting 5–9 related items into each of the 5–9 categories—that's 25–81 items total.

■ Perform a "top of the mountain" review after every hour or so of discretionary time. Ask yourself:

- Where am I and where am I going?

- Is what I am working on the best use of my time right now?

- Is this task the most worthy of my time and attention or is there something else more important that I am ignoring?

- Am I staying on task?

- Am I working with flow or am I allowing interruptions to distract me?

- Am I completed my subgoals in a timely fashion? If not, what is interfering? Should I take time and attention to manage the interference?

■ Use intentionality, mindfulness, and focus to live each day on purpose and increase your ability to concentrate and work effectively (Kabat-Zinn, 2011; Siegel, 2007). See specific directions for meditation practice and mindfulness exercises as described in Part 4 of this book.

■ Some suggestions for mindful review of goals:

- What do you need to do today to increase congruency between your ideal life, as represented by your Pyramid of Power, and your actual life? Consider that what you need to do might be something small, such as writing for half an hour daily.

- What are the most essential tasks that relate to your mission and vision that need to be done today (if you like to use the VAST list)?

■ Once or twice a week, remind yourself to keep perspective. These questions might help you stay on your intended course and prevent being distracted by the tendency to search for what is wrong with your life:

- If you had all the money you need, what would you do?
- If you knew you could not fail, what would you do?
- If you had a fatal illness and knew you would die in five years, how would you live?
- If you knew you only had 24 hours to live, what would be your regrets? What music is still in you that has not yet been played? Sometimes I feel like I'm playing "Sixteen Tons" when I would rather play "Girls Just Want to Have Fun."

Align Your Space with Your Goals

Urban legend has it that the average business executive searches for lost objects eight hours a week. I would venture a guess that some of the more absentminded professors that I coach spend even more time than that looking for lost keys and class notes. One faculty member lost an entire set of term papers and did not find them until three years later when she cleaned out her car to sell it. Unless searching for your own lost treasure is a hobby, align your work space for better work flow, and use the time you have been spending on those scavenger hunts for productive work or fun instead. Evidence is building from the field of neuroscience that good work space design supports high productivity (Epstein, 2011). Design your environment to compel you to do your high-priority tasks as easily as possible.

The ABCs of a Productive Desk

Imagine that your desk is divided into zones designated by how far they are from your reach when you are seated. For the present moment, I am going to imagine an average office desk with no computer or monitor on it (we'll deal with the computer in a minute). Label as the "A" section that section of the desk formed by the space inside your hands when you sit at the desk and place your hands comfortably on the desk where the armrests reach the desk. The A section will measure about 16 inches wide and 16 inches deep from the edge of the desk. The "B" area of your desk is a rim, 8–10 inches wide, arcing around the A area. The "C" area is the rest of the desk. On large desks you won't be able to reach the C section unless you stand up and lean over the desk.

Here is how to use your desk space as you work.

- Use the A section of your desk for what you are currently working on, the B section for "next priorities and projects," and the C section for the level after that.

- When you finish with the materials of your current work project in the A area use the "cracker crumbs" technique mentioned earlier to capture the ideas you are working on so that you save start up time the next time you work on the project.

- Move those materials to the B area if you are coming back to the project later that day or to the C area if you are going to work on it the next day. If you are not going to work on that project again in the next day or two, move it to the front of your desk file drawer.

- When the project is completely finished, archive it in the least accessible drawer of your stand-alone file cabinet—usually the top drawer (the one you can't reach unless you are standing) or, the bottom drawer (if you stand to file). If you will need the materials in a week or so, file in one of the middle drawers of your file cabinet, the ones you can reach from either sitting or standing.

- Work on the next priority project and its accompanying materials, which should be found in the B area of your desk.

- Repeat the steps until close to the end of the workday or until you finish your to-do list.

- If all of your intended work in areas A and B is completed before your work session is over, grab something from the C area to work on.

- At the end of your office time, you can order your projects in stacks in the A, B, and C zones for the next day or clear the desk and file things in that same order in the front of your desk file drawer. At my campus office, I cleared because I didn't want student materials loose on the desk; in my home office, I stacked because only I used that space.

Most readers will have computers in their offices, so here are my suggestions for how to have both computer space and free work space.

- Aim for either two separate flat surfaces or an L-shaped desk. While a single desk can work if you set the monitor back on the desk with the print enlarged so that some of the A area is available for working, two separate dedicated surfaces, one for computer and one for other work, allow for a better work flow.

- An L shaped desk is ideal for most people; one surface serves as a dedicated work zone and the other (usually the smaller) as a computer work station. On the working desk follow the suggestions listed earlier for A, B, and C work areas.

- If you can't get an L-shaped desk from your department, ask to have an auxiliary computer table brought in and set it in an L position to your main desk. If the department can't afford it, get one yourself at the office supply store for less than $30. Set it as a right angle to your desk so you can swivel effortlessly from one desk to the other.

- If your office space won't allow the L arrangement, an alternative is to position a flat table or credenza on one wall and a desk on the other with your chair in between. You face one to use the computer, and then swivel to use the desk with the A, B, and C working spaces.

- Be fussy about the ergonomics of your arrangements. Always sit facing the computer or work space. If you sit at an angle to your monitor, you risk discomfort, which will tire you more than the work does. Your eyes should look straight or slightly down to the monitor. Your hands should set on the keyboard at a right angle. None of these rules can be followed with a laptop. If you use a laptop, get a docking station so that the laptop becomes the CPU with an auxiliary monitor, keyboard, and mouse. The cost of $200–300 for the docking station and auxiliary equipment will save you from hunching over a laptop which causes pain, decreases productivity, and sends you into physical therapy.

Feng Shui in the Office

Feng Shui is the ancient Asian art of arranging space so that it is conducive to its use. Walk into your office as if you were a visitor. What is the atmosphere and use of this space? Pleasant, serious work area? Archive in the Smithsonian basement? Sorting area at the recycling center? Scene from the *Hoarders* show?

Arrange your furniture in the most attractive, practical way possible. Eliminate the paper clutter by keeping up with filing and tossing. The best filing system is one that is easy for you to use. If you haven't yet developed yours, these suggestions will make a quick but noticeable improvement in your office filing system.

- File in ways that allow you quick retrieval. You don't need fancy colored folders unless those really help you. What you do need is a filing system that is arranged in response to this key question: "How will I look for this material the next time I need it?"

- If you have a stand-alone four-drawer file cabinet, designate the drawers by accessibility from the position you will use them. If you like to slide your wheeled office chair over to the file cabinet, the highest-priority drawers are the middle two. If you like to stand when you work with files, the top two drawers are the highest-priority drawers. The least accessible drawer should be reserved for seldom used materials.

- An alternative system is to designate file drawers by roles and responsibilities—for example, one drawer for teaching, one for research, one for service, and one for advising.

- On your file labels, use a topic/subtopic system—for example, Committee/Curriculum Committee/P&T. All of your current committee files should be in the same place with the specific committees in alphabetical order. Similarly label your teaching files—for example, Teaching/Victorian Literature/Fall 2013, Teaching/American Literature/Spring 2014, and Teaching/Women's Literature/Spring 2014. Apply this practice to your research files as well.

- If you have a desk file drawer, use it only for current projects, committees, and courses.

- Establish a similar priority system for your bookshelves, with your most frequently used books easiest to reach in the way you use the shelves, either seated in your desk chair or standing. It may seem common sense that the best book arrangement is by topic, but I consulted once with a professor who had his books arranged by size; this system would have been fine if he could remember whether the book related to his most recent research was 3" × 5", 5" × 8", or 8½" × 11". Finding a book was a one-hour hunting expedition. It could have been worse, though: I recently saw a photo in a high-end furniture store catalogue that had the books on the bookshelf arranged with the pages toward the camera and the bindings out of sight.

- Review all your file drawers (especially the desk file drawer) at the end of the semester. Move this semester's class notes to the teaching file drawer. Throw out irrelevant folders, and clear out your desk drawer for the next semester's projects and courses. If you do this activity at the end of each semester it will take less than an hour. If you have never done this, well, get help the first time.

- Get everything off the floor (that includes auxiliary file boxes). Hang up coats. Declutter the walls and bulletin boards, leaving only things that support your work.

Thinking in Your Office

Faculty need "thinking time," time allocated to high-demand brain activities such as preparing content material for classes and working on scholarly research. These activities should be done in an environment free from distractions. What is your best space for thinking time? Home, office, or a third place?

Is your office conducive to "thinking time"?

- Do you share a space? Then your office is probably not a good space for thinking time.

- Is your office located in a distracting place near the building entrance where it is mistaken for the building information center? If so, can you turn your desk to a wall to prevent appearing available to passersby?

- Do you let messages go quietly to voice and e-mail, and do you close your door until posted office hours while you are advising students or working on high-concentration tasks?

- Is your office neat enough to keep you focused or are you distracted and stressed by clutter or undone tasks (Epstein, 2011)?

- Do you have necessary equipment nearby: computer, research files, and so on?

Thinking at Home

Some professors like to do their thinking at home, either for convenience or because their home office is quieter than their cubicle or shared space on campus. If you do wish to work at home, how do you protect that space and time?

- Do you have a dedicated home office? If not, you need a special corner that can be dedicated to your work, perhaps in a guest bedroom or the basement. One chair at the same dining room table where the kids do their homework does not count as a home office.

- Educate your housemates that you need to spend a block of time in the home office to better do your job. Establish clear boundaries so they know that you are working. One professor wore a baseball cap with his university logo when he was working.

- Don't procrastinate on your real work by answering phones and e-mail, and don't clean house or pay bills during designated work periods. Use those potential distractions as rewarding breaks for completing work tasks.

If neither office nor home is good work space for you, consider a third space, perhaps a carrel in the school library, or a coffee shop or fast food restaurant where you can work with anonymous noise in the background and without interruptions from a wait person.

Robison's Rule
Arrange your time, space, priorities, and even your interruptions including breaks to support your work flow.

Chapter 11

Align Your Work Habits for Success

THIS CHAPTER WILL help you establish work habits that will support you as you become a peak-performing professor. When you set appropriate standards and connect your daily activities to your bigger vision, your work life will become more productive and happy.

Work from Strength

Do more of what you are good at and what already works; do less of what doesn't. When Chris Peterson systemized the measurement of strengths drawn from his study of the key character traits of cultures and philosophical systems around the world, he equated virtue and strengths. This would have pleased Oscar Wilde, who said, "One is not always happy when one is good; but one is always good when one is happy."

As you live your mission, look for ways to use your self-rated top strengths, and you will boost your happiness and productivity (Wood et al., 2011). If that gets boring, reach down further into other things you are good at, and find projects that tap those strengths. Your energy level is the test; do more of what jazzes you. Delegate or eliminate tasks that are outside your strengths or that deplete you unless they are absolutely necessary to achieve what is important to you.

Connect Your Daily Goals with Your Vision

Continue to dream big, set goals, and move to action. Long-term happiness depends on your ability to tolerate a healthy alignment gap between current achievements (*to-date* accomplishments) and what you still wish to achieve (*to-go* goals) (Koo & Fishbach, 2008). Connecting daily and long-term goals will help you maintain focus. Loss of focus causes us to procrastinate on activities that would bring better return on investment for us and our institutions while we plod through a day's worth of administrivia that seem urgent at the moment but are not all that important in the long term.

The happiest, most productive people are those who see the complex tapestry of their lives as all one fabric. To keep yourself on track, reconnect with your Pyramid of Power periodically to remind yourself of your purpose, mission, and vision—why you are doing what you do. When those activities no longer seem relevant and you feel that you are just going through the motions, review and rewrite your Pyramid of Power. Here are some reminders about how to use the power of purpose to continue working in your peak-performance zone:

- Align your tasks and time to your unique mission rather than just to a set of to-do lists by intentionally deciding what you are doing with your time on a monthly, weekly, and daily basis (see techniques in the next section of this chapter).

- Use intentional attention to give each task your full energy, staying focused on one important thing at a time until its completion.

- Work from intrinsic motivations (autonomy, competence, and relatedness), which are more powerful than extrinsic motivations (fame, money, and favorable outward appearance) (Chancellor & Lyubomirsky, 2011; Ryan & Deci, 2000). Make good choices to spend your resources by saying "Yes" to opportunities that connect to your values.

- Define specific goals rather than general ones (Halvorson, 2011). Goals that take only 15–30 minutes are easier to accomplish in the tripartite job description of the professor than global goals that carry over from list to list, staring at you, making you feel guilty and ineffectual.

- Increase the probability that you will complete a goal by using if-then planning, in which you plan for what, when, how you will work on the goal and what you will do if something goes wrong or you are tempted by interruptions and distractions (Gollwitzer & Brandstätter, 1997; Gollwitzer & Oettingen, 2011; Halvorson, 2011).

- Increase your chance of success by using implementation strategies, in which you plan how you will implement your goal, along with mental contrasting, in which you keep in mind what you want in the future and where you are now (Duckworth, Grant, Loew, Oettingen, & Gollwitzer, 2011).

- Expect the completion of your goals to be difficult though possible; people who do so are more successful than those who presume that creating the goals is the hard part and completing them is the easy part (Gollwitzer et al., 2004; Gollwitzer & Oettengen, 2011).

- Arrange your environmental circumstances to stimulate goal completion and decrease temptation so you take the load off ego depletion. This is the strategy of people with good self-control; they use less self-control because they use it at the front end to make choices from the array of options, thereby lowering stress and minimizing crises (Crescioni et al., 2011).

- Expect that you will always have more goals than you can complete; the key is to act from your priorities.

The combination of these strategies will help you narrow the alignment gap and eliminate alignment anxiety. Exercise 11.1 gives you a short-cut method for making your goals less onerous.

Many activities, such as completing a Ph.D., writing a book, or rearing children, that lead to long-term successes and a deep sense of long-term satisfaction are often challenging to work on in the short term (Baumeister, 1991; Lyubomirsky & Boehm, 2010). These activities require grit, the ability to persevere for long-term goals that one cares about (Duckworth, Peterson, Matthews, & Kelly, 2007). Personally, I have never regretted any of these sacrifices. My Ph.D. led to having had a great time in my career, I've written several books including this one, and I'm lucky my kid turned out all right. By the way if you find any typos in this book, they're her fault.

Adopt a Growth Mind-set

Openness to new experiences promotes creativity. Buddhist teacher Thich Nhat Hanh (2007) wrote, "Our idea of happiness can prevent us from actually being happy. We fail to see the opportunity for joy that is right in front of us when we are caught in a belief that happiness should take a particular form." Psychologist Carol Dweck (2008) has studied how people with growth mind-sets, who believe that a skill can be learned and who are open to learning it, are happier than individuals with fixed mind-sets, who presume that one is born with whatever talent one will ever have. Her current research demonstrates that people with growth mind-sets do not get as tired from their efforts; they do not experience the ego depletion of people with fixed mind-sets (Dweck, 2012). If hope and optimism are important components of happiness, it makes sense that a growth mind-set, offers more control and possibilities for the future. You will more likely to keep a hopeful mind-set if you see that every problem you encounter offers an opportunity to grow, learn, and succeed. These questions might lead you to develop more of a growth mind-set:

- If you had unlimited intelligence, what would you do with it?
- If money were no object, what would you try?
- If you could be famous for one thing, what would you want it to be?
- If you knew you could not fail, what would you try?

EXERCISE 11.1

Leap Frog

Think of a goal you have been wanting to complete but can't because of some obstacle, such as a lack of a skill, money, or energy. Imagine how you might work on the goal if you felt better or less blocked. Now pretend that you can leap over feeling blocked and already feel better with all the resources you need; how would you start?

So, do that: start. You may find that you didn't really need to have the obstacle removed or that starting on the goal actually removed some of the obstacle.

Set Standards and Benchmarks

One of the mistakes that hard-working professors make is to use the same high standards on all that they do. They overuse the maxim, "Anything worth doing is worth doing well." If you aim for the highest standards on all you do, you will get very little done. Instead, increase your productivity by diversifying your standards. Some things are worth doing badly, some are worth doing well, and some are not worth doing. As an example, when you mop your kitchen floor, getting up the sticky lemonade spills might be good enough most of the time. Aiming to keep a perfectly cleaned floor robs you of time that you could have used to outline a scholarly article. Many goals can be *satisficed*, meaning that you get by with the minimum so you can move on to the goal at hand. For example, writers who "satisfice" on their first drafts get more writing done than those who aim at perfect drafts (Flower & Hayes, 1980).

If perfectionism is a challenge for you, experimenting with a range of standards will require a new way of thinking: for many of your goals, perfect is the enemy of good, good enough is the friend of done, and done is better than perfect. One of the bad effects of perfectionism is that you set overly high standards for too many goals, leading to several negative consequences. Either you may complete fewer goals at those high standards or you may feel so overwhelmed by the goals and their high standards that you avoid the whole mess. With the first effect, your productivity will be too low to survive an academic career. With the second, you will procrastinate on important goals and then either not complete them or slam them together at the last minute, causing both high stress and low quality. It is no accident that professors in my workshops who seek a cure for procrastination often claim to be perfectionists. The key variable that predicts procrastination is impulsiveness. Perfectionistic professors who dash from one fire to the next get less done than those professors with high standards who stick to one task at a time (Steel, 2007). Aiming for done at a certain standard is better than aiming for perfect because perfect is just not possible. Every class, article, or meeting could be always improved.

In contrast to perfectionists, peak performers select from a range of standards and benchmarks so that they integrate task requirements with their values. These performers accomplish many goals at diversified standards appropriate to the goals. The path away from perfectionism and toward peak performance has many stops along the way (Burns, 1999).

Consider constructing a performance rubric for your work roles and responsibilities the same way you might use a grading rubric for your class assignments. How would you describe a 30% performance? How about a 50% performance? What does mastery at 90% look like? Defining the benchmarks to be attained along the path to mastery will encourage your progress. A mastery-level execution of a skill will earn a 90%, but the first time use of that skill might result in a grade of only 30%. Expecting to leap to mastery in one jump is to ignore the learning processes necessary to grow a skill. One of the early motivation psychologists, David McClelland, found that high achievers improve their performances by setting goals with a 50–70% chance of success, figuring out what to do to correct mistakes, and trying again, while their less successful counterparts aim either too high or too low (McClelland, 1988). Setting low goals seem intuitive; low goals ensure success with little effort. Setting high goals, however, ensures an excuse for not succeeding—namely, aiming too high to even have a chance at success. In both cases, low achievers deprive themselves of the satisfaction of reaching a challenging but doable goal.

Here is an example of a political science professor's rubric for his scholarly writing imagining that "perfect" is 100%

- 30% ideas collected, put into a mind map, an outline with a bit of a flow, sketchy but logical order, a few examples and citations.

- 50% smoother writing in a logical order, more examples and citations and ready to be sent to friendly readers.

- 90% all ideas organized into an excellent flow, good examples, relevant citations, writing style concise but interesting, manuscript well-edited, ready to be sent to journal editors.

One way to beat perfectionism and procrastination while you increase your productivity is to audition some of your 30% material or skills by incorporating them into an already exemplary class plan filled with some of your 90% material. That way, new material will be integrated into an already predictably good product. The opposite action will also be a helpful strategy: the first time you teach a course, consider including relevant mastery-level material from another class along with the brand-new, untried material.

Performance professionals in all fields use these strategies to build their confidence in their performances. When comedian Chris Rock filmed his most recent HBO special, he prepared for a year by trying out new material at small neighborhood comedy clubs around the country. He studied the audience response to each story, rewrote it until it zinged (his benchmark), and then included only the best of the best in his final show. Academic researchers such as psychologist Heidi Grant Halvorson often publish many articles and chapters (Grant & Dweck, 2003) before integrating them into a book (Halvorson, 2011).

Use your performance values to set standards and benchmarks for your rubrics:

- What are the barest minimum standards I need to aim for in the lowest-priority areas of my life and work?

- What are the barest minimum standards for the starting point in my highest-priority areas and how can I improve over time?

- In what areas can I satisfice in the short term to develop a great product in the long term?

- What standard would I like to hit with this next project (class, paper, presentation)?

- What simple measurement can I use to evaluate my performances: 1–10 scale, 0–100% letter grades? What verbal descriptors fit the score points?

- What benchmarks do I need to complete to feel satisfied about my productivity on this project, task, or to-do?

- What is the cost-benefit ratio for my standards on this project?

- What objective criteria (student evaluations, annual reviews with chair or dean, and so on) can I apply to test the reality of my self-ratings so that I'm not fooling myself into thinking I am doing well when I'm not, or vice versa, improving an already wonderful performance to make it even more "perfect"?

Setting reasonable standards that match your values and the situation will add to your productivity.

Instill Structures and Rituals

The way you structure your life can add considerably to your effectiveness and well-being. Following a weekly schedule that includes all your role responsibilities reasonably distributed across the week takes the strain off of your brain and increases your productivity. It is very freeing to turn all of that decision making into one up-front decision in which you set all your activities into your tracking sheet, clock, and calendar. Then you don't have to decide when to sleep, when to grade papers, or when to prepare for class. My favorite grocery shopping time is Tuesday evening at 7 pm; supplies have been replenished from the weekend, the store is not crowded, and I don't have to make a new decision about when to shop each week.

Reduce decisions about wellness activities by scheduling them on automatic pilot: for example, you might schedule a run with a friend on Monday, Wednesday, and Friday; a yoga class on Tuesday; and a spinning class on Thursday. With such a schedule you are supporting your fitness needs through aerobics, stretching, and strength training without overthinking it. Habits reduce the need for willpower because they act like computer subroutines that run automatically in the background while the main program is doing taxing new work (Baumeister & Tierney, 2011).

Similarly, get more professional writing done by scheduling regular sessions when you have the time, place, materials, and tasks predetermined. A daily schedule also allows you to structure your rhythm so that you are working in short sprints on work followed by short rests, a pattern of pulsing and pausing known to produce high performances in athletes and office workers alike (Loehr & Schwartz, 2004). People who plan when and where they will engage in their goals are more likely to complete them (Gollwitzer & Oettingen, 2011).

Rituals are another useful tool to support your well-being and happiness, especially rituals that are social and spiritual. Friday night Shabbat is a wonderful way for a family to end one week and begin another. Sunday after-church brunch reconnects family members with one another and their spiritual beliefs. Having season tickets to the symphony gives you a regular date with your spouse or best friend without having to exert the effort to think up an activity, plan it, and spend the time searching online for tickets.

Increase Your Perception of Abundance

Decide how much is enough in various aspects of your life. Then set goals for how to match those guidelines.

- How much money do you need in your savings account to feel secure?
- How many scholarly publications do you want to produce this year?
- How much time with your friends and family feels good?
- How much recreation time do you want, when, and how?

Answering those questions will provide the boundaries within which to contain your life. For example, applied to your finances, this practice will help you perceive that you have enough money if you lop off some items from your spending plan and enjoy what you already have. Similarly, you will immediately increase your sense of time abundance, the perception that you have enough time to complete your goals, if you make fewer goals. It may sound contradictory to read in a productivity book that you should decrease the number of goals that you have, but expecting less from yourself relieves stress and gives you more focus on the high-priority goals. Ultimately, people with focused goals actually complete more of them than people who feel scattered by working on lots of goals simultaneously.

Celebrate Success

Professors can be so driven by their many goals they don't pause long enough to enjoy their success. Don't wait for the completion of a huge project to celebrate. Instead, celebrate reaching benchmarks. If you are working on a book, celebrate every chapter as you complete it.

Share your successes with relevant people who have supported you, such as your mate, students, boss, and others. Celebrations don't have to be elaborate. After completing a goal, enjoy a special candlelit dinner in the dining room with your mate. Perhaps send thank-you notes to colleagues or an invitation to a book signing to people who have helped you with your book. (See further suggestions for enjoying your success in Part 3 of this book.)

The day after the celebration, review your Tracking Sheet on the project so you don't fall into the trap of being so impressed with your success this far that you forget the work that will finish the project, take it to the next level, or build on it with another project worthy of your time and energy (Koo & Fishbach, 2008). If you have a tendency to move on too quickly from a success to your next set of goals, move the sticky notes on which you've written your goals to the back of the Dream Book pages when you complete them, so that you can review your accomplishments every few days, weeks, or months. Pause from time to time to remind yourself of those accomplishments and how they connect to the development of your current successes.

Robison's Rule
Free your brain for creative thinking: decide on good work habits,
then "set 'em and forget 'em."

Part Three

Connect with Mutually Supportive People

The purpose of human life is to serve, and to show compassion and the will to help others.

—Albert Schweitzer

MANY PROFESSORS VIEW people, personalities, and politics as a distraction from the professors' jobs. This perspective harms you in two ways. First, avoiding the "distraction" of other people means you are not developing the ability to connect quickly and well with others, a skill that is a big part of the tripartite faculty job description. Teaching itself is a people job, requiring that you connect well enough with students to establish a good learning atmosphere (Walvoord, 2008). Scholarly work often requires collaboration with colleagues and editors (Gray, 2010). Good interpersonal skills help you find role models and get mentored, as well as earn promotions and create collaborations. Most service opportunities—advising, committee assignments, and leadership positions—involve working with others to make decisions, often under duress (Boyatzis & McKee, 2005; Burns, 2010; Goleman, 2006; Kouzes & Posner, 2003).

Second, if you hold the attitude that people and their idiosyncrasies are annoying distractions or "campus politics," you place the problem outside any control or influence that you might exert. Of course you can't control other people, but you do have control over how you approach your relationships and also on how you offer positive influence to others.

While your accomplishments demonstrate that you are already smart and skilled in the area of your subject matter, school smarts are not the only way you need to be smart in this profession. The techniques and skills of a discipline account for only 33% of the likelihood of success in most fields, whereas social connection accounts for 66% (Goleman, 2006).

Unfortunately, the autonomy that academics value so much can be taken to the extreme, leading to iconoclasm, isolation, lack of support, and helpful accountability. Humans are wired to be social, to live and work in communities. Survival of the individual and the species depends on our ability to connect with others for mutual benefit (Haidt, 2012). When professors ignore the importance of building and maintaining relationships, they make their work harder, their moods cranky, and possibly their behaviors uncivil, all of which undermine career success.

Applying social skills to your job does not mean that you must be best friends with the people at work or become a party animal. You merely need to connect well enough to work with others toward common goals such as the quality of education, the welfare of students, or the discovery and promulgation of knowledge. Employees who are fortunate enough to develop friendships at work, however, do engage more enjoyably in the job (Gallup Foundation, 2009; Peterson & Park, 2006), live longer and better (Buettner, 2010; Oz & Roizen, 2008), manage stress better (Taylor, 2002, 2008; Taylor et al., 2000), and experience greater happiness both in the short and long term (Kahneman, Krueger, Schkade, Schwartz, & Stone, 2004; Park & Peterson, 2009; Seligman, 2011). Social skills are a necessary part of success on the job. Fortunately, they can be improved very quickly with a bit of practice.

You know that learners learn best when they have a simple framework. Part 3 lays out the major social intelligence skills required for good collaboration with colleagues in a structure that simplifies human relationships as a logical progression of skills. This part of the book asks you to imagine that you are following a hypothetical professional relationship from first encounter through to a successful and mutually supportive relationship. Relationships are more complicated than this simple model portrays, but as a teaching tool, this hypothetical relationship will emphasize skills for developing and maintaining collegial relationships. These same skills can also be applied to relationships with students, friends, and family (see Part 5 for those applications). The three stages of this hypothetical relationship are as follows:

1. Engaging each other at the start of a relationship through meeting and greeting skills.

2. Collaborating for mutual benefit.

3. Creating a productive and satisfying relationship that flourishes in spite of the normal conflict inevitable in any relationship.

Some of the skills presented in this structure will be familiar. You just might not have ever thought about them as part of a systemic whole. In addition, this simple model may also challenge you to learn new skills. As with the skills presented in other parts of this book, don't try to do everything at once. Each day presents opportunities for you to try out these skills and improve your approach to relationships.

How Part 3 Will Help You Become a Peak Performing Professor

This part of the book will help you acquire the following skills:

1. Use social intelligence to make connections and build a community of support so that you can work better and live better.

2. Enjoy and be good at networking.

3. Develop and maintain collaborative collegial relationships.

4. Approach relationship problems and conflicts with ease and confidence.

Chapter 12

Engage Others: Meeting and Greeting

ANSWER HONESTLY, ON a 1–10 scale: How much do you love networking events, faculty receptions, cocktail parties, and teas?

If you are like most faculty, you cringed in response to this question. Whenever I ask this question to faculty audiences as a true/false question, only 3% are excited about networking opportunities. I believe part of the response is due to a phenomenon I have observed in my workshops but can find no empirical studies to verify, namely, the higher proportions of introverts (as measured by the Myers Briggs Preference Inventory) among faculty (75% compared to 25% extroverts) compared to the U.S. split (75% extrovert to 25% introvert) or the world split (50/50) (Tieger & Barron-Tieger, 1993).

Scoring higher in introversion does not mean you don't like people or lack social skills. According to Carl Jung's personality theory (Tieger & Barron-Tieger, 1992), it merely describes how people gain and renew their energy when they are tired. Extroverts replenish their energy through social stimulation, whereas introverts express a preference for being alone or hanging out with people with whom they are already acquainted. For introverts, the thought of gearing up at the end of the day to meet new people at a social event makes them want to take to their beds. Introverts have an experience and go home to process it alone; extroverts haven't had an experience until they process it with others. The tips in this section will help introverts build relationships without having to change their personalities. The same tips will also be helpful for extroverts who sometimes struggle with finding topics to talk to strangers about.

Most professors dread meeting new people at loud, crowded events. They also dread the perceived social requirement of those events, making small talk, an activity that intellectual professionals disdain. I used to be one of those professors—until I learned a few tricks I will share with you about networking that will guarantee that you will never have to make small talk again. Not only will these skills easily move your professional conversations from small talk to big talk, these skills will also be helpful to teach to your students so that they are better prepared to network when they enter the business and professional worlds.

While it is clear that people can develop e-mail and online relationships, for our purposes we will emphasize relationships that begin with a face-to-face meeting. Instead of thinking about networking as an activity that only takes place at dreaded, crowded, noisy receptions, consider that you already have been networking in many settings your whole life. We will start by studying what you have already done to meet people and to develop mutually supportive relationships. Then we will make the process less haphazard and more systematic.

1. With whom have you socialized in the past six months?

2. With whom have you discussed matters important to you in the past six months?

3. Name someone who has been important to your work life in the past six months.

4. Name someone whose work life you have been important to in the past six months.

5. Name someone who would be influential in obtaining approval or resources for an important project you want to work on.

As you answered those questions, it might become obvious to you that you already have networks of people whom you influence and who influence you. If the people in your network all know one another, you have a *closed network*. If they do not, you belong to multiple *open networks*. There are advantages and disadvantages to both kinds of network. People in closed networks compose a stable group of people working together to support one another's agenda. People in open networks bring in fresh information and perspective and enrich one another's professional growth. One reason to meet new people is that you need both types of networks to support your productivity and happiness.

When it comes to maximizing professional opportunities, it is better to have a large number of weak ties (casual acquaintances) rather than a small number of strong ties (close friends) (Granovetter, 1973). You are more likely to be considered for professional opportunities when you are connected to several influential people with key professional relationships rather than to just one or two close friends. This does not mean you should not have good, close friendships. Rather it means that you also need a variety of casual professional contacts with whom you can share resources such as research information or introductions to other possibly supportive colleagues. Luck favors the well-prepared and well-connected.

The surest way to conquer shyness about networking with strangers is to structure your interactions with others. Following these simple rules will make networking events less stressful and perhaps even enjoyable (Baber & Waymon, 2007).

- *No small talk:* Use the same basic interviewing skills described later in this chapter to transform networking events from torture to tolerable or even to terrific.

- *No big groups:* Until you are comfortable with your skills, stay away from groups of people conversing. Instead look for individuals to talk with—especially people who look more uncomfortable than you feel. Your job will be to help them feel at ease.

- *No strangers:* Look for people who have interests similar to yours. For example, at a professional conference look for others who attended the same workshop you attended earlier in the day. Instead of conversing about the weather or the conference in general, ask them what they learned in the workshop that applies to their campus roles.

- *No forgetting:* If you exchange business cards with someone you just met, take a moment to write on the back of the person's card some memory joggers about the person, his or her interests, and the gist of your conversation.

There are four skills important to successful networking:

1. Form a quick impression of the other person and make a good first impression.

2. Turn small talk into *big talk* for mutual benefit.

3. Listen deeply and remember what you hear.

4. Use interviewing skills to lead into interesting conversations.

Form a Quick Impression of the Other

Like an intriguing movie plot, the meeting of two strangers is really two stories told from two points of view. During this first encounter, both people play two roles simultaneously: that of impression-former and that of impression-giver. At the same time as you are making an impression about your trustworthiness, social class, and intelligence, the other person is giving you data to aid in the formation of your impression of him or her.

First impressions matter. Even before two people speak, they gather visual data about each other's faces and bodies. Whether we like it or not, we judge others, and they judge us. Our brains prevent us from becoming easily overwhelmed by using streamlined systems for quick assessments of people, often forming an impression within the first four minutes of a meeting (Zunin & Zunin, 1994).

The ability to quickly separate friend from foe was a question of survival for our cave ancestors. In modern society, our brains persist in making each meeting about survival. Extreme situations like campus shootings aside, most academics don't have to worry about the threat of physical danger from students and colleagues. Yet other, nonphysical dangers lurk—the danger of competition, the danger of being bested by someone, the danger of contract nonrenewal, or the danger of student complaints to the dean. Our brains' self-protective quick circuitry can't tell the difference between life-threatening and ego-threatening events, so we often respond in similar ways to both kinds of event.

Although most colleges have statements on their websites about not discriminating against people due to their personal characteristics, it is a struggle to be inclusive, because our brains are hardwired to exclude nontribe members from our tribal activities. Territoriality is merely an extension of our tribal tendencies; we think, "This piece of land, river, or lake is a resource for my tribe to plant on, sail down, or drink out of. You can't have it for your tribe." This predisposition, outdated as it might seem, is the social-biological basis for racism, sexism, and international wars (Haidt, 2012).

Fast-forward through the history of mankind, and you will see that territoriality in academic life becomes "this funding, lab space, classroom belongs to my tribe for our use. You can't have it for your tribe."

Our long-term success as professors depends, however, on our ability to override that territorial hardwiring with software that leads to true inclusiveness, the ability to extend our tribe to include diverse others. This inclusionary mind set looks for similarities of background or interests and allows us to work successfully with diverse colleagues and students who might not, at first meeting, strike us as similar to ourselves.

After we decide whether a person is a friend or foe, as in "my tribe versus the other tribe," our brains move on to the second question "Can I trust that this person is really who s/he say they are?" If trust for our cave ancestors involved evaluating that others would not harm them, trust in the academy might be about whether a job candidate can work with the rest of the department without a lot of conflict and drama.

Several findings from neuroscience can help you understand others and your reactions to them.

■ Pay attention to your mirror neurons. These neural wifi cells pick up the behavior and emotions of others to provide you with a shortcut into what the other is doing or feeling (Di Pellegrino, Fadiga, Fogassi, Gallese, & Rizzolatti, 1992).

■ Guard against mood contagion, the down side of mirror neurons. While your neural "tuning fork" mirrors the vibrations of others' moods, you still need to be able to distinguish your own feelings from the experience of others (Barsade, 2002; Goleman, 2006), or you will be prone to physiological linkage, bodily changes that occur when one person's upset triggers a heightening of stress arousal in the other. Marriage researchers found that if you are too much on the same wavelength and share a physiological linkage with your stressed spouse, you may miss the chance in the short run to do effective problem solving because of emotional flooding, and you may be at increased risk for stress-related health problems in the long term (Kiecolt-Glaser & Newton, 2001; Levinson & Gottman, 1983).

■ Learn to read microgestures. Essential to forming quick but accurate information about people is the ability to read fleeting facial expressions and the emotions they convey (Ekman, 2007). Attending to these powerful yet subtle cues helps you assess trustworthiness and authenticity. You can test your ability to read faces and practice the skills by going to Paul Ekman's website (www.paulekman.com).

■ Train yourself to notice body language and emotions by observing speakers, conversation partners, or even TV characters. Turn down the volume on a soap opera, and you will probably be able to guess most of the plot.

■ Increase your brain's ability to read people through the regular practice of meditation, which can help you override the unconscious tendency to judge people negatively. Buddhist monks who meditated on compassionate feelings toward others were more easily able to act compassionately toward them (Lutz, Brefczynski-Lewis, Johnstone, & Davidson, 2008).

Make a Good First Impression

When we meet people for the first time at a faculty reception or in class, we are anxious to make a good first impression. This is the reason you may have had those typical teacher nightmares about showing up for class dressed in your pajamas or about getting lost on the way to a conference presentation.

This normal social anxiety can be so overwhelming as to be debilitating and can cause people to avoid social functions. You do not need long-term therapy to fix this problem. Learning some practices that structure interactions will help you approach all social functions with more purpose and less anxiety.

Appearance

When you encounter someone for the first time, you need to give information that is consistent with the person you really are. Your posture, hygiene, dress, speech pattern all create an impression of you. Dressing like the other tribe members gets your relationships off on the right foot.

Follow the behavioral norms for your campus and professional associations on how to act, including how people address one another (Professor, Dr., Mr., Mrs., Ms., first names). Match the norms on how professors arrange their office hours and contact one another, and whether they eat together or alone in their offices. When you are new, try to fit in. You can individuate later, but don't start out with a chip on your shoulder that says, "This is my style and that's it." Find "someone in the know" who seems to know names, is well-liked, and acts confidently. Ask this person for guidelines about the culture. Socialize just enough to get acquainted with your fellow faculty, but don't hang out in the faculty lounge; you have too much work to do.

Meeting and Greeting Skills

Now that you know that networking is not beneath you but rather a step along the way toward developing mutually supportive relationships, let us turn our attention to setting up a structure for your social interactions.

Clarify Your Purpose for Each Social Situation

Defining outcomes for a social event will help structure your connections there.

1. **What outcomes do you want from this function?** Examples might include the following:

   - Get some snacks to hold off hunger.

   - Find Alice and see whether she has finished her dissertation.

   - Look for someone on the program committee and volunteer for next year.

2. **What do you want to give at this function?** Aim at creating relationships of mutual support by imagining that you have something wonderful to offer people that will benefit their careers or lives, such as an introduction

to a journal editor or a recommendation for a local eatery. Although others may express gratitude by offering benefits to you, that is not the point. Instead, by offering others help or information without expecting immediate returns, you will become known as a friendly and generous person. Evidence is accumulating that suggests that such an attitude of generosity, when managed well, will increase your chances of success (Grant, 2013).

Assign Yourself a Role for Each Event

Did you ever notice that when you have a job to do at a social function, like taking coats or checking people in at the door, you don't feel as anxious? A role distracts you from the self-focused feeling of "how am I doing?"— a feeling that undermines social confidence by focusing your attention on how awkward you feel (Zimbardo, 1990). First, you notice that your shoes are scuffed. Then you notice that your heart is pounding, and pretty soon it is pounding even if it wasn't pounding to begin with. Taking on a role at an event decreases social anxiety by distracting you from that intense self-focus.

In addition, when you have a role at a networking function, you have guidelines on how to act, because the role prescribes the behaviors. If you are serving appetizers, you say, "These have cheese, and these have shrimp"; if you are working at the registration desk, you say, "I don't see your name on the registration list, but let me add it."

Even if you don't have an official job at an event, you can give yourself a job. At any networking event, you could assign yourself to be the unofficial greeter, whose job it is to welcome people who look lonely and lost. At a professional conference or your school's back-to-school faculty retreat, you could decide to welcome newcomers, introduce yourself, and use the suggestions given later in this chapter to connect through conversation. You can later connect a couple of newbies by walking them over to other newbies and introducing them, highlighting what they have in common, and then slipping away while they continue to talk about their common interests.

Providing structure to your interactions through this self-appointed greeter role will reduce anxiety by calming your amygdala, the structure in your brain that acts as a danger assessment center. Once your amygdala is assured that the other person is not dangerous, you will relax and show your usual wonderful self to the new person that you are meeting.

Greet People with a Smile, Eye Contact, and an Offer of a Handshake

To our cave ancestors, an open, extended hand signified a hand without a concealed weapon. If people you meet don't offer a hand back, don't take it as a rejection; they may be getting over a cold or come from a culture where touch is not given to strangers.

Introduce Yourself Clearly

1. **Speak your name slowly and clearly**, as if the other person has never heard it before—because he or she hasn't. Don't mumble your name as if you are answering roll call. A good formula is to repeat your first name: "Hi, I'm Susan, Susan Robison." Say your name slowly and highlight a memory trick for the other person, such as "That's Hough, like a hue of a color. Some people thinks it rhymes with *tough* but we Houghs are more colorful than we are tough."

2. **Introduce yourself** with a brief, two-sentence description that is interesting and customized to the setting. Ask yourself, "How do I want to be known in this setting?" For example, at a psychology conference, you might introduce yourself as a cognitive neuroscience learning expert, because others at the conference understand that vocabulary. At a campus faculty event, however, you might introduce yourself as a psychology professor who teaches courses on how the brain influences learning. At your son's PTA meeting, you might introduce yourself to another parent as a college professor who teaches the scientific but not the therapy part of psychology. In each situation, you have adapted your introduction for the setting. For practice in customizing your introductions see Exercise 12.1.

Not only can you customize your introductions related to events, you can use this same tip to customize your bios for presentations. An introduction read before your presentation at a scientific professional association needs technical terms and publication landmarks. An introduction before a talk on the future of higher education at a higher education conference needs to emphasize the specific credentials in higher education that make you qualified to give that presentation, such as being a department chair or publishing articles in higher education journals. Don't have your introducer read your entire curriculum vitae while your audience goes to sleep unless that is the norm for that group. Instead, make your bio short and sweet, even including a bit of humor appropriate to the occasion.

Use Strategies to Remember Names

If you are one of those folks who feels that your brain is a sieve when it comes to interpersonal information, you can improve that part of your memory by learning about people the same way you learn things in your field or for your hobbies. You pay attention, review the information, and try to use it.

■ When you are introduced to a new person, say the name aloud: "Nice to meet you, John." If the person mumbles his name, ask him to

EXERCISE 12.1

Introductions

Write out a two-sentence introduction for three situations in which you might be meeting new people in your work life or your personal life. Ask yourself what the people you meet need to know about you in that context to connect easily with you.

Situation 1

Introduction:

Situation 2

Introduction:

Situation 3

Introduction:

Notice how each introduction is different, but each accurately represents you. Practice speaking these introductions aloud so that they sound smooth and clear. Before your next networking event, rehearse the introduction you will use until it rolls off your tongue.

repeat it. As the person teaches you their name, picture the name written across the person's chest as in a mug shot or above his or her head like a headline in the newspaper. Try to repeat the name back to the person and take a millisecond to associate the name with something physical, as when you notice that Professor Foxx has slightly pointy ears or when someone you meet named Barbara looks like your neighbor Barbara. Using the person's name at least once in the conversation will move the name deeper into your memory.

■   Introduce your new acquaintance to someone else at the event and bring up some common interests if you can. "John Fox, this is Mary Elizabeth Murphy. She is also working on a grant." You will be practicing linking their names while at the same time you are helping them transition to a conversation about grants. Once they continue talking you can slip away to meet other people knowing that you have done your job as "chair of giving people a good time."

■   The very act of writing down names and common interests on a sticky note or business card will help you remember the person and the conversation afterward.

Making Connections

1.   As you meet new people, listen to the other person's introduction and look for places where you can connect your interests and the other person's. What puts you in the same "tribe?" Do you live in the same part of town? Do you both eat lunch at the student café because they have better food than the faculty cafeteria? Do you have joint research or teaching interests?

2.   Share information relevant to the setting and conversation without getting excessively personal. Avoid discussions about campus politics and gossip. Be aware that even subtle unconscious facial expressions about sticky topics can reveal personal emotions. Stick to uncontroversial topics. Be sincerely interested in getting to know the person. Inhibit behavior that turns people off, such as talking at length about yourself and your interests or using language that might better fit poker night with the guys.

3.   Move the conversation from small talk to big talk by asking powerful questions—that is, open-ended questions that allow people to talk about how interesting they are. Small talk is talk about trivia—for example, "What did you think about those snow showers the other day? Unusual for these parts in April, isn't it?"—not exactly scintillating conversation. When you ask a powerful question, the person will often say, "That's a really

good question," because it causes the person to pause to make connections he or she doesn't usually make. Although these questions will usually get others talking about their favorite topic, themselves, the goal of big talk is to lead the conversation to topics of mutual interest rather than just inviting others to ramble about themselves.

Ask questions about professional roles that help you get to know people and their circumstances better without prying into their personal lives. You are aiming for individualized questions that are not so personal that they would make a person uncomfortable, such as questions about marital or parenting status (Baber & Waymon, 2007). An example of a good question is "What is the best part of your job?" You can also plan a few questions related to the event you are attending—questions that can't be answered with "Yes" or "No"—such as, "How would you apply the techniques of today's plenary speaker to your classes?" These questions are reliable conversation movers.

Don't fire questions in rapid succession like a Law and Order detective grilling a suspect. Instead, good interviewing skills require that you learn to listen well and then summarize; "So what you are saying is that . . ." If you are at a loss how to do this, tune in to network TV and watch one of the masters, such as Barbara Walters, do an interview. Instead of watching the celebrity as the camera guides us to do, watch the interviewer to see how he or she directs and paces questions, asks a follow-up question, or segues to a new question altogether. Here are some questions that can be adapted to conversation with any professor.

- What led you to this campus (or conference)?
- How did you decide to go into your field?
- What do you like best about your job?
- What is most challenging about your job?
- What is a typical day like for you in the office, class, lab, clinic?
- What project are you working on that you are most excited about?
- What or who has influenced you in your career choice, research topic, theoretical orientation?
- What advice would you give someone from your experiences?

For conversation-starting questions that you could ask other faculty attendees at a teaching conference, see Exercise 12.2.

Your goal in interviewing and conversing with colleagues is to share relevant work information about one another's roles, responsibilities, and interests in order to find common professional interests. After the other

EXERCISE 12.2

Asking Powerful Questions

Look for opportunities to practice asking powerful questions to find points of connection between yourself and the other. Add some questions of your own relevant to specific interests of the people at the event. For example, the following questions might relate to attendance at a teaching conference:

- What new teaching methods have you implemented lately?
- Have you found any grading methods that cut down on your workload but have good pedagogical outcomes for student learning?
- What books on teaching do you recommend to new assistant professors?
- Have you ever collected research on your teaching methods and presented here?

    Add similar questions you might use at a conference in your discipline.

person answers the powerful questions and you summarize, pause to watch what the other does with the obvious connections you are making. Can that person make similar connections and ask follow-up questions? If the other person asks you questions about a shared area of research, it will give you some clues about possible connections that might prove fruitful, such as collaborating on a joint area of interest or, at least, providing resources for each other. If the person fails to show such enthusiasm, direct the conversation elsewhere with another question: for example, "What are your top priority projects this year?"

You won't fear that these conversations will be too "personal" if you stick to the sort of information that you could get from a person's curriculum vitae. Information beyond the c.v. is culturally bound. For example, although in U.S. culture it is customarily not appropriate to ask a person what his or her salary is, that question could be appropriate in other cultures.

4. If the conversation really begins to connect, relate the next steps of the connection to the setting of your meeting. Next steps might be partly determined by the norms and circumstances of the meeting place. During a five-day conference, you might suggest that you sit together at the next meal to continue the conversation. At a reception for new faculty on your campus, you might exchange business cards and arrange a follow-up meeting. In any setting, once you have decided on follow up, wrap up the conversation by exchanging contact information and saying something like "It's been so good meeting you. I look forward to our brunch meeting on Thursday."

Employ graceful exit strategies. If the conversation has not led to a decision to have further contact, say something like "I've enjoyed meeting you, and I know you will want to meet some others today, so enjoy the rest of the reception." You can extend well wishes related to the conversational topics that came up, such as "I hope you are able to straighten out that difficulty with your dissertation committee."

Don't try to work the whole room. An event is worth your time if you make only a few contacts with whom you can build mutual support.

5. Maintain boundaries appropriate to the nature of the relationship. Picture a diagram of concentric circles representing levels of intimacy from least intimate (outer circle) to greatest (inner circle). The circles determine the behavior that matches the level of intimacy.

- Stranger—a person you are just meeting.
- Work acquaintances—you share common interests or goals but usually do not socialize outside of work.

- Colleagues—you know more about each other, perhaps meet each other's spouses casually at social events.

- Social friends—you socialize regularly with one another; meet one another's mates, children, and parents; and visit one another's homes.

- Close friends—you are social friends and, in addition, you share confidences and help one another out in crises.

- Best friends—you are close friends, participate in one another's lives, and establish interdependency around family celebrations and personal crises.

- Life mates—you are best friends and, in addition, share your household, finances, intimacy, and perhaps children.

Misunderstandings and hurt feelings can be prevented by matching your questions, conversation, and commitment to the level of intimacy of the relationship. You will save yourself from awkward moments, such as when a professor who was an immigrant to the United States gave his lab assistant a Valentine's Day present without realizing that in the United States, Valentine's Day is a romantic holiday for lovers.

When work colleagues confuse a good working relationship with an intimate friendship or romance, trouble abounds. Interactions may not only become awkward but can also, in the case of a romantic involvement, cause legal difficulties. Proceed slowly, and check out expectations with the other person. If you feel things are moving into the next level of intimacy too quickly, kindly state your needs and limits.

There are other cases when conversations about expectations are helpful. For example, Amy was hurt because Kirsten, her colleague from the same department, was not in the audience for Amy's presentation at a conference they both attended. While Kirsten was happy Amy was presenting, Kirsten chose to attend another session that matched her own research interests. If Amy had told Kirsten ahead of time what it meant to Amy to have Kirsten's support at the presentation, Kirsten would have been happy to oblige.

You don't have to change your personality to practice the skills found here. You can adapt the same meeting and greeting rules to any social interaction—whether with students, colleagues, in-laws, or your child's third grade teacher. The structure described here allows you to stay true to any introverted need for alone time while at the same time increasing your confidence that you can walk into a roomful of strangers and talk comfortably to anyone for at least for a few minutes. You will find all social events less intimidating because you will be open to meeting interesting people, starting and deepening relationships for mutual benefit, and actually finding receptions and networking events worth your professional time.

Robison's Rule
Strangers are just friends you haven't met yet.

Chapter 13

Collaborate for Mutual Benefit

IN OUR HYPOTHETICAL relationship, a networking encounter can present an opportunity to turn into a collaboration. To transition those meetings and greetings into successful collaborations, you need to know how to do the following:

- Manage your information about people
- Expand your network and make further contacts
- Continue conversations
- Develop mutual goals

Manage Networking Information

Take advantage of the time you put into meeting people at networking events by managing their information with economy of effort. You want to deepen those relationships that will be most mutually beneficial without spending lots of time communicating your interest. Fortunately, modern electronics helps you manage the information relevant to those relationships with these steps:

■ Soon after the event, capture the relevant information from each person into a database such as your e-mail program. Include contact information and also notes about where you met, the topics of conversation such as common research interests, and any promises you and the other person made to follow up. Capture a photo from the person's department web page so it can jog your memory later.

■ Make a notation about any future contact you would like with each person, such as the projects or collaborations that you talked about. Send out a short note thanking the other for the interesting conversation and include appropriate follow-up information such as articles you promised or possible times to continue the conversation by phone. Review these professional relationships on a monthly schedule with a sticky note on your paper calendar or a signal in your electronic system.

■ With those who respond to your initiation of further contact, extend the initial conversations. Move those who don't respond into an inactive database.

■ Once communication warms up about a project, include occasional phone conversations with "firm up" e-mails to summarize action steps. Phone calls allow for quick brainstorming of ideas and decisions about action plans. This "call first, then send summary e-mail" policy limits both potential misunderstandings and the number of e-mails in your in-box.

Expand Your Network Related to Your Goals

Not only does it take a village to raise a child, it takes a whole village to support each adult as well. You may need different villages to support your varied goals.

■ Every time you pull a new project out of your Dream Book, ask yourself what kind of people with what kind of skills can support you on this project.

■ Use your database to set up a subfile of people who can help.

■ Make clear requests about people's roles, how they can help you, and what you are willing to do in return. Your village may include some mutually supportive people and some people whom you pay for service. For example, if you are writing your first book, your writing village might include a writing mentor or coach, one or more writing buddies with whom you can exchange work for support and critique, or a mastermind group that helps you design and execute a marketing plan. Paid help might include an intellectual property attorney who reviews and amends your contract or an editorial assistant. The key elements are that each person is competent and trustworthy in the role that you are asking them to play.

■ Clean your database from time to time eliminating contacts who are not relevant to the goal of mutual support. Move "inactive" contacts into an inactive folder just in case they contact you about something that interests you. For those who remain, periodically update their contact information.

■ If you do not find the right people in your database for a particular project, expand your network.

- **Mine the gold of your own village to find out whom they know**. We have all experienced how small the world seems to be when we meet someone who knows someone we know (Travers & Milgram, 1969). Although it is urban myth exactly how far removed we are from others—guesses range from three to six people—the application of this social psychology research is that at networking events everyone you encounter potentially "knows a guy who knows a guy," when the "guy" you are looking for is a key resource for your next project.

- **Visit other villages**. Expand your encounters from closed networks, in which all of the people know one another, to open networks by occasionally targeting a new group or event to attend. Meeting new people exposes you to different resources and opportunities, which raises the probability of the right people being in your network when you need them. For example, consider expanding your network by alternating attendance at a conference in your discipline every other year with attendance at a college teaching conference.

Make Further Contact to Continue Conversations

■ Periodically send updates with links about your professional news such as publications and awards to those whom you know would be interested. When others announce their accomplishments, ask permission to circulate that information to your network. Connecting others with similar interests is a great way to earn social capital.

■ Prepare for the next campus event or conference where you are likely to run into the folks you met last time by reviewing your networking information and goals beforehand.

- Review your database for photos and threads of common topics so that you can continue the conversations you began last time.

- Set an agenda for yourself. Do you want to meet new people or reengage with those you have meet before? What can you give and what do you want to get in the interactions?

- Remember to give yourself a role. Think of yourself as "master networker" or "unofficial goodwill ambassador."

■ Greet people you have already met and reintroduce yourself within the context of the previous encounter: "Hi, Fred, I'm Bob Smith. We met at the teaching conference last year. As I recall, you were working on revising an interdisciplinary course. How did that turn out?"

■ Be ready to ask powerful questions. With people you have already met, ask follow-up questions to the previous conversation: "I remember you were having trouble with students texting during class. How did you decide to handle that problem?"

■ Listen well. Listening involves two steps: paying attention and summarizing what the person said.

- Pay attention with your brain and your body. Make eye contact. Shut out the distracting noise, both auditory and visual, that is attacking your brain. Use your mirror neurons to make some guesses about what the other is feeling. Check out the person's face for those unconscious micro gestures about what she is feeling. If you match your face to hers, your mood will begin to match hers and give you helpful information about her experience.

- After a few sentences, summarize what the person has said so far using active listening. If this skill is new to you, use this formula: "You are feeling _____ because _____." As your skill increases, this response will get easier and you will use more creative wording, such as "So you really like what you have been working on this year but you want to produce more publications in the next two years."

■ After you have listened well, ask another powerful question or insert information about yourself.

■ There are no correct rhythms to these conversations, but the goal is reciprocity with each person having approximately equal floor time.

■ As you summarize what the other is saying, highlight the common areas: "It sounds like we both enjoy collecting data on our teaching methods."

■ If the mood is right, it may seem natural to extend the connection to a next step: "Since we have both studied the effects of multiple submission term papers in our classes, would you be interested in partnering on a presentation on that topic for next year's teaching conference?" Often it will be so natural to move to the next level the other person will suggest it.

Conversation connects us to others, so that we feel part of a greater whole, and increases our collective wisdom (Wheatley, 2009). When people don't connect well, their experience is that of detachment, distrust, and invalidation (Cloud, 2006). If some of these skills are new for you, expect to feel awkward when you first try them. As you build new neuronal pathways in the social association part of your brain, these skills will become more automatic and no longer take such conscious effort. The fine art of conversation takes time and practice but will pay off in building mutually supportive relationships.

Form Bonds and Alliances Around Common Goals

You are getting better at remembering names, keeping in touch with people, and listening well. Now you are ready to use these skills to form bonds and build alliances. A bond is a connection between two people formed around a common interest, goal, or shared experience. You can have a bond with someone whom you do not know very well, as long as the common goal is mutually defined, such as working on a committee assignment with another professor.

More general than bonds, alliances are cooperative relationships for mutual benefit, providing mutual support on a variety of goals (Higgerson, 1996). You do not have to be best friends with alliance partners; you just need them to support your causes and agenda. An example of an alliance is a faculty member in your department who shares your passion about quality teaching. The alliance might result in collaborating on pedagogical research or workshops, or it might result in your colleague supporting your application to a special teaching institute with a letter of recommendation.

- The motivation for these alliances comes from the perception of mutual benefit. Use the skill of identifying common ground to continue to build and maintain a database of possible alliance candidates.

- Once you have an alliance around a common goal, have a check-in system for setting goals, assigning deadlines, and including others in projects related to the common goal.

- On the theory that one is known by the company one keeps, be cautious about linking your name and reputation with people and causes that do not represent your deepest values. Maintain integrity throughout all your alliances, avoiding gossip, dishonesty, and trash talk about rivals.

Create Productive and Satisfying Relationships

While it is not easy working with others, the payoffs of good collaborative partnerships are satisfying and productive. Partnerships lead to a synergy of creative thought not possible with solo work and ease the isolation often felt by faculty working autonomously. In addition, they enlarge your networks, an effect which brings more opportunities.

When partnerships don't work out, they bring a lot of heartache. An ounce of prevention is worth a pound of cure. Developing your social and emotional intelligence for collaborations will pay off in rich rewards. Take these steps to lay the foundation for successful collaborations:

- Pick a good partner.
- Be a good partner.
- Be clear about partnership agreements.
- Be clear about accountability and progress.
- Prevent the common pitfalls of collaborations.
- Prepare to handle negotiations, problems, and conflicts.
- Develop skills in remediation in case it is necessary.
- Be ready to let go when necessary.

Pick a Good Partner

If you have been networking successfully, some of your relationships will begin to move into potential collaborations.

1. Screen carefully for potential partners by looking for people with common professional interests.

2. Do some background checks on the potential partners. It is not paranoid to study what kind of a professional each is. This is relatively easy these days because so much information is available online. Believe only half of it, however. Check campus faculty websites for curriculum vitae information, such as publication and educational history. Google the name to see what comes up. Use the social networking sites to see how they present themselves. Ask other colleagues discreetly what they know about the person and the history of other collaborations.

3. Interview the person about the possibility of collaborating with you. Ask about interests, availability, and work habits.

4. Ask about their other collaborations. If you hear repetitive scenarios about dramas, traumas, and tragedies, run the other way. Be on the alert if the story always stars your potential collaborator as the innocent victim who is injured by others, because that will predict how this relationship will end no matter what you do.

5. Spend some time in the person's company at conferences or over the phone to see how you feel in his or her presence. Sometimes talented people make great collaborators—with someone else. Trust your gut about how comfortable you feel; if you feel on edge, something isn't right.

Be a Good Partner

The intense people skills requirement of the professoriate can challenge those who find themselves not as skilled as they would like to be in managing their side of relationships with colleagues, administrators, or students. Since these skills are learned, they can be improved by anyone. The goal in the beginning of a new partnership is similar to that of both courtships and job interviews, namely, to increase the probability of good outcomes by presenting yourself honestly and favorably.

1. Decide on how you want to be known by colleagues and work to align your behaviors with those values. You have a good bit of control over your public persona by aiming to be your best self. Are you the fun guy, the serious one, the cranky one, the absent-minded professor who forgets deadlines, or the one who can be counted on?

2. Be clear about your motives for the collaboration: Why this person? Why now?

3. Manage your emotions in the interactions (see the suggestions at the end of this chapter).

4. Use good listening skills, especially summarizing what you hear.

5. Be clear and redundant in your communication.

6. Underpromise and overdeliver.

Be Clear About Partnership Agreements

1. Communicate your expectations for the collaboration and listen to those of the other. Use the personal pronoun "I" when clarifying your goals for the relationship, whether they are publication, funding, emotional support, or fun. It is not selfish to talk about what you want and what you don't want. Be clear about what you have to offer such as grant money, lab space, statistical skills, or networking connections to supportive people.

Use your interviewing skills combined with powerful questions and active listening to encourage a frank talk about the other's needs (Bolton, 1979; DuBrin, 2001). You might ask:

- "If our collaboration went well, what would you hope would happen?"

- "If our collaboration did not go well, what would be your worst fear?"

Use your active listening skills to summarize what your partner expects. Make some umbrella summaries that link common goals—for example, "I hear that we both want to build this research protocol so that it could lead to funding. Is that also your perception?"

2. Don't let initial enthusiasm carry you too far before applying the discernment questions from Part 2 of this book. Ask yourself and your potential partner how this project fits in with each other's personal priorities, mutual goals, and collegial and institutional priorities outside the project. You will prevent later problems if you become clear about motivation by working from purpose. Generate mutual enthusiasm by tying in the goals of the project with each person's short- and long-term goals at this career stage.

3. Get explicit about how you want the project to go. Define the scope of the project and the partnership by setting mutual goals and boundaries, planning, and prioritizing (Rock, 2009). Discuss the desired outcomes, task assignments, and ownership (authorship) of the final product.

Say "No" gracefully to tasks that are outside your skill set. Discuss the possibility of delegating some parts of the projects to paid or unpaid help such as assistants, students, or tech people.

Summarizing the intentions of each collaborator at the beginning of the project will save a lot of heartache later about the order of authorship, ownership of discoveries, creation of techniques and equipment, and urgency about publication.

4. Ask the other how he or she likes to work regarding pace (slow and methodical, or dashing toward a final push to the deadline), details (broad sweep or fine tuning), and strengths (big picture, small picture, writing, conceptualizing). Lay out your favorite ways of working and be willing to negotiate any differences or, in the case of severe differences, respectfully walk away from the project before difficulties begin.

5. Discuss how you will maintain momentum and accountability to produce results. Will you meet often, send quick e-mails, submit manuscripts to each other, work on a shared online website such as Google Docs or Dropbox, keep tracking sheets, or report to someone else like a department chair, committee chair, or editor about the result of your work?

6. Discuss in advance how you both like to handle conflict. This will be a shocking question because hardly anyone ever talks about this aspect of working together, even though there will be conflicts whenever two people gather. Since we even have conflicts within ourselves among our values and goals, of course we will have conflicts with others. Very few people

realize that they have a style or favorite way to handle conflict. Some styles such as avoiding or screaming are less adaptive than others, such as using the steps of problem solving to work through problems. Tips about handling collegial conflicts are given later in this section.

7. Take notes on your discussions and share the written notes with each other. These notes form an informal contract about how you want to work together.

Be Clear About Accountability and Progress

As the collaboration continues, you will want to make sure you and your partner both stay on track.

1. Use the Tracking Sheet from Part 2 of this book to set up the steps for completion of the project. Name the person in charge of each step. Post it on Google Docs, Dropbox, or your campus shared website. This practice prevents problems with colleagues not getting their assignments done in a timely fashion.

2. Update the Tracking Sheet periodically to assess how the project is going, what still needs to be done, and where the problems are occurring. Nothing keeps people on track like the threat of mild social embarrassment.

3. Have regular feedback sessions about the working relationship. Be sure to emphasize positive feedback. Because of our brain's negativity bias, we are primed to look for what is wrong in situations. That bias sets up a curious phenomenon. Our brains only perceive a relationship as going well when there are 2.9 or more positive interactions for every negative one (Fredrickson & Losada, 2005). When the ratio of positive to negative interactions falls below 2.9, we perceive the relationship as going badly. The exception to that law is in marriage, when the required positive ratio needs to be closer to five or six positive interactions for one negative interaction, probably because more is at stake in marriage (Gottman, 1994).

4. Take responsibility for regulating your own emotions so you can manage stress, especially the stress of negative emotions such as jealousy and competition (Kabat-Zinn, 2005). (You will find more tips on this topic in Part 4 of this book.)

5. Celebrate the completion of stages of the project and review the plans for the next phase. Clink teacups, give high fives, or treat yourselves to a lunch at a special café. Academics are so hard working and task oriented that

we often forget a basic law of learning—namely, that behavior that is reinforced will increase in probability of occurrence. Being able to savor progress and accomplishments by taking in the good of those experiences is a low-cost way to deepen happiness and renew energy (Hanson & Mendius, 2009).

Prevent Common Pitfalls

1. **Drama:** Work is hard enough without exaggerating the aggravations of everyday life. Choose collaborators with the interpersonal, emotional management, and work skills required for managing their part of the project.

2. **Chronic complaining:** Flip the switch from the brain's negativity bias about danger and what is not going well to the positivity bias, the search for what is going well (Baumeister, Bratslavsky, Finkenauer, & Vohs, 2001; Fredrickson, 2009). Have regular feedback sessions with your collaborator to discuss what is going well and what could be improved. It will become easier to discuss problems when they come up once you have established this feedback habit.

3. **Competition:** Prevent feelings of competitiveness with your collaborator by looking at the relative contributions that each of you make to the project. Recognize that both of you are smart and talented, perhaps in different ways, so you can work from strengths by assigning tasks using each person's best strengths, instead of tripping over each other trying to do the same tasks.

4. **Confusion about expectations:** Be as clear as possible about the who, what, and when of how the work is being done. As you divide up the tasks and assignments, make written lists of role definitions (who does what), deadlines for phases and subtasks of the project, and the standards of how tasks should be done. Since not all subtasks need to be done perfectly, be sure to discuss a range of standards for different tasks. (See Part 2 of this book for guidelines on setting standards.)

5. **Overpromising and underdelivering:** By underpromising and overdelivering instead, you will safeguard against the future planning fallacy, the tendency to think that you can get a lot done in a short time only to find out that you can't (Kahneman & Tversky, 1979) and to think that you will have more time in the future, say a month from now, than you do today (Zauberman & Lynch, 2005). Because people do not recognize future trade-offs of time with one task versus another, they can think they have as much as 14 hours more time next week than this week (Troupe & Liberman, 2003). It is far better than to hesitate on commitments until you

discern their relevance than to agree to something you can't do. Deliver your parts of the project early, and you will be a hero to your partner.

6. **Procrastination:** There may be parts of the project that no one has the desire or expertise to do. Instead of pushing yourself to work outside of your strengths, consider how to get help. Would you hire others or ask for volunteer help? Would you pay your helpers, give them research hours credit, third coauthorship, or a thank-you in the footnote? How will you pay for the fee-based help, such as an intellectual property attorney to negotiate a book contract? Will it be a 50-50 split? Will it be out of your own pocket, or does one of you have access to such services on campus, for faculty? Follow the steps to effective delegation discussed later in this chapter whenever you do decide to ask for help.

7. **Unresolved problems:** Avoid letting small problems become big problems by discussing problems immediately with your collaborator. Discussing relationship problems with people outside the relationship becomes problematic for three reasons. First, it doesn't give your collaborator a chance to help you fix what is wrong. Second, discussing problems with others makes you look like a complainer, which damages your professional reputation. Third, complaining to others trashes your collaborator's reputation with a wider public. Instead of complaining to others, go directly to your collaborator about issues using the basic steps of problem solving discussed later in this chapter.

8. **Incivility:** I hesitate to even list this topic, but just this afternoon I coached two professors who are each dealing with mean-spirited collaborators who treat them badly. Some of these problems could have been prevented at the front end of the collaboration using the suggestions listed here. If incivility happens in spite of good agreements, remind the person of the mutual agreements. Give feedback on the behavior you are seeing and your interpretation of the behavior, and inquire whether you are misinterpreting the behavior. This tack gives the person a chance to "correct" your misinterpretation without losing face. If the person confirms your worse fears and continues to behave contrary to your preferences, suggest that the collaboration would go better with a few ground rules in place. If those steps don't smooth things out, you might suggest a mediator to monitor the interactions. Only as a last resort, suggest dissolving the partnership.

When Your Attempts at Bonding Don't Work

Sometimes it seems that even if you do everything right in a relationship, it doesn't go well. Don't take it as a personal failure. Well, maybe you need to take it a little personally. It could be that you are not yet as skilled as you would like to be. Seek wise counsel from a trusted colleague who is a good observer of behavior and can give you feedback about how you come across.

1. Are your micro gestures consistent with your warmth? For example, do you concentrate so hard while you listen that your face scrunches up and looks judgmental?

2. Do you listen attentively by looking at the other person and summarizing what he or she is saying?

3. Can you inhibit any tendencies to interrupt while the other is talking?

4. Are you clear about your needs?

5. Do you connect the dots of the conversation to find the common themes?

6. Do you summarize the needs of the other person and yourself to move goals forward?

7. Are you able to ask for what you want in a clear and nondemanding fashion?

8. Are you able to manage your emotions so that you can stay calm when things get heated?

After you ask yourself these questions about your part in the interaction, you can then apply them to how the other person interacted with you. The answers may explain why things didn't go well. Successful collaboration requires that both people bring their good communication skills and maintain a nonjudgmental attitude.

When you notice a disconnect between someone's expressed interest in working with you and their facial expressions, reflect it back to the person in a nonthreatening way by using an active listening response: "You said you wanted to work on this project with me but you seem somewhat distracted when we meet. Am I misreading you?"

Sometimes the things that go wrong with collaborative relationships come from the baggage people bring to their relationships.

1. **Excessive competitive feelings:** These feelings may arise because of the intense achievement orientation of academic workplaces. Be clear with these colleagues about issues of ownership of intellectual property, so they can relax and work well with you.

2. **Untreated mental health problems:** It is estimated that about 20–25% of faculty may be suffering with a preponderance of negative

emotions, such as anger, anxiety, or depression, or with more serious symptoms, such as paranoia, that interfere with their ability to interact with others in predictable ways (Schwebel, 2009). Their difficulties are neither a reflection on you nor a character flaw on their part, but proceed with caution before making extensive commitments to work with such individuals.

If you are in a position of leadership when someone with such personal problems is causing chronic problems with students and colleagues, it might be your responsibility to suggest that they get treatment. Be kind but firm, describing the problem behavior and its effect on the workplace. Your goal in these cases is damage containment rather than collaboration.

3. Faculty with attachment disorders: Early childhood experiences with a caregiver with whom they had an insufficient positive attachment can lead some adults to feel insecure about the world not being a safe enough place in which to work and love (Bartholomew & Horowitz, 1991; Prior & Glaser, 2006; Shaver & Hazan, 1987).

For the approximately one-third of the US population with such a history, relationships seem like land mines to be avoided. People with insecure attachments either avoid collegial relationships because they are afraid of getting hurt, glom onto others to get affirmation and love, or relate warmly at the beginning of the relationship until conflict comes up, at which point they get "weird," either lashing out with emotional outbursts disproportional to the problem or abruptly ending the relationship, leaving you bewildered about what you did to hurt them so badly.

When this happens, it is most likely not anything that you did or didn't do. Two things are needed when you work with these folks: compassion for the other person's pain and healthy self-protectiveness so that you contain damage to your own productivity and happiness. You might need to back off your expectations about successful collaborations with these colleagues or set firm boundaries about unacceptable behaviors. Introducing such structure can be very freeing to insecure folks who feel they can trust such a frank yet kind collaborator. Many people who are insecurely attached do have corrective experiences in their lives with influential and trustworthy people such as teachers, mates, colleagues, friends, or therapists, but you don't have to appoint yourself the savior of the world.

Robison's Rule
No man or woman is an island.

Chapter 14

Negotiate Mutual Needs: Solve Problems and Manage Conflict

AS A COLLABORATION develops, you will need a third set of skills to continue to create productive and satisfying relationships—skills aimed at giving other people what they need while you get what you need. An old expression points to the benefits of these skills: "You scratch my back, and I'll scratch yours." An even more successful approach is to build social capital by giving generously without expecting an immediate return. Current research is showing that strategy brings greater returns over the long haul than an attitude of immediate mutual reciprocity (Grant, 2013).

If you have ever taken a college course on human relations skills, you learned that there is a technical distinction between situations in which the participants have the same goals and are trying to work on the means (consensus building and problem solving, for example) and situations in which the participants start with different goals and need to decide on common goals before working on the means (negotiation, persuasion, and conflict management). I'm going to make your learning simpler in this context by giving you a template of steps that work as a general process for developing all of those subskills.

Steps for Meeting Mutual Needs

This section is written as though you are using this template with just one other person—the hypothetical relationship begun with networking and developed into a collaboration—but you can also apply it with more than one person and with groups. Things just get more complicated with more people.

Prepare

1. Start with a collaborative mind-set. All of the varied approaches to reach the mutual meeting of needs assume that the two (or more) people involved are searching for a creative solution that gives all parties most of what they want in the situation. Such mutually beneficial solutions are superior to compromise, in which both parties give up much of what they need to find a mutual solution, often leading to resentment as both parties give away so much that neither gets most of what they want.

Your goal in this work is to discern the best path, not necessarily the perfect path. Sometimes the resolution lies in finding a good enough path, as long as it is good enough for both people.

2. Know what you want. Before you start the conversation with the other person, have a conversation with yourself about both the ideal and the minimum solutions that you want to come away with as well as your bottom line and boundaries of what you will and won't do to reach a win-win agreement.

3. Guess at what the other wants. What does your partner probably need to be satisfied? What can that person give and get to reach a win-win agreement?

4. Imagine some possible win-win options. Try to think of possible solutions that might lead to a win-win conclusion, while at the same time staying open to the creative possibilities that might occur during the interaction. Your goal is to increase resonance in which you are in tune with others' needs and decrease dissonance in which you are disconnected with what others need (Boyatzis & McKee, 2005).

Manage the Stress of Conflict

Before you begin negotiations and while you are negotiating with collaborators, some reminders will help you to manage conflicts that may arise.

1. Before negotiations: Remind yourself that you and the other person have some common goals and values that have drawn you into this collaboration. Plan how you might bring up the topic. What would be the best setting and timing for you both?

Rehearse how you might handle the predictable emotional triggers for you in the situation. How might you calm your emotions during the conversation? How might you soothe the other person if s/he is emotionally triggered by your conversation? For example, engaging in active listening has a soothing effect on both speakers and listeners. How would you know whether either of you is too emotionally flooded to continue, so that you would both benefit from taking a brief time out? Consider the predictable sidetracks and dead ends that you might encounter and how you might handle those.

2. During negotiations: Stay respectful. Treat the other kindly. The other is not the enemy, although the issue might be. You are collaborators in a quest for projects, policies, and procedures that will help both of you get more of what each wants.

Set parameters, limits, and ground rules about the atmosphere of the proceedings—for example, how long the first meeting will last, what guidelines to follow.

Manage your emotions, especially your frustration, by reminding yourself that both the issue and the partnership matter to you. If negotiations seem to hit a wall or you lose your ability to think clearly because of excessive emotionality, push the magic pause button. Taking a break can calm everyone and prompt fresh ideas.

Clarify What You and the Other Want

1. Speak clearly. Present your point of view briefly, clearly, and assertively when it is your turn to speak. Ask for what you need as gently but clearly as possible. Don't undermine your point of view by muddling around, but stay away from a demanding, ordering tone. If you are a woman, avoid expressions like "sort of" and "kind of," which women often use but which make the speaker sound tentative instead of confident, and which may cause you to lose ground in negotiations.

2. Ask the other what s/he wants for an ideal solution. Speak about your ideal. See how much overlap there is with the other's ideal solution and where the differences are. Express willingness to negotiate differences.

Listen Effectively

1. During the conversation, listen to the other person. Use your self-awareness and your mirror neurons, the brain cells that pick up the subtle cues as to what others are feeling, to match the mood and the pace of the other so that you get on the same wavelength. The combination of clarity about your needs and compassion about the other's needs prepares you to listen empathetically.

2. Reflect what the other says. Use words and body language to reflect back to the other what you heard before you give your own viewpoint. Think of yourself as "buying the floor" through your effective listening, by summarizing what the other is saying and feeling. The speaker is the judge of whether the listening is effective.

Use the Steps of Problem Solving

1. Define the problem in terms of needs. Sometimes, what appears to be a conflict is merely two different descriptions of the same problem.

- Use "I" messages, which show you are willing to step up and recognize the problem even if the other person isn't willing to do so. You might say, "Since I haven't gotten your pages to review, I have been feeling stressed by trying to reach that deadline we set."

- Give the person a chance to actively listen so that s/he understands how you see the problem.

- Then it is the other's turn to give his or her perception of the problem while you actively listen, summarizing what the other is saying before speaking.

- Summarize the problem with both points of view included. Don't proceed to offer possible solutions until you have a common understanding of what you are working on.

In conflict, two people have different goals. By contrast, in problem solving, they agree on the goal but do not have a clear path outlined for reaching it. When there are two different perceptions of the problem, active listening and summarizing are essential skills, allowing the parties to listen deeply for the conflicts and communalities of the two points of view until they can be merged into a common goal to be worked on.

Conflict management is not an all-or-nothing matter. Many conflicts are too complex to be solved as a whole, but they can be managed by resolving small pieces of the conflict at a time (Gottman, 1999). The cumulative effect of solving pieces of the conflict will make the whole conflict more manageable while at the same time strengthening a collaborative mind-set with your partner.

2. Brainstorm alternative solutions. The idea of brainstorming is to create a storm in the brain that leads to as many ideas as possible. While refraining from censuring or evaluating any ideas, aim for 8–10 possible solutions. Don't be afraid to generate outlandish solutions. Be open to each other's suggestions. Quantity and out-of-the-box thinking brings quality solutions to the surface. Record the solutions on tape or on paper so you don't forget any of them when you get to the next step.

Extend your creativity by using value clarification, a problem-solving technique in which you change an aspect of the situation to see what solutions emerge. For example, what if money were no object? What if time were no object? What if we knew that we could not fail? What if we could get all the support we need? This exercise often highlights the real problem behind the problem, such as lack of funds or fear of taking risks.

3. Critique possible solutions. This process is not like the critical reviews you learned to do in graduate school, but rather an analysis of the pros and cons of possible solutions. What would solve the problem? How much would that cost? What would it take for that solution to work? Keep in mind your two goals: solving the problem and preserving the relationship. See all brainstorming ideas as generated by the team, not by the individuals. You are aiming at a two-winner solution, in which both people get most of what they need, rather than compromises, in which both people give up what they want for a solution neither wants.

4. Engage in action planning. Decide which solutions you might want to try. Your plan may require combining aspects of the various solutions into a creative solution that was not even mentioned during the brainstorming session. You may also be surprised when a solution appears that was not part of the list. Get very specific about the "who, what, where, when, and how" of the solution. Set up a plan for communicating the solutions proposed and acted upon in the various phases of data collection or writing.

5. Execute the action plan. Track your progress: have some way to report in to each other and revise as you go. New solutions as well as new problems often evolve as ideas are tested.

6. Evaluate the success of the plan. Did the plan solve the problem or at least chip away at the original conflict?

If the problem seems to have been solved, do two things now: celebrate your success and record how you solved the problem so that you can learn from the experience. Keep these records in your Dream Book so that you can access them later.

If the problem is not solved, repeat these six steps.

If a problem has not been handled well interpersonally, here are some tips to repair the damage:

- Don't overreact. If you have a history of losing your temper or of being easily hurt, see tips at the end of this part of the book to learn how to regulate emotions and manage stress.

- Give your partner a chance to explain and apologize and be ready with an explanation and apology of your own for your part of the misunderstanding.

- If the problem is the other's responsibility, let him or her take responsibility while you listen attentively. Don't make your collaborator wrong by blaming. By remaining gracious and taking your share of responsibility, you allow the other to save face, which increases the chance that the other will graciously take or share the responsibility for what went wrong.

- If your partner comes to you with a problem, actively listen before jumping in to defend yourself. Even if s/he is exaggerating, listen to the truth inside of the rant. Find a legitimate way to agree with that kernel of truth so that you can see the problem from your partner's point of view (Burns, 1999).

If the solution has not worked to both people's satisfaction, repeat the process. What new information appeared that is needed to solve the problem? Was the problem defined well enough? Were the ideas in the brainstorming adequate? Which ideas could be used now that had been discarded earlier? What is still needed to solve the problem? Avoid competition or power plays. Don't make anyone wrong. The partnership is solving the problem. People who feel that they lack power try to keep power and control; those who feel personally powerful are able to let go of the need to be in control in order to promote creative problem solving. Paradoxically, letting go increases these people's value to the team because they show an investment in the team rather than just in their own view of things.

Additional tips for good collaboration:

- Make sure you have room for new projects by saying "Yes" to ones that really fit your priorities and "No" to those that are not integrated with your mission and vision. Better that you disappoint potential collaborators by saying no on the front end than disappoint collaborators you have committed to by not coming through for them.

- Be generous but don't make unhealthy sacrifices that burn you out.

- Encourage civility in yourself, your colleagues, and your students through an attitude of collaboration.

- Think "win-win" in conflict. If anyone loses, everyone loses. A short-term victory turns hollow as resentment builds.

- Keep thinking outside of the box to find creative ways for everyone in a conflict to get the best possible solution.

Case Example: Problem Solving with a Collaborator
You are working with a research collaborator who likes to wait until the last minute to turn in materials for grants and articles. You value his

expertise and reputation in the field but have a hard time with his work habits because you like to work ahead on deadlines, pace yourself, and leave room for those unexpected family and student emergencies, and he doesn't.

> **You:** *Tim, the grant we are working on has a due date of March 1. When can you get your sections to me so that I can revise the entire proposal and send it back to you for your final approval?*

> **Tim:** *Probably around February 25 or so. I have some other things I am working on.*

> **You:** *So you would like to get it to me around the 25th. Let's look at the schedule. That leaves us one day for me to revise and integrate the section, one day for you to revise or approve my revisions, and one day to ship it to our grants office for official university approval. Does that sound realistic?*

> **Tim:** *Hmmm, I guess not. What if I get it to you a day earlier?*

> **You:** *(Silence)*

> **Tim:** *I guess that won't work. What do you propose?*

> **You:** *I was thinking a week for each phase might be good. Planning backward, that means in order for the grant office to have a week to work on it, they need to get it on February 21. That means that you have to have it back to me with final revisions on February 20, then I should send you my revision and integration on the 14th. That means that I need your sections on February 7 to do my revision and integration in a timely fashion.*

> **Tim:** *Gee, that's pretty quick on the heels of some of the other projects that I'm running late on. I don't know if I can do it.*

> **You:** *Does your hesitation mean you want to consider withdrawing from this project? I can decrease the scope of the study and submit it myself in this time frame.*

> **Tim:** *No, no, I want to do it. I just don't know how.*

> **You:** *So you have to work out the logistics of the rest of your schedule. Would you like to think about the commitment overnight and see what you can arrange in your schedule before we firm up our collaboration?*

> **Tim:** *Yeah, it's a big, prestigious grant, and I really want to work with you. I might have to let some other things go to do this. Let me get back to you tomorrow.*

> **You:** *When tomorrow, and should I expect an e-mail or phone call?*

> **Tim:** *I'll e-mail you by 3 pm.*

> **You:** *Good. I'll suspend working on this project until I hear from you.*

Manage Emotions in Relationships

As you deal with other people and increase your interpersonal skills, you may still get tripped up because of your own emotional management issues. Here are some suggestions to handle your emotions so that you can stay in control while chaos is swirling around you. There are two main problems which can cause you difficulty: getting drawn into other people's emotions instead of hanging on to your own and succumbing to compassion fatigue.

1. Be kind to yourself and others. There is a difference between being "kind" by showing thoughtfulness to others while respecting your own needs and being "nice" by making huge sacrifices for others at great cost to your own needs. Weigh the pros and cons of your various proposed actions to see which can benefit both yourself and the other with the least cost to either of you.

2. Manage your moods so that you are cheerful, upbeat, and positive most of the time. Of course there is a time to be serious, and of course there are times you will be stressed. To paraphrase Eleanor Roosevelt, no one can upset you without your cooperation. Study the material in Part 4 of this book on wellness and well-being to find ways to care for yourself so that it is more likely you will maintain a positive default mood. Mindfulness practices can train your brain to stay calm in tough situations by quieting the amygdala, the danger alert center, and to stay mindfully present no matter what happens (Amen, 2006; Siegel, 2010).

3. Help others have good moods by choosing civility. Choosing civility can make a big difference with students as well as with colleagues. Many episodes of student incivility can be traced to the perception on the part of the students that the teacher was not acting civilly to them—even when such behavior was unintentional (Bray & Del Favero, 2004; Forni, 2003; Twale & De Luca, 2008). Be warm to your classes while at the same time being clear about your expectations about classroom decorum, and your students will be more likely to return your civility with their own.

- Practice the "Platinum Rule"—that is, instead of doing unto others what you would want done unto you, do unto them what they really want done. That means asking others what they want, including whether they want your help. Watch out for the tendency to rush in to help those who might find your help to be an intrusion or, worse yet, an insult to their competence.

- Be generous with praise.

- Encourage those who rely on you for feedback, such as students, children, employees, and friends, to increase their own efforts at kindness.

- Refuse to gossip. Instead, come to the defense of someone being made fun of or put down.

4. Separate your emotional reactions from those of others. To keep your mirror neurons from leading you to overempathize with others, ask yourself, "Whose problem is this?" You can participate in helping others without feeling their emotions. Just because they are having a reaction to something you did, you do not have to take responsibility for those emotions, unless you did something to offend. In that case, apologize quickly and sincerely, and ask what needs to be done to repair the rift.

When you are clear that you had nothing to do with the emotional upset, center yourself: take a deep diaphragmatic breath, stay calm, and modulate your voice. Use your active listening skills to summarize what the other is saying. Take the content in small chunks so you can pace your intake of information and so you can show the other person that you understand. This approach will help you think clearly and will have a calming effect on the other person.

5. Protect your work-life boundaries by letting others know the best ways—e-mail, office telephone, cell phone—and hours to contact you. Open door polices are a recipe for burnout. Instead, protect your off-work time and your home life by turning off those methods of contact during your personal time.

6. When others try to take up your office hours with their serious emotional problems, set limits on your availability for those kinds of sessions. Tell the visitors gently but firmly that you have work, students, or colleagues to attend to. With students, consider referring them for counseling or advising to the appropriate places on and off campus. Your school may even have policies requiring that classroom teachers make such referrals so that disturbed students get help. Even if you have training in counseling, don't—I repeat, don't—try to counsel troubled students yourself if you are their classroom teacher. With distraught colleagues, consider referring them to your college's employee assistance program for help. You also might consider telling the department chair or the dean about your observations of the problem and its effect within the workplace. This action does not constitute whining or tattling; instead it alerts those in authority to observe patterns if a faculty member needs help. If need be, get mentoring or coaching yourself on how to handle sticky situations.

If you use the social skills from this section as you meet and work with others, you will be well thought of by many wonderful people.

Robison's Rule
Don't burn bridges; it's a small world.

Part Four

Energize Yourself for a Long and Happy Career and Life

In the long run, we shape our lives and we shape ourselves. The process never ends until we die. And the choices we make are ultimately our own responsibility.

—Eleanor Roosevelt

THE PROFESSORIATE, ALTHOUGH a demanding career, can be rewarding—if you take care of yourself along the way. Faculty are such hardworking and self-sacrificing professionals that they often think of self-care and self-renewal as something to be earned through spectacular achievement, deferred until the semester is over, or deferred until even later, when they retire. Many feel guilty about taking time for relaxation and hobbies.

Blame it on Descartes, or maybe the Greek philosophers, but professors often treat themselves as though they were disembodied intellects unattached to a brain, heart, and other organs. This mind-body split and its subsequent delay of self-care is misguided, because the result of ignoring the whole person is increased risk of burnout, disengagement, premature aging, and health problems (Lee et al., 2012; Oz & Roizen, 2008). Although you might have raced through graduate school as if you were running a sprint, continuing at that pace is a recipe for burnout. Instead, you need to manage your career and life more as though you are running a marathon, pacing yourself as you go. Now that retirement from the academy is no longer mandated at age 65, you can stay in your job long past the ages that people retire from other jobs if you sustain yourself and your energy.

About one-third of participants in my workshops on work-life balance attend hoping that I will work magic on "them"—namely, the administrators—so that teaching loads will be reduced, research requirements will be lightened, and salaries will be raised. These faculty are convinced that all of their work-life balance woes would be remedied by improving what career researchers have called "work hygiene factors," a term coined in 1959 by Frederick Herzberg and still used today to refer to work conditions and pay (Herzberg, Mausner, & Snyderman, 1959; Herzberg, Mausner, & Snyderman, 1993).

The truth is that even if work hygiene factors were ideal, professors would still have problems with job requirements unless these professors develop practices for self-care. Herzberg demonstrated in his two-factor theory of work satisfaction that motivational factors, such as the work itself and recognition of achievements, have much more of an influence in employee motivation than the hygiene factors (Herzberg, 1987).

The other two-thirds of workshop participants are concerned with the basic question, "How do I stay energized for a lifetime of this work?" They frequently voice concerns like these:

- "I'm tired of working all of the time. I wish I could get a break once in a while."

- "I worry all of the time about whether I will get tenure."

- "How can I relax at the end of the day? I'm always working in my head."

- "How do you stay energized and motivated to face students year after year?"

- "I try to hide out in my office so I don't have to talk to cranky colleagues."

- "I can't seem to stop gaining weight, but eating is the only hobby I seem to have time for."

- "I know I would feel better if I exercised, but I don't have the time."

Even those faculty who want to take better care of themselves mistakenly worry that time and effort put into self-care will subtract from their productivity. Compelling research from the wellness and neuroscience fields suggests that only by keeping yourself and your systems working well will you have enough energy for a long fulfilling career and a rich satisfying life (Loehr & Schwartz, 2004; Oz & Roizen, 2008). Busy professionals who ignore themselves to steal time to work harder will experience lower productivity in the short term as well as risking burnout and health problems in the long term. Abraham Lincoln said it well: "If I had four hours to chop down a tree, I'd spend the first hour sharpening the blade."

While noting that institutional policies can impact faculty productivity and happiness, the goal of the Energize practices of PACE described in this part of the book is to empower faculty to increase their productivity and happiness with a set of peak performance practices that will help you attain work-life balance the only way it works—from the inside out. Although convenient communication often requires that we talk separately about a person's various organs and functions, my goal is to present an integrative approach to the body-mind question—namely, that in reality the body, mind, and spirit of a person are all part of the same holistic system. This view is gaining recognition on campuses as colleges explore contemplative approaches to both teaching and faculty development (Bach & Robison, 2011; Lee et al., 2012).

Don't overwhelm yourself with these practices by making a new list of "Susan's Shoulds." Instead, sample the practices that address your most pressing needs at this time, integrate them into your life and your habits, and then come back later for more. Choose the wellness chapter, choose the well-being chapter, or start anywhere you wish. As with any health information, consult with your health care provider to adapt these suggestions for your individual circumstances. Building each day around minimal self-care and effective work habits will save you time, improve your concentration, increase your productivity, and extend healthy middle age well into your elected retirement years (Oz & Roizen, 2008). Follow the advice of the flight attendants to "put on your oxygen masks first," by prioritizing yourself before you attend to your students, classes, and research, and you will maintain the energy to do great work.

Long-term happiness is an additive proposition. While wellness and well-being practices support vitality and mood management in the short term, they combine with the other peak performance practices, such as working from purpose and developing mutually supportive relationships, to help faculty cumulate productivity and happiness in the long term. It is that deep, enduring sense of life satisfaction and long-term happiness that sustains peak performers even on their bad days.

How Part 4 Will Help You Become a Peak Performing Professor

In Part 4 we will look at two sets of practices that help peak performers flourish in body, mind, and spirit:

1. Wellness: These are evidence-based practices of healthy eating, regular exercise, and restorative pauses that keep the biological machinery healthy and energetic. Residents of longevity cultures where an exceptional number of people live well and long into their 90s and 100s have given us models for what to do to live well and long (Buettner, 2010).

2. Well-being: These practices involve positive mood management coupled with appropriate challenges that will give you life satisfaction, boost your productivity, and model living well to colleagues and students.

Chapter 15

Wellness

PROFESSORS ADMIT TO not taking good care of themselves, sometimes sacrificing their health and supportive relationships in a misguided attempt to be productive (Astin et al., 2011). This effort is misguided because wellness activities actually rebuild our capacity to do good work without wearing ourselves down (Robertson & Cooper, 2011). Wellness involves activities that promote the physical, mental, and emotional fitness and stamina that lead to high energy for your great work and your great life. To support good stress management and energetic living and to recover from the strain of all that you do, you need to ingest good nutritional chemicals, exercise away the toxic residue of stress, and rest and relax.

The higher the level of stress and the more demands made on the body-mind system, the more one needs the wellness practices of peak performers to achieve the following benefits:

- Better energy

- Higher productivity as your brain operates at its best

- Greater engagement with the job—less likelihood that you will burn out, rust out, or blow out

- Fewer sick days, less illness, and a longer life

- Higher job and life satisfaction

Have you ever noticed that people vary widely in their energy levels, health problems or lack thereof, and rate of aging? I have been curious about those phenomena since I was a child and noticed how some adults like my dad were doing cartwheels with their kids in the backyard while other dads could barely finish reading their evening newspaper without dozing off. Those in the first group were energetic, enthusiastic, and seldom sick; those in the second complained of being tired all of the time, suffered from frequent illnesses, and aged more quickly. Was it family heritage, or something they did? It was probably some of both, but how much?

With interests like that in childhood, it makes sense that I would find a professional home in psychology, where the body-mind question is one of the essential areas of study. Across my career as I continue to take professional education courses on genetics, wellness, nutrition, neuroscience and longevity, I have studied fascinating research that now provides some partial answers to many of those body-mind questions. This chapter represents an attempt to organize a huge buffet of those evidence-based wellness and well-being recommendations into palatable nibbles to help readers live long and continue their great work as educators and scholars.

For a well-written expansion of the scientific basis for the practices in this chapter, consult Oz and Roizen's (2008) excellent *You: The Owner's Manual*, as well as the sources cited in this text. If you want an extra challenge, take Oz and Roizen's wellness survey at www.realage.com. Based on wellness and longevity research, this questionnaire analyzes the risk and protection factors from your family history, illness history, and lifestyle practices to calculate your "real age," the age determined by these factors rather than by your chronological age. If you have already incorporated wellness practices into your life, you will see how they predict a lowered statistical risk of disease and premature death. If you haven't yet incorporated such practices, your score might motivate you to start doing so.

Healthy Eating

In one of my recent continuing education courses on wellness, the instructor presented a cartoon picturing an anchorwoman at her desk announcing, "This just in: all food is bad for you." On her background screen was picture of fruits, vegetables, milk, and other foods in a circle with a red line diagonally across it.

Do you sometimes feel like you just don't know what to eat to keep yourself healthy? Barely a month passes before some news announcement tells us that a commonly ingested food is bad for us. In that same month the latest fad diet appears, recommending that you eat only lychee nuts for the first week followed by a week of a cocktail of soy sauce and ginger root, followed by only crackers for the third week. Maybe I'm exaggerating a bit—but when it comes to eating well, what's a person to do? While the food researchers sort it all out, we still need to eat. The wellness field does have a number of evidence-based recommendations to make about healthy eating that, if followed, will likely increase your present energy and your potential for good energy lifelong. For summaries of the science behind these and other evidence-based recommendations, see the books by Hyman (2012), Oz and Roizen (2008), and Whyte (2012).

These evidence-based recommendations represent a list of ideal eating practices. You don't have to suddenly change your whole diet to match them. In fact, it is dangerous to do so, since your internal environment needs time to adjust to new dietary items. Be reassured that not every one of your 21 or more meals per week has to be exemplary in terms of nutrition. Even small changes toward a life-long healthy eating plan, however, such as limiting sugar intake, will place your nutrition well beyond the Standard American Diet (SAD), the diet that has led to a national obesity crisis and underlies many illnesses, including heart disease, diabetes, and some forms of cancer. Just as your car needs a good quality gasoline to keep running, your body needs the correct chemical composition to sustain itself for building, repairing, and maintaining itself for the long term.

1. **Eat a balanced diet of protein, fats, and carbs** in foods close to their sources, that is, foods that have not been processed into frozen, canned, or dehydrated form. To get the right chemicals into your body, you need to take in the following daily:

- Eight glasses of water.
- Five to nine half-cup servings of fresh fruits and veggies. Nine servings seem like a lot until you do the math. A small salad contains about three half-cup servings (lettuce, tomato, and cucumber); a larger one may have more than half a cup of each ingredient. Add some fruit in morning, noon, and evening. That's six. Now a veggie for lunch, another for dinner, and carrot sticks for an afternoon snack, and you have your nine.
- Two to four servings of unprocessed whole grains.
- Two to four small (four- to six-ounce) servings of meat, nuts, milk products, tofu, and other sources of protein, an amount that fits into the palm of your hand as a giant meat or tofu ball.

Make your food types proportional on your plates and they will automatically be proportional in your diet. Fill half your plate with vegetables, one-quarter with grains, and one-quarter with a protein source such as meat, cheese, or bean burgers. Add fresh fruit for dessert, and you will find the whole confusing mess about what and how much to eat getting clearer. Notice, there is no room left on that plate for chips.

To keep your body chemically sound you need to limit or avoid the following:

- Processed sugar (especially high fructose corn syrup), flour, cereals and products made from the same

- Alcohol beyond moderation (one small drink per day for women, two for men)

- Caffeine beyond moderation or 400–800 mg a day depending on sensitivity

- Fried foods (choose broiled or grilled whenever possible; switch from butter and other oils to olive or canola oils)

2. Pace eating to your caloric needs so that you stay energized all day. Ideally, consume the amount of food and energy units (calories) that you need during each day. Front-load your protein and your calories early in the day to fuel your activities all day instead of back-loading your protein and calories at dinner where they turn to sludge during the night. Overeating is not good for obvious reasons. Also not helpful, however, are calorie-restriction diets, because your body interprets the loss of calories as the beginning of starvation and will compensate with two effects: signaling your body to lower its metabolic rate and then to eat more to make up the calorie difference once you go off the diet. The latter effect explains why most lost weight is gained back.

In cultures where people live to healthy old age, they undereat in terms of appetite and move around a lot. In Okinawa, a longevity culture that has no obesity, the people say a blessing before meals that roughly translates to: "May you eat until you are 80% full." That makes sense because it takes about 20–30 minutes after a meal for your blood sugar to rise sufficiently to shut off your hunger mechanism in the hypothalamus. If you eat until you feel full at the end of a meal, you will feel stuffed a short time later.

Don't ignore weight gain. Many faculty are concerned about the inevitable middle-age weight gain that results from their sedentary workday, spent sitting in the office and meetings. You can maintain a healthy lifelong weight, however, by eating just what you need and by exercising regularly (which burns calories, allowing you to eat more than you would burn when you sit for most of the day).

3. Enjoy your meals more and lower your stress by eating mindfully, slowly, and deliberately, chewing 15 times while you enjoy the texture and taste before swallowing.

Pause to talk with others at the table instead of shoveling the food in so fast that it misses your taste buds. Rest between courses.

4. Summary. In *Food Rules*, a short, very humorous, but scientifically informed book, Pollan and Kaiman (2011) summarize the current wellness nutritional advice in a pithy sentence: "Eat food, mostly plants, not too much." Pollan and Kaiman emphasize that while plants are real food, anything made in a plant is not. To elaborate, avoid eating things made in plants, especially chips, snacks, sugar drinks, and ground-up breaded nuggets formerly known as meats. Avoid anything that is called a "chip" even if it has a plant name in front of it, such as "zucchini chip."

Exercise

One of the best energy-promoting and stress-reducing strategies is exercise. Exercise provides the following benefits:

- Helps you dissipate the products of stress. The stress response prepares your body for flight, fight, or freeze. Moving relieves the tension from built-up stress.

- Builds your capacity to handle future stress in healthy, productive ways. Exercise makes you stronger, more flexible, and better able to expend and recover energy, and exercise keeps your "real" physiological age below your chronological age (Oz & Roizen, 2008).

- Induces the brain to produce an array of chemicals that it loves, including endorphins, serotonin, dopamine, and norepinephrine, as well as two recently discovered compounds: brain-derived neurotrophic factor (BDNF) and nerve growth factor (NGF). Both BDNF and NGF promote cell health and development in the brain, stave off the ravages of aging and stress, and keep the brain in tip-top condition (Arden, 2009).

- Makes you smarter by improving cognitive capacity (Schwartz, 2010). This is great news for professors who make their living from their ability to think.

- Improves emotional well-being (Schwartz, 2010).

- Improves your self-discipline in others areas of life (Oaten & Cheng, 2006).

Tips About Exercise

1. **Pant, stretch, and lift**. For overall fitness and stress management, you need to include three types of exercise: pant, stretch, and lift.

- *Pant:* Engage in aerobic exercise such as running, walking, swimming, rowing, or dancing to increase your heart rate for 20–30 minutes so that you are breathing deeply. While three times a week will keep you fit, a daily dose will lower your stress levels.

- *Stretch:* Yoga, tai-chi, and other gentle nonbouncing stretches will keep your muscles and connective tissue working more efficiently and prevent injury.

- Get up from your desk to stretch every 90 minutes. Prevent "old professor slump" caused by slumping over your keyboard by stretching in a doorway with both hands raised on either side of the doorway molding. Lean forward slightly so that your hands and arms are supporting your weight. Hold for about 10 seconds. As you walk away from the doorway, maintain your arms in that position without the help of gravity.

- Hang forward gently reaching for your toes. Hold for 10 seconds and roll up slowly through a rounded spine.

- *Lift:* Using light weights with many repetitions will build your endurance, keep your bones strong, and maintain core strength so that your whole body works as a unit to support your activities.

  - If you don't want to buy weights, use textbooks or soup cans.

  - If you get serious about strength building, visit the weight room at the college school gym and ask the trainers for advice on how to use the machines. Many universities, such as Brigham Young University, are offering health insurance discounts for faculty who exercise regularly.

2. **Schedule exercise**. You won't "find time" for this activity any more than you will find time to prepare for class or do scholarly work. Self-discipline is not a magical part of some people's personalities. Instead it is the learned capacity to schedule activities that matter to you and then to block work and other obligations around the time designated. You will more likely succeed in building a habit of exercising (just as with any other habit) if you figure out the specifics of when, where, and how you will exercise (Halvorson, 2011).

3. **Exercise with a buddy**. Having an exercise buddy will increase commitment, lower boredom, and increase accountability.

4. **Include movement that doesn't seem like exercise**. Take the stairs instead of the elevator. Put on some upbeat music and dance while you mop the floor. Walk 10,000 steps each day (five miles). Walk whenever you can, from the far end of the parking lot to your office or inside the building at lunchtime. Add some stairs for increased aerobic challenge.

Rest and Restoration

When your cell phone battery runs down, you recharge it. When your energy runs down, how do you recharge yourself? Peak performers know that rest is as important as hard work to achieve success (Loehr & Schwartz,

2004). Just as driving your car effectively requires a balance between the gas pedal and the brake, your brain needs a balance of neurotransmitters, the chemicals that regulate mental alertness and mood (Robertson, 1997).

The gas-pedal chemicals of dopamine and norepinephrine rev you up and energize you, whereas the brake-pedal neurotransmitter, serotonin, slows you down and relaxes you. Too much of the former, and you will feel like the three giant lattes you drank on the way to work have caught up with you. Those symptoms can range from over-the-top energy, racing thoughts, and feelings of pressure, all the way to debilitating anxiety. Too much serotonin and you will feel sleepy and lazy, good feelings for vacation or a day off but not so great on a workday when you want to get things done. The ideal brain balance is to rev yourself up when you need to be revved up and wind yourself down when you are finished revving. You want to bring good energy to your tasks through effective rest both by taking breaks during the day and by winding down effectively at the end of the workday. There are three sets of strategies that will help you rebalance your energy: rest, relaxation, and re-creation.

Rest

When I started doing workshops on work-life balance, I was shocked to learn two things about my fellow professors and sleep: they don't have bedtimes, and they never consider that their low motivation and energy are caused by chronic sleep deprivation. They go to bed when their heads hit the keyboards for the third time and they are getting little Chiclet marks on their foreheads from the key imprints. Although they surprised me, I also surprised them by pointing out the following:

- Sleep deprivation is the real reason these professors feel tired all the time. They get far less sleep, an average of six hours a night, than their bodies and minds need to function well (seven to nine hours sleep is recommended by the National Sleep Foundation, www.sleepfoundation.org.)

- Sleep deprivation causes high stress and low productivity.

- Natural biorhythms make sleep easy and effective if you go to sleep and get up at the same times each day.

- Chronic sleep deprivation contributes to premature aging.

Signs You Are Not Getting Enough Sleep

There is a wide range of individual differences as to the hours that constitute adequate adult sleep, between seven and nine hours. You might not know how much sleep you need. In addition, U.S. adults overestimate the amount of sleep they get (at 7.5 hours) versus what they actually get (6.1 hours) (Lauderdale, Knutson, Yan, Liu, & Rathouz, 2008). That amount matches the average of six hours that I see on professors' time logs when we coach about energy problems and time management. The following signs can indicate that you are not getting enough sleep:

- You need an alarm to wake. When people have enough sleep they wake on their own and feel refreshed.

- You are tired during the day—not just a midafternoon slump but dragging through the whole day.

- You feel on edge and chronically cranky.

- You fall asleep in lectures, sometimes your own. If you do nap, you feel like you could sleep forever and have trouble waking.

- You fall asleep at night within minutes. Well-rested individuals usually take 10–20 minutes to settle down to sleep at night.

- You think about sleep during the day. (This is my personal favorite. When I start staring at a horizontal surface, like the floor under my client's chair, imagining it as a place to sleep instead of paying attention to what my client is talking about, I need to readjust my sleep schedule.)

- You suffer from lowered functioning in several areas including attention, executive function, working memory, mood, quantitative skills, logical reasoning, and even motor dexterity (Medina, 2008).

- You make more mistakes and are less productive in your work. Sleep experts suggest that sleep deprivation is responsible for the following tragedies: 100,000 deaths a year related to medical mistakes; industrial accidents such as Chernobyl, Exxon Valdez, Bhopal, and Three Mile Island; and more than a million auto accidents a year (Colten & Altevogt, 2006).

If you aren't currently getting enough sleep, where will the hours come from? Is it worth the sacrifice to trade some waking work hours for sleep?

The Payoff

Aim at adequate sleep for one week. Judge for yourself whether the benefits of higher-quality performance, better alertness, and fewer slumps of energy are worth trading time spent doing other things for more sleep. If you don't experience the following benefits, go back to your old schedule.

1. **An increase in peak performance**. Contrary to the hard-working habits of many professors, peak performers actually take more regular

breaks and naps. Researchers studying such diverse performances as music, sports, and military leadership found that peak performers sleep more at night than their counterparts who do less well in the areas of their performance (Ericsson, 2009; Mah, Mah, Kezirian, & Dement, 2012).

2. **Feeling rested and smart**. Researcher Sara Mednick found that adults who had eight hours of sleep showed superior performances on memory and visual tasks, while those with that much sleep who added a midday nap performed even better (Mednick et al., 2002). The biggest gain my clients report after a week of adequate sleep is that they get more done in less time because they feel less foggy during the workday. In brief, they feel smarter, more creative, and better able to make decisions.

3. **Better mood management**. When you are well rested, your ability to manage your emotions leads to the following benefits:

- Frustrations roll off your back, and you bounce back more quickly when life throws you curves.

- You have an increased ability to keep perspective and gain joy from the simple things in life.

- Other people's moods seem better because you are more tolerant toward others.

- You lower your risk of anxiety disorders and clinical depression.

4. **Wellness benefits**. Getting adequate sleep changes how your cells function (Prather et al., 2011). Physically, you will see the following effects:

- A more youthful appearance, because adequate sleep prevents premature aging

- Easier time maintaining healthy weight without cravings

- More physical energy, ambition, and ability to initiate

- Improved immune functioning, therefore, fewer illnesses and less time lost from work

- Improved sexual functioning, including increased drive and enjoyment.

The Sacrifice

In order to get adequate sleep you may need to make some sacrifices.

1. Some prime time TV.

2. Some badly done work. It takes twice as long to complete an intellectual task when you are tired; in addition, the quality of that effort suffers.

3. Your image. If you like to think of yourself as the beleaguered professor in the tattered tweed jacket slaving over yet another set of badly written lab reports, you will have to adjust your image to your new suave, thinner, rested self, smiling while you work.

Restoring Natural, Restful Sleep

Most sleep-related problems reverse themselves once you start getting adequate rest. Here are some suggestions for restoring good-quality sleep.

1. **Find your own sleep biorhythms**. Experiment with rising and sleeping times to see what works best for you. About 10% of the population are larks, those who rise at dawn full of energy, while about 10% of the population are owls, those who come alive after dark. The rest are hummingbirds, those who rise after the sun rises and do their best work from midmorning to midafternoon. The right amount of sleep is the amount you need so that you can wake without an alarm.

2. **Rise at the same time each day, no matter what bedtime you end the day with**. A set rising time establishes a good sleep rhythm because it locks in your circadian rhythms of appetite, elimination, alertness, and other bodily functions. If you get to bed later than desired, get up at your regular time even if you have to use an alarm clock. Tolerate the fatigue during that day or take a short power nap and resume your normal bedtime that night.

3. **Practice good sleep hygiene**. Sleep in a cool, dark, quiet room. Don't fall asleep with the TV on. Its noise and flickering light, while not actually waking you, will disrupt the depth of your sleep. Cover or turn off lights such as the alarm clock display. Protect yourself from other interruptions by turning off your computer and phone.

4. **Avoid the following for a few hours prior to bedtime:**

- Caffeine
- Vigorous exercise (exercise earlier in the day will improve the brain chemistry that makes you sleep well)
- Adrenalizing excitement (arguments, suspenseful novels, movies, or TV shows)
- Big meals (although a light snack is fine)
- Light from an electronic display, such as a computer, tablet, electronic reader, or smartphone.

5. **If you do have an occasional bout of insomnia, get out of bed and worry productively**. Use paper and pencil to write all your worries

and begin to problem-solve on them. You won't figure them all out in the wee hours of the morning, but your notes can be preliminary to a daytime problem-solving session. When you feel tapped out, go back to bed and think of a pleasant nature scene that you have visited or would like to visit. Breathe deeply, especially emphasizing slow exhalations with each breath.

6. Limit naps to 20 minutes in the early afternoon (siesta). The human race has a universal need to nap sometime between lunch and midafternoon. Many non-U.S. cultures plan commerce and other activities around that need. Limit yourself to a 20-minute power nap to increase your productivity in the later part of the day (Medina, 2008), since longer naps interfere with the normal four sleep cycles per eight hours of nighttime sleep. Instructions for taking a power nap are very similar to meditation instructions, except that for nap purposes you need a more comfortable position that actually allows dozing off, whereas in meditation you want to be upright and alert. Here are instructions for effective power napping:

- Prime the pump of creativity by thinking or writing out a question before the nap.

- Set an alarm just in case. Don't get too comfy in a quiet, cool, dark room since those are the cues for deeper sleep. Instead, sleep in a desk chair with your feet up or put your head down on your desk.

- You may or may not actually fall asleep. You are aiming to "phase out," lightly sleeping while being aware of your environment.

- For the first couple of minutes, just notice your breathing. Deepen your breathing by breathing in through your nose and breathing out through pursed lips, emphasizing your exhalation by drawing it out slowly.

- Observe your thoughts without entertaining them. Thoughts will fly at you: "This is dumb, I probably won't be able to do this." If you invite the thought to take up space, you might continue thinking, "Yes, it is a dumb idea. Hope my department chair doesn't find out I have my head down. I better check my e-mail." In contrast, observing the thought goes something like this: "That's an interesting thought, maybe it will or won't work, now back to the breathing." Eventually you will be able to notice periods of time when you are not aware of any thoughts. If you notice your muscles twitching slightly it means you are in hypnogogic sleep, the state of consciousness between alertness and sleep. All you need for a power nap is a light level of sleep.

- When the alarm goes off, move around, stretch, reach for your toes, shake out the kinks, and then do something interesting, such as a very challenging intellectual task perhaps returning to the question or issue you posed just before the nap. You will be pleasantly surprised how sharp your thinking is immediately following your power nap. Jot down insights you might want to use later.

Interested in the evidence for these recommendations and an online quiz? See www.sleepfoundation.org.

Relaxation

People misuse the word *relaxation* to include anything that is a nonwork diversion, including television, eating, and drinking alcohol. None of those activities actually produce relaxation, the specific body state that is opposite to stress and which gives the body-mind system a chance to recoup from emergencies (Benson & Proctor, 2003).

The stress response is not a bad thing—in small doses. The stress response is effective for self-protection in emergencies. The stress response is triggered by the sympathetic nervous system, which increases arousal, with elevated heart rate, blood pressure, and muscle tension—body-mind reactions conducive to handling emergencies. The relaxation response rebalances the body-mind system through the complementary parasympathetic nervous system, which decreases heart rate, blood pressure, and muscle tension. For detailed instructions on a procedure that will usually produce a relaxation response see Exercise 15.1.

Balance between stress and relaxation has been a protective mechanism for humans since the days of our cave mothers and fathers. Stressed by the sight of a saber-toothed tiger coming down the forest path, our cave ancestors responded with their entire body-mind system geared for fight or flight. After the emergency was successfully dealt with, they recouped and rested.

Living in modern times, our stressors are no longer likely to be environmental dangers like scary tigers but are more likely to be internal stressors, such as fears about scary department chairs or difficult students. In either case, the body-mind system doesn't distinguish between acute dangers and prolonged stressors. When concerns are unresolved and become prolonged, our brains never receive a signal to end the crisis, thus leading to a chronic state of arousal, which prevents the necessary rebalancing that recharges our energy and boosts resistance to illness. Prolonged stress also increases the production of cortisol, a stress hormone similar to adrenaline that is also secreted by the adrenal glands. While adrenaline energizes us to deal with a short-term stressor such as slamming on the car brakes to avoid

EXERCISE 15.1

Relaxation Response

Here is a quick meditation exercise which can usually produce the relaxation response in just five minutes.

1. Sit upright on chair or on pillows on a floor.

2. Draw in a deep diaphragmatic breath to the count of four (one thousand one, one thousand two, and so on).

3. Hold the breath very briefly, and then exhale slowly and completely to the count of eight (one thousand one, one thousand two, and so on).

4. Force the exhalation a little more and then just let go. Don't try to inhale. It will happen automatically, and as it does so it will trigger a release in your vagal nerve, the third cranial nerve that runs from your head down through the center of your abdomen. When you let go, you may feel a slight "pop" in your tummy. That vagal release rebalances your nervous system from being controlled by stress (sympathetic nervous system) to being controlled by relaxation (parasympathetic nervous system).

5. Repeat the slow breath and vagal release a few times and then just breathe slowly for a few minutes.

6. Notice the thoughts that come and go during the time you are concentrating on breathing. Let the thoughts come and go without letting yourself get pulled in to actually thinking them (for instructions on how to make the distinction between observing thoughts and thinking the thoughts, review the steps for power napping listed earlier).

7. Finish the meditation by imagining your heart wrapped in love, maybe from your spouse, your mother, or a divine being whom you believe loves you.

8. Set an intention for the rest of day, whether it is to finish a stack of papers you are grading, to spend some good time with your children or friends, or to greet colleagues with a smile. Continue breathing while you set that intention.

9. Return to the environment by noticing your surroundings with its sights, sounds, and smells.

an accident, cortisol boosts your ability to deal with a prolonged stressor, such as working for a difficult boss.

On the down side, cortisol is implicated as a culprit in several stress-related diseases, including heart disease, elevated cholesterol, and autoimmune diseases such as some forms of arthritis. Cortisol also causes body fat to be accumulated around the midsection. While belly fat might cause you a fashion problem, it is an adaptive response to stress; a stressed body likes belly-fat cells, which have more steroid receptors than subcutaneous fat cells, allowing fat to move to the liver to be converted to energy when stress demands a sudden output of energy (Dallman, Pecoraro, & La Fleur, 2005). Your belly fat is your body's way of telling you, "You're stressed, and we're going to deal with it by storing a reserve of fat for the next time stress comes along."

To counter this chronic stress even if the stressors continue, regularly elicit the calming effect that comes with activating your peripheral nervous system, the branch of your autonomic nervous system that slows down stress and rebalances your body-mind system (Hanson & Mendius, 2009). Doing so leads to the following benefits:

- Lowers your heart rate and hormones back into baseline mode

- Lowers risk of chronic sympathetic arousal

- Lowers arousal, so that you can work with increased creativity and problem-solving ability

  These are examples of activities that can evoke the relaxation response:

- Aerobic exercise (not during the exercise, but after its completion)

- Meditation

- Progressive relaxation

- Deep breathing

- Body movement, slow stretching, and posture relaxation methods such as yoga, tai chi, and qi gong

Re-creation

A third way to re-energize yourself is through activities that re-create your energy and renew you on a more spiritual and psychological level. Such activities do not necessarily produce the relaxation response, but they refresh you because they rebalance your body-mind system in other ways. Here are the principles of re-creation:

1. Choose activities that re-create you. An activity that might bore or stress one individual might re-create another. For example, practicing a musical instrument may re-create a history professor but might seem too much like work to a music professor.

2. **Pulse and pause** (Loehr & Schwartz, 2004). Balance a spurt of hard work with a break. Hit the brain-pause button every 90 minutes for 5–10 minutes, have a longer pause at the end of an eight-hour work day, take some refreshing time at the end of a five- to six-day work week, and indulge in a few days off from work at the end of each semester (Goleman, 2005; Loehr & Schwartz, 2004).

3. **Rebalance the body-mind system with contrasting activities**. If you have been sitting too long, get up, stretch, take some deep breaths, or go for a walk outside. If you have been standing too long, stretch your body, put your feet up, have a healthy snack, and drink water. Balance intellectual work with physical activity such as yoga or aerobics and physical work such as working with hospital patients or standing in class or lab with intellectual activities such as reading or working on family genealogy.

4. **Renew yourself mentally**. Rebalance overused parts of your brain with parts that are underused. For science faculty, this process might entail balancing the logical, orderly activities of your left brain with the free-flowing creative activities of the right such as drawing or dancing. For faculty in the arts, it might mean taking in a lecture, completing an online course, or reading in a field outside of your discipline.

5. **Enliven yourself emotionally**.

- Change your pace. Vacations and overnight and day trips provide a break in routine and a contrast to your normal place and pace. Professors at rural campuses might spend off-work time in the nearest big cities while those at urban colleges might re-create themselves at their lake cottages.

- Repeat predictably refreshing activities. Go for a run, read an inspirational book, or listen to music that you know will refresh you.

6. **Strengthen nourishing social and family connections**

- Focus on positive experiences. Talk with colleagues about what you enjoy about your work and life. Taking the time to foster those relationships will lighten your load, provide a place to connect, and give you a place to be heard. Of course, exercise good judgment about what you share. Save the divorce and surgery stories for your best friend or therapist. And avoid the gripe sessions in the faculty lounge.

- Reconnect with family and extended family on vacations and at holidays. Vacations provide the shared adventure of new environments, sights, and even getting lost which can form memories for years to come. Holiday rituals are short-cut reminders about our intimate connections.

- Create social play without even leaving home. Games can bring everyone together. Play basketball outside or on a Wii with your family. Our family has a four-generation tradition of playing charades. Kids are included and are helped to read the prompts until they can read by themselves. Being "on stage" builds confidence. It is a great family game because everyone can be silly, even adults who get a momentary break from being authority figures.

7. **Plan an academic sabbatical around work that will refresh and renew you.**

8. **Refresh yourself spiritually by enjoying Sabbath time on a regular basis.** While the world's major religions teach that a Sabbath day off every seven days is a desirable break for the weary body and mind, professors who are not religious can benefit from a secular version of Sabbath time, that place where your body and mind intersect and where you renew yourself to continue doing good in the world. Some suggestions:

- Take it on the weekend or in the middle of the week.

- Balance the "noise" of e-mail and upsetting news with soothing media that uplift you, such as reading, music, plays, or movies, or with an electronic-free Sabbath, a period of time where you exchange being plugged in for time spent in quiet reflection.

- Get outdoors to observe and enjoy nature.

- Enjoy dinner in the dining room with family or friends followed by game night or movie night.

- Reconnect with your meaning and purpose in life. Take a few minutes to reflect on your Pyramid of Power and especially how your work is a privilege and serves a greater purpose.

- Experience art at an art show or by creating something.

- Volunteer for a cause that you care about. Include your family and friends for double benefit.

Robison's Rule
Take care of yourself; it's the only one you have.

Chapter 16

Well-Being

> Happiness is the meaning and the purpose of life, the whole
> aim and end of human existence.
>
> —Aristotle

POETS AND PHILOSOPHERS have been writing and teaching about it for centuries. Songwriters sing about it. Whether you call it joy, life satisfaction, well-being, or positive emotions, happiness has always been, along with love, one of the two most interesting topics to students in Psychology 101. Although students in decades past were surprised to find out that psychologists had very few answers to their questions about happiness, today's students can find a large body of research about happiness and well-being, which has been developed since the mid-1990s.

Over the past 15 years, the leadership of American Psychological Association president Martin Seligman and the persistence of well-being researchers such as Ed Diener and Mihaly Csikszentmihalyi have brought about a seismic shift in psychology's view of human behavior, from a focus on healing pathology toward an exploration of what makes for a high level of life satisfaction in people around the globe. This new field of positive psychology has contributed some partial answers to questions about what factors are correlated with happiness and whether you can do anything to increase your happiness and well-being. Some of these research findings may surprise you. A few of them may already be out of date as you read them, because this field is moving quickly toward better answers about what makes people happy.

What Is Happiness and Well-Being?

Lest you are concerned that being a happy professor means pasting a fake social smile on your face, positive psychologists use the terms *happiness* and *well-being* to describe the state of people who flourish and feel satisfied about their lives. Researchers continue to debate the nuances among the terms *happiness, well-being,* and *life satisfaction.* For example, Ed Diener describes well-being as having three characteristics: high life satisfaction, high positive affect (or emotional mood), and low negative affect (Diener & Rahtz, 1999; Diener, Suh, Lucas, & Smith, 1999).

In this chapter, I will use this distinction between happiness and well-being: happiness is a deep, enduring sense of well-being and satisfaction that comes when people experience great work and great lives in the long term (beyond six months), while well-being is the shorter term positive physical and mental health resulting from energy management practices that effect a positive outlook in the short term (three to six months). In a sense, a person's well-being gives a current weather report, while a person's happiness describes the broader climate.

Let us explore the definition of happiness (a deep, enduring sense of well-being and satisfaction that comes when people experience great work and great lives in the short and long term) in more detail.

- *Deep* because surface conditions do not determine it. Long-term visions for great work and a great life lead to a sense of meaning and purpose (Seligman, 2002) even when current work isn't yet satisfying. This sense of meaning and purpose encourages the development of self-control and grit, two aspects of personality that allow professors to persist towards long-term goals (Baumeister & Tierney, 2011; Duckworth et al., 2007).

- *Enduring* because it cannot be ruined by a bad day, bad week, or bad semester. While their daily happiness ratings ebb and flow, happy people whose lives are grounded in meaning and purpose rate their overall lives as better than they rate any individual day or experience (Kahneman et al., 2004).

- *Sense of well-being and satisfaction* in the sense of supporting the body, mind, and spirit (Oz & Roizen, 2008).

- *Great work and great life,* which combine to give people the best satisfaction in life (Pillemer, 2011; Stanier, 2010).

- *Short and long term,* with many pleasurable moments enjoyed in the present, along with cumulative success and satisfaction that results from doing the right things across a lifetime (Lyubomirsky, Sheldon, & Schkade, 2005; Sheldon & Lyubomirsky, 2007).

By bringing more balance into your life, well-being practices cumulate towards a deeper life satisfaction in the long term. This kind of balance is not the equal mixing of aspects of your life but rather a synergy that comes from mind-body balance, work-life balance, and the balance of performance and process orientation in daily activities. Neuroscientists such as Dan Siegel (2007, 2010) and Rick Hanson (Hanson & Mendius, 2009) are exploring specific methods for experiencing better overall balance of the brain structures and its functions by increasing the vertical integration in which the higher centers control the lower centers and the horizontal integration in which the left and right hemispheres of the brain work more in unison.

Both short-term well-being and long-term happiness are likely results of employng the PACE practices described in this book: the power of working and living from meaning and purpose (the "P" or power in PACE), the authenticity of matching your activities to your purpose (the "A" or alignment of PACE), the connection of mutually satisfying relationships, both personal and professional (the "C" or connection of PACE), and the positive energy of good self-care resulting from mindful practices that promote a higher preponderance of good feelings while dealing with the challenges of life (the "E" or energy of PACE).

Happiness and the Life and Work of the Professor

Both you and your institution should care about your happiness, because work productivity and engagement are affected by life satisfaction (Lyubomirsky, King, & Diener, 2005). When you and your colleagues focus on activities that boost a sense of well-being, you are in a better position to influence your institution to pay attention to some of those work hygiene factors mentioned earlier, such as salary. The rewards for workplaces that do pay attention to happiness can be summarized in two sentences: Happy workers work better. Happy workers live better.

Happy Workers Work Better

Hard-working faculty erroneously believe that productivity and happiness are exclusive of each other. As one biology teacher said to me during a workshop, "Work is a four letter word. It's not supposed to be fun, that's why it's called work." Faculty who overemphasize productivity to the detriment of their satisfaction may actually achieve less than they had hoped for in their work lives.

Higher Productivity

Current productivity research shows that the happier you are, the more productive and creative you will be, because happy brains work better (Ledford, 1999; Wright & Cropanzano, 2004). There is a weaker relationship between the two variables the other way around. Reaching your goals is an important contributor to your long-term life satisfaction, because if people see time slipping away without accomplishing the goals that they value, they experience an erosion of their sense of meaning and purpose.

Reaching your goals does not account for the bulk of your happiness, however, since it is goal attainment in combination with the other variables discussed in this book that increases overall satisfaction.

Happiness is not easy because it is not the natural default mode of our brains. Left on its own, our automatic brain processing focuses on immediate emotions related to survival of self and species. The survival of our ancestors and their descendants depended on their ability to scan for and deal with danger (Hanson & Mendius, 2009). Hence, our brains are usually on the lookout for the fulfillment of short-term needs for food, safety, and a date.

Over history, the human race previously found more adaptive value in attending to what wasn't working and what fulfilled immediate needs, instead of what was working and what would assure attainment of future needs. This is the reason you pay more attention to preparing for tomorrow's class than to writing an article that you have wanted to write for several years and that would build your tenure portfolio. Like a riderless elephant, our automatic brain can run amok, causing us to eat until we get stuffed, scan for dangers to the exclusion of creative thoughts, and mate with inappropriate partners in inappropriate situations. Saddle up the elephant, take control of the reins, and your brain will aim at the benefits of healthy nutrition, creative thoughts, and long-term, committed relationships. Urgency trumps importance unless you make intentional, mindful choices to blend both into your priority system.

While scanning for danger is an occupational requirement of firefighters and air traffic controllers, professors do their best work when they are motivated by compassion and creativity rather than by vigilance. Engaging your prefrontal lobes, the creative thinking and planning center of the brain, gives you the best chance at being smart and productive. This Wizard, as I like to call it, is smaller and less developed than its more primitive cousins in the lower brain centers, centers we share in evolutionary schemes with the reptiles and the mammals. Amygdala action in the mammalian brain trumps prefrontal lobe planning and problem solving because responding to immediate danger is more crucial to survival than long-term planning (Hanson & Mendius, 2009). Once your amygdala takes charge, you will be flooded with negative emotions, particularly fear, and temporarily lose your ability to think clearly and solve problems, two skills much needed in your everyday work. Operating out of fear causes your reptilian brain to get defensive and your mammalian brain to get aggressive. To experience productivity and happiness over the long haul, your Wizard needs to tame your reptile and mammal. This is not easy or natural. As Hanson & Mendius (2009) explain, our brains are Velcro for bad news and Teflon for good news.

Working while stressed is expensive for the brain. Your Wizard tires easily while trying to manage your moods and think at the same time (Muraven & Baumeister, 2000). Chemically, stress causes your brain to "melt down" because of excess norepinephrine and dopamine, which overemphasize amygdala-striata connections instead of prefrontal lobe engagement. In other words, stress makes people act less intelligently. Since emotional management operates in two modes, automatic pilot and intentionality, it is far more efficient for the Wizard if you set a course of positive emotions and work more directly on the higher cognitive tasks required in your profession, allowing routine and ritual to guide your tasks on a day-to-day basis.

Brain studies have shown that there is a positive synergy between well-being and productivity, especially in work that involves extensive contact with others, such as teaching (Zapf, 2002). Those faculty who habitually maintain a positive outlook are able to work more effectively, thus lowering their stress about undone or badly done work and leading to increased well-being (Robertson & Cooper, 2011). They are less likely to burn out and more likely to be more effective leaders (Boyatzis & McKee, 2005; Fredrickson, 2001). They are also more cooperative, less self-centered, and more willing to help other people because they are less distracted with monitoring for danger. Working better with others lowers stress even further by lowering interpersonal stress and eliciting social support. As researcher Shelley Taylor (2002) found, tending and befriending others in times of stress lowers our own stress. Faculty who connect well to colleagues (see Part 3 of this book) will likely find their days feeling less stressful than those who work in isolation (Taylor, 2008). It is a case of the rich getter richer.

Better Focus

Happy brains perform better because they are better able to use strategies such as prioritization and goal setting to effectively attend to key tasks and stay undistracted from emotional issues. The most effective, least time-consuming training technique to increase focus and concentration is the practice of meditation (Dalai Lama & Cutler, 2004; Davidson & Begley, 2012; Raffone & Srinivasan, 2010). These studies on the long-term effects of meditation practices show more efficient brain functioning on challenging tasks—a great benefit for professors who make their livings from their brain power.

Increased Engagement

Employers benefit from increased employee satisfaction because it leads to employee retention and motivation, which affect the bottom line and the mission of the organization (Harter et al., 2002). Low faculty turnover avoids the high costs of recruiting, rehiring, training, and incorporating replacement faculty. It is easier and cheaper to keep people engaged who are already in a system than to recruit new members of the system. This rule applies across the academy, to customers, students, faculty, and donors. Furthermore, happiness is bidirectional and synergetic (Kenrick, Griskevicius, Neuberg, & Schaller, 2010). Happy people are more prosocial, seeking out and getting along better with colleagues, an orientation that raises life satisfaction, which in turn increases prosocial tendencies. In addition, having a satisfying personal life allows one to do more creative work, which leads to additional opportunities that heighten the quality of life.

Happy professors with good well-being practices have the energy to teach better which shows up in their capacity to care about the students and their learning (Walvoord, 2008). These professors collaborate more easily with research colleagues (see Part 3 of this book). Happy professors emphasize civility in their interactions and develop leadership skills (Kouzes & Posner, 2003).

Happy Workers Live Better

Optimism is correlated with well-being because optimism leads to hope, a positive emotional state that acts to moderate the workplace stress that can lead to health problems, such as cardiovascular disease. Hope protects against stress created by such factors as low social support, little decision-making authority, and imbalances between effort and reward, factors that are related to increased risks to hypertension, diabetes, upper respiratory infection, and unhappiness factors (UC Irvine Center for Occupational & Environmental Health, 2005).

Health Benefits

Here are some additional positive health outcomes for happy workers:

- Happy workers have less sickness, less severe symptoms when sick, and greater longevity (Buettner, 2010).

- Happiness decreases absenteeism and health insurance usage (Parks & Steelman, 2008).

- Happy workers are more resilient. They are less affected by change and situational stress. They more easily broaden and build their skills, a benefit for themselves and for their employers through job sharing, reassignment, cross training, and flexibility with processes and procedures (Fredrickson, 2009).

- Good mood and perspective taking slows aging rates and keeps quality of life higher as people age (Oz & Roizen, 2008).

- Married (or coupled) workers with happy relationships reap the benefits of better personal health, wealth, and longevity (Waite & Gallagher, 2001).

Increased Resiliency

Negative emotions are not all bad; they serve the very useful purpose of calling attention to dangers and other factors we should be acting upon. It is the resiliency to recover quickly from negative emotions, however, that predicts high productivity and happiness (Davidson & Begley, 2012). Any time we can successfully attend to the issue at hand and take appropriate action, we triumph over our brain's wiring in which the default mode is to scan for danger. Resilience promotes the brain flexibility to quickly return us to the creative part of the brain where we produce good work. Happiness increases your flexibility and increases your resilience to stress by allowing you to do the following:

- Envision outcomes and break down these visions into tangible and reachable goals (Halvorson, 2011).

- Take appropriate risks, increasing self-efficacy, life satisfaction, and willingness to take additional appropriate risks (Lyubomirky, 2008).

- Develop a good relationship with time, by simultaneously learning from your past, planning for your future, while living in the here and now (Sheldon, Cummins, & Kamble, 2010; Zimbardo & Boyd, 2009).

What We Know About Happiness and Well-Being

We have learned a few things about what happiness is, and what happiness is not. This section discusses some of these findings.

What Happiness Is Not

1. Happiness is not merely the absence of negative emotions. Happiness and general mood correlate but probably not in a simple, causal fashion. Negative emotions can be effective signals for your body-mind system to call attention to an aspect of your life that is not working. However, excessive anger, anxiety, depression, guilt, and jealousy take their toll on health, marriages, and jobs. We now know that while effective treatment of psychological maladies will decrease the preponderance of negative emotions, the process does not make people happy. Even the best all-around self-help book for mood disorders, David Burns's *Feeling Good* (1999), is too optimistically titled; it should be titled *Feeling Better* because it emphasizes how people who suffer with excessive negative emotions can learn how to decrease the frequency and intensity of negative emotions. The new positive psychology adds to that psychological wisdom by showing how people can increase their capacity for joy.

2. Geography doesn't seem to have as much direct impact on happiness as common sense would predict. While common sense might predict that living in a beautiful tropical area might make you happy and shivering in an icy one would not, geography is not as important for happiness as perspective. The warm, wonderful country of Bhutan is one of the happiest countries in the world but so are Denmark, Norway, Finland, and Iceland, located in the northern part of Europe with long periods of light scarcity. The common factor of these happy countries with differing environments seems to be the high quality of life related to social connection (Lyubomirsky, 2008).

However, order in one's immediate environment does relate to well-being. Walking back from class into a clean, well-organized office might set you into a better mood than walking into a scene from the *Hoarders* television show (Epstein, 2011). Faculty who get help with organizing their paperwork do report that they feel better and work more effectively.

3. Money may or may not make you happy, even though people think it will. The research is not definitive on the relationship between subjective well-being and earnings. Some studies have shown that there doesn't seem to be a direct causal relationship once income rises above poverty level. However, the causal relationship between rising income and happiness may be true only in the United States; poor people in Los Angeles are less happy than poor people in Calcutta, India, even though the people in Calcutta live in more dire circumstances (Easterbrook, 2004). On the other hand, other research has shown that there may be a relationship between happiness and income level, with higher income bringing more satisfaction (Easterlin, McVey, Switek, Sawangfa, & Zweig, 2010).

A recent analysis of a series of worldwide data sets by economists Stevenson & Wolfers (2013) led those researchers to conclude that the relationship between money and well-being is a linear-log relationship and that no satiation point has yet been shown. Accumulating money may not increase happiness levels directly. Instead, money tends to buy the perception of safety and of increased choices as long as you are not presented with too many options. While purchasing power in the United States has doubled in the past 50 years, life satisfaction levels have stayed flat. Researchers suspect that this finding has to do with levels of happiness being lowered when people have too many product options, setting off a hedonic treadmill. The more pleasure and stuff you get, the more you desire: "I like this car but a bigger car will make me feel even better" (Schwartz, 2004).

While the researchers sort out the mathematical relationships between money and happiness, the conclusion for regular people is that to get the most out of your money, you should use it for goods that are consistent with your values, experiences that build good memories for you and those close to you, and charitable contributions to causes you care about.

4. Focusing directly on happiness doesn't work. The pursuit of happiness in and of itself does not produce happiness directly. This is especially true if you seek a hedonistic lifestyle, which emphasizes a focus on oneself (Gruber, Mauss, & Tamir, 2011). Rather, happiness is increased indirectly by pursuing goals that usually lead to happiness, particularly goals that get you outside of yourself (Lyubomirsky, 2011) such as many of the goals you outlined under your various vision statements in Part 1.

What Happiness Is

1. While happy people aren't happy all of the time, their general approach to life is positive. One counterintuitive finding of positive psychology is that the most productive people are happy in the long term but not extremely happy at any given point along the way, while those with the highest happiness scores (higher than 8 on a 10-point scale) in the short term are less happy over the long term. Researchers speculate that the moderately happy subjects do better because they are realistically optimistic about the ups and downs of life, whereas the extremely happy are overly optimistic about what they can expect from themselves and others and therefore are bound to be disappointed (Oishi, Diener, & Lucas, 2007).

Research is making it clear that there needs to be a balance between positive experiences in the short term and difficult experiences or emotions necessary to achieve a higher good and leading to higher happiness in the long term. When author Gretchen Rubin (2009) embarked on a year to get happier by applying happiness research findings to her own life, her happiness project led her to conclude the following: "To be happy, I need to think about feeling good, feeling bad, and feeling right in an atmosphere of growth." That is a nice summary of the balance of emotions and the importance of setting challenging goals in ways that bring individual meaning and purpose!

2. Happiness levels can be altered. Originally it was thought that people have a fixed set point for happiness. However, studies of people who won the lottery and people who became paraplegics have revealed that although those events dramatically affected immediate happiness levels, both groups of people had returned to their previous level of happiness a year later. We adapt quickly to life circumstances, particularly good ones (Frederick & Loewenstein, 1999; Lyubomirsky, Sheldon, & Schkade, 2005) unless we consciously continue to appreciate them (Lyubomirsky, 2011). Current thinking is that there is a happiness "set-range," with 50% of the variability around happiness scores accounted for by genetics, 10% by life circumstances, and 40% learned and changeable (Lyubomirsky, 2008). The research-based practices discussed later in this chapter will give you many approaches to choose from to alter the 40% of the happiness variability that is under your control.

Paths to Happiness

Pick one or two of the paths to happiness that appeal to you, experiment to see whether they work for you, and then practice them until they become routine. Just a couple of small changes can make huge differences in your day-to-day life.

I have divided these practices into two groups, those that tend to improve short-term mood and well-being and those that increase deeper, longer-term happiness. There is considerable overlap in these effects, since many short-term strategies, when practiced on a regular basis, contribute to long-term happiness, especially when attention is paid to some of the other factors of happiness: purpose, alignment, and connection.

Increase Short-Term Well-Being

1. Every day, plan one pleasurable activity for yourself. It could be a workout, a bubble bath, listening to jazz music, or a long-distance call to a favorite friend.

2. Practice self-awareness . . . but not too much. Check in with your feelings by asking: What is going on in my body right now? And where in my body am I feeling that? Using this quick trick keeps you from being blindsided by emotions that take you by surprise in stressful situations, like cartoon character Charlie Brown, who once exclaimed, "My mind and my body are at war with each other!" Notice good feelings, and do more of what produces them. Research suggests that just by naming negative emotions you will be taming them (Siegel, 2010).

Beware of excessive self-reflection, however, since it can lead to rumination in which one obsesses about one's weaknesses (Lyubomirsky & Tkach, 2003). Thinking and journaling too much about bad experiences can exacerbate negative emotions and decrease your functioning. If not stopped, ruminating becomes a vicious circle: ruminating leads to lowered confidence, which leads to taking fewer actions to reach your ideal life, which leads to increased bad mood, which leads to rumination to find the cause of your bad mood. Paradoxically, faculty who are asked to worry, but only on paper or on a screen, actually decrease their problem list over time, in part because writing the list makes their problems finite and fixable. Once people notice patterns of the same several problems repeating themselves, it is possible to break the cycle by shifting from rumination to problem solving, finding potentially effective solutions to problems, and taking action, all of which lead to a better mood (Nolen-Hoeksema, Wisco, & Lyubomirsky, 2008).

To strengthen the observing function of the brain, you can begin to incorporate mindfulness meditation into your life by practicing on a daily or almost daily basis using the same technique suggested earlier for relaxing into a power nap—but with the caveat that you not get so comfortable that you fall asleep (Davidson & Begley, 2012; Davidson et al., 2003). Picture Julia Roberts sitting on her meditation cushion in *Eat, Pray, Love*. Picture yourself observing your thoughts without judging them—not easy to do, but a fruitful practice nonetheless.

3. Prevent and minimize the effects of stress such as fatigue, bad mood, and stress illnesses by finding techniques that de-stress you such as yoga, tai chi, relaxation, or meditation. Practicing mindfulness-based stress reduction helps you soothe yourself by training your brain to observe your thoughts and feelings without judging them. These mindfulness practices help you in the short term by quieting the amygdala, the brain's alarm system, while these practices ultimately change your neural wiring, strengthening the ability to stay calm in the heat of a moment (Davidson & Begley, 2012; Kabat-Zinn, 2005).

4. Keep an optimistic perspective. Optimism is not, as popular belief would have it, always seeing the glass half full. It does not involve denying that bad things happen and that our intended outcomes do not always match the results. Optimism involves practicing opening your mind to allow you to identify and solve problems while at the same time keeping the problems in perspective with the good happenings of your life. To develop a more optimistic viewpoint, try to see good events as related to the results of your efforts rather than a matter of luck and expect good things will continue to happen in the future (Seligman, 2006). When bad things happen, pause to see if anything needs to be learned from the experience, and then move on to continue working on your goals while expecting positive results.

An optimistic mindset affects body and mind; both our physical immune systems and our emotional capacity for stress are increased by maintaining a positive outlook. The regular practice of positivity increases neurotransmitters such as dopamine that ensure likelihood of performing at our peak (Fredrickson, 2001, 2009). Positive psychologist Martin Seligman has found that realistic optimists feel happier, make more money, marry well, live longer, and live better as a result of the combination of paying attention to tasks that enhance their lives as well as to tasks that avert disasters (Seligman, 2011). One way to keep this balance is to use the VAST daily to-do list from Part 2 of this book to track your vision goals along with your goals for averting disaster.

5. Savor good experiences as much as possible. When something pleasant happens, pause for a moment to savor the experience and allow it to enter your memory system, so that you can recall it later in the day when you are reflecting on your experiences and accomplishments. It is especially helpful to reflect on the day's significant events close to going to sleep. The practice of reflecting on what is going well in your life will increase both short- and long-term happiness as you attend to how the accumulation of good short-term experiences leads to a lifetime of happiness.

Journal about fun times, put photo albums together, and reminisce with those that shared the experience. Those activities help a meaningful experience last longer (Sheldon & Lyubomirsky, 2012). James Pennebaker at the University of Texas has found that journaling about experiences deepens the experience, both by helping to form memories and, in limited doses, to lower emotionality (Gortner, Rude, & Pennebaker, 2006). Using reflection this way cements experiences in your memory, because you are slowing down enough to allow your brain to rehearse and store the memory.

Enjoy the fruits of your productivity by savoring your accomplishments and taking in the good of how productive you feel so that it generalizes to a positive mindset of agency and competence (Hanson & Mendius,

2009). Frequently, hard-working academics are quick to wrap up a goal and move on to the next one without pausing to take in the good.

6. Practice economy of emotion. If you do get stressed, decide how upset you want to become to handle this stress, and don't emote any more than the situation requires. The Alexander Technique in dance and movement therapy teaches dancers to expend only the minimal amount of energy needed to get from one place to the next—any more is a waste. Happy people do not avoid negative emotions. Instead, these people use negative emotions as a signal to notice what might need attention. Start with the lowest level of energy to handle the stressor. For example, instead of screaming at the dry cleaning lady about your ruined blouse, merely ask her to pay for a replacement. If this step doesn't work, increase the amount of energy you expend to take the next step, such as asking to see the manager.

When you find yourself upset with someone in the workplace, these tips may help.

- Figure out what is really bothering you; to name it might tame it (Siegel & Bryson, 2012).

- Ask yourself what you need to make it better.

- Learn to ask for what you want instead of just describing what is bothering you.

- Take the risk to ask for what you need directly. Subtle hints can come across as manipulation and often fail to communicate what you really need.

- Aim to be flexible and easy to work with.

Look for areas of your life that you can bring under control instead of worrying about what you can't control, like other people's behavior. Especially don't waste your time and energy on the predictably bad behavior of others, such as lateness for meetings. Either request a change or ignore the behavior, and get on with your own agenda without the distraction of excessive negative emotion.

7. Engage in activities that bring joy both at work and at home. Mihaly Csikszentmihalyi reflected, "How we feel about ourselves, the joy we get from living, ultimately depends directly on how the mind filters and interprets everyday experiences. Whether we are happy depends on inner harmony, not on the controls we are able to exert over the great forces of the universe" (Csikszentmihalyi, 2008). Use your brain's natural tendency to scan for the novelty of delightful surprises, and be willing to wonder at them. Nature, art, music, and children are sources of this kind of pleasure.

8. **Increase your resilience by doing hard things with grace**. Stretch yourself; try new things and new ways of doing old things. When you stretch yourself by operating just on the edge of your comfort zone where your strengths match the challenge of the task, you increase your flow and increase your skills. With too much challenge relative to your skill, you will feel anxious; with too little, you will feel bored. While it is not always possible to hit that sweet spot of flow, balancing a boring task such as desk cleaning with an interesting one such as writing will help to increase the possibility that parts of your days will have flow.

9. **Take good risks within your value system**. Playing it safe doesn't develop your gifts; taking risks does. Be 10 times bolder. If you knew you could not fail, what would you do? Explore new activities and new ways to do the usual activities.

Faculty leaders who increase their personal resilience remain more open to the rapid rate of changes happening in the world and have more potential to influence their institutions of higher education (Lee et al., 2012).

10. **Choose "long cuts" in some places in your life instead of "short cuts"** to experience a momentarily slower pace. For example, make bread by hand instead of using your bread maker or occasionally drive to work on the side roads to see the spring blossoms in the yards.

11. **Multitask only when you are working on low-priority, low-concentration activities** (Hallowell & Ratey, 2011). Do not try to multitask when you are working intensely on a high-priority task.

12. **Choose media carefully**. Think of it as food for your brain. Limit your exposure to bad news that you can't do anything about anyway. Take media breaks; try two hours of working at your desk without checking e-mail or answering the phone. Go to a "third place" like the library or Café Joe's to do thinking work without media distractions. Instead of depressing news, read uplifting books and helpful periodicals and news sources. Seek daily sources of inspiration, such as reading autobiographies, praying or meditating, or engaging in artistic endeavors. Read your Dream Book backward to remind yourself of all your accomplishments. File and read notes of appreciation you receive from those you have influenced, including your students, colleagues, and loved ones.

13. **Avoid social comparisons**. There is always someone who is better-looking, smarter, or more competent or who makes more money than you do. By the way, happy people do occasionally compare themselves to those less fortunate and as a result feel appreciative for what they have. So if you are going to compare, compare down instead of up. And if you need to compare to see how you fit in with social norms, pick a reference group that is similar enough to yourself to provide a fair comparison. Compare yourself to other faculty in your field with similar lifestyle choices and responsibilities or professors in similar family and personal circumstances. Instead of worrying what everybody thinks of you, set up appropriate accountability to people who matter such as your boss, mate, or 12-step sponsor.

14. **Sacrifice for your goals but proportionally to the outcome**. Take care of your needs as you make those sacrifices so you don't burn out or harbor resentments (Kenrick et al., 2010; Lyubomirsky & Boehm, 2010). As Abraham Maslow (1954) observed, if your basic needs are met, you will have the energy to attend to the more complex needs, such as those for social affiliation, status, self-esteem, and intimate partner acquisition and retention. For example, safety is so important that it has found to be highly related to life satisfaction in 145 nations (Tay & Diener, 2011). No wonder faculty get nervous about salary and benefit cutbacks.

15. **Get outside of yourself regularly**. Altruism, the feeling that comes from doing acts of kindness, results in a happiness paradox—by thinking of someone else's needs, you will actually increase your own happiness. Researchers have found that the maximum effect of altruism on happiness is experienced with one big kind act or three to five small ones per week (Lyubomirsky, King, & Diener, 2005). Fortunately, as a professor you are in a position that allows you to do acts of kindness on a regular basis such as tutoring a student who is struggling or mentoring a colleague.

16. **Contain the long-term damage of common negative emotions by recognizing and using those emotions effectively**. For example, if you find yourself anxious about the future, ask yourself what possible bad events you are worrying about, how likely it is that they will occur, and in the unlikely event that bad events do occur, how you would respond. Rehearse your resilience strategy, and then let go of the worrying since you are now prepared.

Another common emotion is shame, the feeling that we have when we feel so embarrassed by a mistake or transgression that we generalize the embarrassment to feeling unworthy. Shame is a common feeling of academics; as we present our performances in teaching, research, and service, we feel vulnerable and susceptible to ridicule. Think back to the last time you read peer reviews of your scholarship. A daily practice that combats the potential for being laid low by shame is to remind yourself of what a worthy human you are no matter what you have succeeded or not succeeded in doing. In other words, learn to separate your behavior from your personhood. For further suggestions on how to combat shame, see the research of fellow academic, Brené Brown, who claims to be a frequent sufferer herself (Brown, 2010, 2012).

Increase Long-Term Well-Being and Happiness

The practices just listed are short and can be done almost daily. Your brain has limitless capacity to change, but what fires together wires together. The long-term effect of positive and physical health brought on by wellness and well-being practices will be to increase overall happiness. You can change your brain to function better by practicing habits that lead to vertical and horizontal integration (Siegel, 2010). Vertical integration results from practices such as meditation that help the rider (the prefrontal lobes of the brain) direct the elephant (the lower mammalian and reptilian centers of the brain). Horizontal integration results from practices that balance the left and right hemispheres, such as balancing a sedentary day with physical activity or a highly verbal activity with visual or musical activities.

The following are additional practices that influence long-term life satisfaction. These practices are listed in a rough order of their potential for the greatest impact on your happiness (except for gratitude, which is listed last but is one of the most impactful practices). Most of these require more extensive effort and commitment than the quick well-being activities listed above.

1. Develop and maintain a sense of meaning and purpose. People who feel that their lives matter rate themselves as being more satisfied with their lives. According to Martin Seligman (2011), anchoring one's life with meaning and purpose predicts more than its share of the many pathways to happiness, since this practice accounts for 60% of the portion of happiness variability that is under our control.

It might initially appear that professors should excel on this factor, because our jobs have the potential to have meaning and purpose built into them. We help students learn. We create, analyze, and disseminate knowledge. Then why are we sometimes so cranky? In my experience, there are two reasons, both caused by a lack of attention and intention.

First, we don't know that we should intentionally include paths to happiness, both the short- and long-term well-being practices, in our happiness plans. Second, we get caught up in the default mode of attending to our day-to-day duties and forget to connect our activities back to our deeper sense of meaning. Wandering through life in a reactive mode risks the despair of having wasted resources on an unfulfilling life.

The remedy requires living intentionally, being proactive about applying resources (talents, time, money, and attention) to create a life that matters, makes a difference, and builds capital according to your deepest values. Two people doing the same job, one with a sense of meaning about the job and the other without, will have entirely different energies surrounding the work (Csikszentmihalyi, 2008).

2. Look for opportunities to serve friends, family, and your institution. Cultivate good interpersonal relationships and increase your social and psychological capital by living the full life of service. It takes a village for all of us to succeed. Seligman (2011) himself was most surprised when his research revealed that the best prediction of life satisfaction was the number and quality of relationships. Those of us who knew his colleague, the late Chris Peterson, often heard him say that his best summary of the happiness research was this: "People matter. Period!" The satisfaction of relationships involves both the giving and the receiving of social support. Given that many professors claim to be introverts, it is important to emphasize the quality rather than quantity of our relationships. The best principle to guide relationships is to give before you get. Altruism and generosity bring short-term pleasures that raise immediate happiness levels as well as leading to long-term satisfaction (Lyubomirsky, Sheldon, & Schkade, 2005). Learning to forgive others by taking their perspective contributes to longevity in relationships. However, forgiveness does not mean forgetting, nor does it mean condoning bad behavior. Limit contact with toxic people, and seek out good finders who see the best in you.

3. Commit to institutions—your college, place of worship, family, or community. Seligman also found that the happiest people committed to institutions in addition to people (Seligman, 2011). Engage your mission with your institution's missions, and invest your time, talent, and treasures for mutual success. Some of the happiest professors I have met on campuses increase their institutional commitment as they take advantage of the perks of discounted faculty tickets by attending campus plays, concerts, lectures, or sports events that they enjoy. As you move through different circumstances and life stages, you will probably change your commitments or their emphasis. In addition to personal satisfaction, professors' own expanded community connections may also benefit their students with internship and job opportunities.

4. Aim for legacy. At the end of their lives, no one laments not working harder, but many do lament not accomplishing enough of lasting significance (Pillemer, 2011). What is or will be your legacy professionally and personally? What do you want to be known for? If you were receiving a lifetime achievement award, what would it be given for? What will you leave behind after you are gone? If you died tomorrow, what would you want your obituary to say about you? If you died in 10, 20, or more years, what would you want the obituary to say? What small activities today and tomorrow will get you to that goal?

5. Keep perspective. Knowing that there is something or someone bigger than yourself helps to keep the end in mind by prompting questions such as these: "How much of my personal capital of time and energy do I want to spend on this? What return on investments do I want to make? Does this matter in eternity? Will this matter after I'm gone?"

6. Cultivate an attitude of gratitude. Selfishly, an attitude of gratitude is good for you; it is the single most powerful short-term well-being practice that contributes to happiness (Seligman, 2011). Gratitude forces you to bypass the ancestral hard wiring of pessimistic scanning for danger and to override it with an optimistic scanning for the good things in life. The gratitude habit extends your life expectancy and promotes a high-quality life.

- Count your blessings. Every night for two weeks list three things that went well during the day. They can be specific events—for example, your partner stopped for milk on the way home from work—or more global elements of your life—for example, the general thoughtfulness you receive from your partner. Research subjects who did this gratitude exercise raised their general happiness level more than those who did not. Ordinary things that you have never noticed before take on a sweet pleasure when you tune up your awareness dial. After the initial impact of the two-week daily gratitude exercise, most people will find that they need to switch to doing the exercise twice a week to prevent losing the impact of a grateful feeling, a research result that surprised researchers (Fredrickson, 2009). If you add a few notes each morning about what activities you are looking forward to and which you are dreading, and a few notes at night about what went well and not so well, you will have within two weeks a rich collection of data to guide your choices. If you add a notation about why each item went well, you will also see patterns. Then you can intentionally increase the activities that feel like blessings and contain those that increase negativity.

- Expressing gratitude is a good way to build relationships and stay connected to the people who matter to you so they will stay engaged with you. In an increasingly unpredictable world, being connected to others who help you survive has survival value.

  - Express gratitude to others. Today notice how often you say thank you to others and see if you can double the number tomorrow. Thank the bus driver when you get off at your stop. Thank your significant other for a meal you didn't have to prepare. Thank your mother for her phone call. According to William James, the father of American psychology, nothing seems to reach people more that the feeling of being appreciated.

  - Appreciation is also a good professional strategy. If you show your bosses, colleagues and employees appreciation, you build social capital, making it more likely that people will be willing to help you meet your needs in the future.

  - Appreciate and give credit when people make sacrifices for you, and let others close to you know when you are making a sacrifice for them unless you have a good reason to do so anonymously. This allows them to appreciate what you are doing and prevents you from building up resentment.

  - Express gratitude to an intimate in a special way. Consider writing out your appreciation and delivering it in person—maybe for a birthday or an anniversary.

New research in wellness and well-being is proliferating as I write this book. I expect this chapter to be the one most likely to be considered dated. This is good news because it means that professors who seek work-life balance will have an even richer collection of evidence-based practices to guide their life choices.

Robison's Rule
Your future self sends a thank-you for all you are doing today to make a better tomorrow for yourself.

Part Five

PACE Your Roles and Responsibilities

The main purpose of life is to live rightly, think rightly,
act rightly.

—Mahatma Gandhi

IN THIS SECTION, we will apply the PACE (Power, Align, Connect, Energize) practices to each of the most common roles in the tripartite faculty position and to several common personal roles. The most frequently asked questions by professors in my workshops are how to teach well and get their research done without working 24 hours a day, seven days a week, and how to give service without being overwhelmed by too many service obligations. The first four parts of this book helped you apply the PACE model to create a life management system that lowers your stress and increases your productivity and happiness. This last section applies the PACE model to your professional and personal roles.

The point of this part of the book is not to teach you everything that you need to know to function well in each role. There are many wonderful books and workshops that can help you in your quest to master these roles. Instead, the goal of this section is give you tips about maintaining better work-life balance while you fulfill your responsibilities in your professional and personal roles.

How Part 5 Will Help You Become
a Peak Performing Professor

This part of the book will help you learn to do the following:

1. Manage your career as though you are self-employed.

2. Teach well while saving time.

3. Complete scholarly work more easily.

4. Serve well in strategic service opportunities.

5. Create a personal life that is supportive and reenergizing.

Chapter 17

The Professor

PROFESSORS WHO WORK at their personal peak in each of their roles exert a minimum of effort yet produce what is expected in their roles and enjoy their jobs better than professors who struggle with their responsibilities (Bain, 2004; Boice, 2000, 2011; Gray, 2010; Walvoord, 2008). Lest readers misunderstand my intent and think I am advocating laziness about the important responsibilities of your roles, I want to remind you of the scholarship cited throughout this book that supports the notion that when it comes to fulfilling the responsibilities of knowledge professionals, it is a matter of the rich getting richer. Professors with less effective strategies risk struggling with long work hours, low productivity, burnout, and dissatisfaction while those with more effective strategies are happier and more productive.

The synergy of both styles, peak performing and struggling, increases over time. The struggling state can worsen over the course of a professorial career, leading to what Bob Boice calls his "MADF" or "Middle Aged Disillusioned Faculty." In what I call his "grumpy old men" study, he found that faculty who fail to incorporate what strategies he found "exemplary new professors" or "quick starters" used at the start of their careers may track on a trajectory to cynicism and disenchantment in the later years of the job. These "terrorists," as Boice called them, act uncivilly toward students and colleagues, give bad advice to new faculty, complain to their chairs, and spend their writing time responding to litigation instead of producing scholarship (Boice, 2011).

Boice's finding was that those disillusioned faculty have career histories exactly opposite to his "exemplary new professors" or "quick starters," those successful faculty who at the beginning of their careers handle their responsibility with high effectiveness and low risk of stress (Boice, 2011). This finding is the faculty development version of one of the principles of chaos theory, that of "sensitive dependence on initial conditions" (Wheatley, 1994), in which conditions which exist at Time 1 become entrenched or exaggerated at Time 2. Boice's research underlines the cost-benefit ratio for faculty development. While those with less exemplary work habits become unhappy, negative influencers in their institutions, "quick starters" began their careers handling their responsibilities with

EXERCISE 17.1

Professorial Roles

Use the following questions to assess how you are doing in your many roles.

- What are your current roles?

- Which ones do you value the most?

- How are you doing in each role? (Give yourself a quick self-rating on a 1–10 scale.)

- What are the responsibilities of each role?

- How do you keep track of your responsibilities so that you complete or maintain them in a timely fashion?

- How do you stay focused and free from distractions?

- Where can you take shortcuts without shortchanging anyone or anything?

high effectiveness and low stress and, as their careers progress, continue to benefit themselves and their institutions. Use the questions in Exercise 17.1 to assess how you are doing in your professional roles.

The following questions will help you assess how the PACE model can help you stay on a positive trajectory in your career:

- Where is my power in this role? What is my purpose, mission, and vision?

- What activities align with that purpose, mission, and vision?

- What people do I need to connect with to fulfill this role?

- What energizes me to do well in this role? What wellness and well-being practices keep me energized?

The following are some of the benefits that come from applying the PACE model to the professoriate:

■ An interesting and varied life—where else does an adult get paid for learning new things? Each day is different from the one before or after, each academic year a fresh start, with many opportunities to try out new ideas and to enjoy meeting interesting new people.

■ Transfer of training and skill sets from one role to another, which builds self-confidence—for example, leadership experience at the PTA transfers to committee chair responsibilities and vice versa (Marks & MacDermid, 1996).

■ Exposure to a wide variety of people who can support, challenge, and inform you—you get to meet and influence the next generation of students while you influence your peers in your discipline and your college.

■ Buffer against overgeneralizing your occasional failures—when things are not going well in one role, you are still getting good feedback in another. Seeing your name in print on the cover of a book can restore your threatened self-esteem when your hypercritical teenager asks, "Whadda you know?"

Those benefits of multiple roles will be yours as long as you heed these principles.

Principle 1. Know what you are all about. Aristotle said it best: "The most difficult victory is victory over yourself." Aim for the ideal of the peak performing professor: work from meaning and purpose through your Pyramid of Power by defining your purpose and applying your best skills while working on your favorite tasks with your favorite groups of people.

Principle 2. Recognize that life is a long journey and that the roles you emphasize at any given time will vary. Realistic expectations about how balance is defined during different periods of your career and life will prevent frustration before it starts (Buller, 2012). The work-life challenge for younger faculty is how to build a career base while simultaneously building life structures that possibly include mates and children.

Assistant professors need to acquire teaching skills rapidly while they take a programmatic approach to building a body of research. Unless their institution is an extremely service-driven school that rewards service, assistant professors should not be asked to fulfill major service roles pretenure. Especially deadly at this stage is the seduction of "taking a turn" at department chair before attaining tenure.

Associate professors will be coming into their own in teaching while at the same time continuing to build their research agenda. When asked to fulfill service roles, they should pick and choose carefully what fits their Pyramid of Power.

Full professors will be exemplars for younger colleagues, both within the department as well as nationally or internationally, mentoring those who want to improve their teaching and research skills. Having established themselves professionally, full professors can devote themselves to larger service roles such as chair, director, or associate dean positions while enjoying travel and outside interests.

Principle 3. Frequently assess your role effectiveness using questions similar to those in Exercise 17.1 so that you can decide which roles need more attention and which should be downplayed or outsourced. The question, "Did I have a good day (week, month, semester)?" can be answered in any areas that needed improvement. It is also helpful to occasionally get a reality check from other interested parties, such as your students, mate, and department chair.

Principle 4. Clarify how much effort you wish to put into each role and how much return on that investment (ROI) you wish to receive. Life is always a series of sacrifices and rewards. Discriminating small differences in priorities and standards is an essential skill to doing great work (remember the discussion of the perfectionism trap in Part 2 of this book). Invest in high-ROI activities instead of spending your valuable time and energy on tasks or relationships that are unlikely to help you achieve peak performance. Your school needs you to do your best. Don't waste your time and energy on activities that drain you, unless those activities are short term and absolutely necessary to support your core priorities. When you discover duties not aligned with your priorities and move aside, you open the door for other faculty who may be eager to fulfill those duties.

Principle 5. Direct your own career. Instead of thinking like an employee who waits for others' decisions and directions, think like a free agent who fits into the culture but who initiates projects (Pink, 2002). Accept tasks that advance your own agenda within the institutional mission. Think about which initiatives support your long-term goals.

Principle 6. Adopt a growth mind-set about your own professional development in which you feel confident in your ability to learn new things, a mind-set that has been shown to result in more success than a fixed mind-set in which you assume that you are limited in your abilities (Dweck, 2008). Create your own professional development plan that includes reading, workshops, and conferences. Go to relevant conferences even if you have to pay out of pocket. During your early career, read extensively in your field, and expand your reading to outside your field as time permits starting in midcareer. Collaborate with faculty from other departments and institutions. Team-teach to learn new things and to create new educational experiences for your students. Take calculated risks by trying new things, perhaps volunteering to help someone in a new area of interest before committing to a major project in that area.

For example, commit to becoming an even better teacher, familiarizing yourself with the best pedagogical methods, by alternating attendance at teaching workshops in your discipline with attendance at teaching conferences such as the Teaching Professor Conference and the Lilly Conferences on Excellence in Teaching.

Principle 7. Keep track of tasks and time lines for all of your roles in the same place with one tracking sheet, one calendar, one e-mail system synced to your computer, tablet, and smartphone.

Principle 8. Continue to build a network of associates inside and outside your college and discipline. Stay accountable to others especially when trying out new roles and skills. Enlist a mentor, hire a coach, or form a mastermind group to support brainstorming and committing to goals, or join or form communities of practice, in which colleagues gather to study ways to improve teaching or scholarly writing.

Principle 9. Aim at being productive, not just busy. Professors can be seduced by a campus culture of professors complaining about how busy they are, wasting so much time talking about the work that they don't actually get a lot of the work done. While they think they will build their sense of competence and importance through competing with others for the prize in the "busier than you" contest, such professors may be sending an unintended message to their listeners that they are unable to manage things well through either inefficiency or incompetence.

Instead of each semester being an exhausting sprint through lists of tasks you think you "should" do but that don't really matter, imagine your whole career as a marathon where pacing yourself will keep you healthy and in the running. According to psychologist and meditation teacher Dr. Tara Brach, the Chinese word for busy is "heart-killing." Nourish your heart by focusing on your Pyramid of Power activities. You might discover that less is more.

Robison's Rule
As Smokey the Bear says, "Only you can prevent forest fires."
Only you can manage your career.

Chapter 18
The Teacher

GOOD TEACHING IS a skill that can be learned and can be continually improved throughout your career. The goal of this chapter is not to teach you how to teach but to suggest ways to teach effectively while you maintain work-life balance. If you are interested in teaching well, the suggestions in this chapter will provide a template for approaching your classes quickly but thoughtfully. Be open to all resources including the books cited here and the workshops at your faculty development center or center for teaching and learning.

Most professors start out their teaching careers spending too much time working on class lectures unaware of the findings from the pedagogical literature that good teaching is about the students learning, not the teacher teaching (Bonwell & Eison, 1991; Gross Davis, 2009; Nilson, 2010). Surprisingly good teaching also results in less stress on the teacher. For example, developing learning activities that promote student learning will take less time than crafting the perfect lecture. The result is a win-win situation; the students learn better, you enjoy your teaching more, and you will have more time for scholarly pursuits and other responsibilities.

You can develop a repertoire of learning exercises and activities by attending teaching workshops and experimenting in your classes to see which methods work on which material with which students. In time, you may consider sharing your own creative approaches with peers through presenting at teaching conferences or publishing in the SoTL (Scholarship of Teaching and Learning) literature (Hutchings, Huber, Ciccone, 2011; Weimer, 2006). William McKeachie is honored as one of the earliest "master teacher of teachers." His *Teaching Tips*, now in its 13th edition, is a classic book on techniques that has been revised frequently over the many years of his career (McKeachie & Svinicki, 2013).

Teaching Strategies

To learn to teach effectively with the least stress possible, you need to develop reliable practices that help you to carry out your teaching role. These specific strategies will apply the PACE model to your teaching:

1. Design courses to meet your goals.
2. Create classroom activities that are fun and promote learning.
3. Make assessment work for you instead of you working for it.
4. Apply effective work habits.
5. Study the effectiveness of your methods and consider publishing the results.
6. Advise students effectively.

If you have been teaching for a while, the suggestions in this chapter will probably not be brand-new ideas. What these suggestions will do is to encourage you to systemize your teaching practices so that you can fulfill those teaching responsibilities quickly, effectively, and creatively.

Quick Steps to Effective Course Design

There are two stages to effective course design: designing a great course and then communicating that design in a syllabus, the document that tells your students and the dean what the course is about. Naïve early career academics usually rush to prepare a syllabus by looking at course content, texts, and the academic calendar. Instead, pause to take the following steps toward a great course design. These suggestions are based on an amalgam of the wisdom of course design experts (Clement, 2010; Diamond, 2008; Fink, 2013; Grunert O'Brien, Millis, & Cohen, 2008; Richlin, 2006). They are easy to do and will make your course go well.

Connect Your Course to "Cosmic Questions"

Give the power of purpose to yourself and your students by looking at why the class is organized the way it is. You don't have to worry about motivating your students if you help them see the connection of the course material to a bigger vision of the field. For example, Dee Fink's (2013) research recommends that instructors demonstrate the Big Purpose of the course in terms of how the course prepares students for what comes after college and how students can develop a deeper understanding of themselves as a result of this course. When the power of purpose matches for teacher and student, the teaching and the learning get easier. Start the course design process by asking yourself these Big Cosmic Questions:

- Why should a student take this course or learn this material—to get science credit, learn to write a term paper, become a better citizen?

- What are the students' goals besides getting credit?

- What will the course teach them about life or their career areas? Answers might include these: "learn literary analysis" or "think critically about course concepts."

- What do you (or the department or the college) want them to do as a result of this course? See the catalogue description for hints.

- What do they already care about or expect from the course? How could you find out? What should they care about and why?

- What do you care about? What are you passionate about in this course?

- What kind of students will you be teaching—online, lower-level, honors, developmental?

The answers to those questions will shape your philosophy of the course—content, assignments, textbook choices, and grading policies. These answers will also shape how much time you spend on each topic, which chapters of the text to emphasize, and what supplemental readings or experiences you want to design into the course.

When Barbara Walvoord (2008) studied 50 of the highest-rated college and university religious studies teachers in the United States, she found that even experienced teachers have unvoiced expectations that can get easily frustrated when students don't meet them. For example, many teachers who hoped that their students would increase in critical thinking skills didn't always have specific strategies to help students achieve that goal. Instead of keeping your goals secret, hoping that the students will guess and meet those goals, articulate them and plan learning experiences aimed to reach those goals.

Review Evaluations

If you have taught a course before, use the information from student evaluations to make better connections between your "Cosmic Questions" and the syllabus. Consider making major course revisions to two courses each year, with minor touch-ups in between. If you teach an average teaching load of three courses a semester all with different preparations, you can confidently teach the four courses that you aren't revising completely this year by making minor changes as needed and know that you will totally revise all of your courses in a three-year rotation.

- Consider writing very brief "after action reports" to yourself when you return to your office from each class. Daily, it takes only three minutes to review the class and ask what worked and what didn't, but when it comes to course revision, this cumulative wisdom will be invaluable.

- Review course evaluations soon after the course ends, so that you can see whether the students learned the major course concepts. Taking notes from that review session when your course is fresh in your mind will be invaluable the next time you prepare to teach the course and wonder what changes to make to the course design.

- As a general rule, do more of what worked. In the case of what didn't work, revise that content or assignment, or consider eliminating it.

- Keep bad evaluations in perspective. Of bad evaluations, 10% are "outliers," students whose responses are so different that they don't seem to have been in the same class. As the percentage of bad evaluations increases so should your attention to what they are saying. If you get more than 40% bad evaluations, figure out what isn't working and take steps to correct it. Perhaps consult with someone from your faculty center for teaching to help you problem-solve about what went wrong and how to correct it.

Lay Out a Design with Content and Learning Activities

Using a grid format allows you to juxtapose content, course objectives, and competencies. List the content themes from your Cosmic Questions as rows, and the skills needed (critical thinking, definition, enumeration, and others) as columns. I highly recommend Dee Fink's learning-centered approach to course design that begins with identifying learning goals, then matches the type of learning goal to specific teaching and learning activities, and finally evaluates achievement of the learning goals by feedback and assessment activities (Fink, 2013). Insert the learning activity and assessment methods for each cell. These recommended procedures will align your teaching and learning activities with your course purpose. For example, a political science teacher who sets a goal of students caring about their country as they study the history of the U.S. Constitution might ask the students to list the major ways citizens contributed to the development of the Constitution.

Pick Resources and Write Materials

Tie the course resources into your Cosmic Questions. What texts, articles, lab manuals, websites, and audio-visual materials such as videos support your course goals? What do you want the students to do with these materials—for example, skim articles, turn in lab reports, write reaction papers about films, or listen to conversations in the language lab? Skim potential texts to see whether their philosophy and information fits with your design. Make sure you are planning to assign a good portion of the text, say 80% and actually assess the reading so the students feel that the purchase price is worth the investment. Start the semester with all your handouts and worksheets prepared.

Plan How You Will Assess Learning

How will students demonstrate their competencies? Class discussion, one-minute papers, random quizzes, and term papers are all very different experiences from the students' point of view. Not all assessments have to become labor-intensive on a professor's part to be effective (Nilson, 2010; Walvoord & Anderson, 2010). Match assignments with your course goals and make that connection obvious to the students (Banta, Jones, & Black, 2009; Suskie, 2009).

In addition to assessing student learning, assess the class and your teaching periodically during the course rather than just at the end of the course. Take any "consumer complaints" seriously enough to change elements of the course design during the current term so that those students benefit from the changes.

Grade yourself on your own performance standards as though you were grading yourself on a rubric. Here is an example of what one language teacher wrote:

- *First time:* a grade of 30% of my eventual highest quality—a pretty good syllabus, classes mostly prepared, and decent assignments

- *Second time:* 60% quality—all of the above plus classes well-organized, some interesting learning activities, well-thought out grading rubrics

- *Third and subsequent times:* 90% quality—all of above plus interesting, well-organized classes, well-thought-out learning activities, assignments, and grading rubrics and effective use of audiovisual and electronic media.

Until you have cumulated wisdom from several experiences with the course, it is unrealistic to aim at 90% quality. Instead, aim to improve the course each time you teach it.

Write the Syllabus

Be sure to double-check the upcoming campus schedule just in case someone moved the term holiday, homecoming, semester start dates, or exam schedules. For a list of elements in a well-prepared syllabus, consult your college's campuswide format for syllabus preparation or one of the books in the reference list. Here are some elements of a well-prepared syllabus that will help you keep your sanity while you help your students learn:

- Information about you, your office, your office hours, and preferred contact methods and information. Clear directions about preferred methods prevent most late-night phone calls to your home.

- A week-by-week or day-by-day schedule of class topics, reading assignments, other assignments, and assessments.

- Specifics about assignments, including term paper guidelines, grading rubrics, due dates, and late penalties.

- Class policies such as attendance, class participation, use of cell phones, texting, recording devices, shopping on eBay, and gum chewing.

- A tone that sounds warm and welcoming rather than nasty and harsh. Does your tone convey a perspective that your class is a "community of learners" with you as one of the learners or that of a prison with you as the warden? One syllabus I reviewed for a coaching client said, "No amount of begging will get me to change your grade if you are late on assignments." We changed it to read, "The best strategy to earn the grade you desire is the timely completion of quality assignments." If you are new to teaching, seek out model syllabi from your department or your faculty development or teaching effectiveness center to see how they set up classroom policies in a friendly yet clear manner.

- Exemplary assignments from previous students (with their permission to reprint and their identifying information removed) posted on the class website. This step will head off many questions because it gives the students examples of what it takes to earn a good grade.

- Office hours—in person and e-mail. Being a good professor does not mean that you have to dedicate your life to students to the exclusion of your own work-life balance. Do not have an open door policy or give students your home phone number. Do list a few hours a week for live appointments and drop-ins and a few e-mail office hours in which you promise to be available for almost instant responses to student e-mail. Defer working on any of your urgent think work during those posted office hours, or you will resent the interruptions. Instead organize your desk by turning some of your piles into files while you wait for phone calls, e-mail, or visitors. For more suggestions on effective office hours, see Nilson, (2010).

- E-mail instructions. Give your students in Victorian Literature 339 a code such as "Vict Lit 339" to put in the subject heading of their e-mails. Set up an e-mail folder for the class and a filter that directs those e-mails into the folder while bypassing your in-box. During your electronic office hours, open the class folder and respond to the e-mail.

- Create a frequently asked questions (FAQs) page on the class website. Doing so up front will save you the time and aggravation of having to write narrative responses. Respond to an inquiry of "How long is the five-page paper?" with the link to the FAQs page, which says, "The five-page paper is usually five pages long."

Ask some wise elders who are known to be good teachers to read your syllabus draft and critique it kindly.

Create a Lively Learning Atmosphere

Even experienced professors wake up in cold sweats with presemester nightmares about arriving for class in pajamas, showing up in the wrong building unprepared, or teaching a class of students who rudely ignore the teacher. This section will help you manage the stress and create an atmosphere conducive to learning through interesting classroom activities.

Easy Guide to a Great First Class

Calm your back-to-school jitters by planning a strong start to each semester (Clement, 2010; McGlynn, 2001; Nilson, 2010). Nothing increases a professor's confidence at the start of the semester like having your goals clear and your work life organized.

Make a good connection (the "C" of PACE) with students at the start of the semester:

- Post your syllabus ahead of time if possible so that the students have time to digest it and come to class prepared with questions.

- Arrive early so that you can greet students, circulate around, introduce yourself, and learn a few names. Calling students by name reinforces their hard work and builds a community of learners. It motivates the other students to be in the "in group." If you race in at the last minute, it may be interpreted as either lack of interest or disorganization.

- Start class on time, even if all the expected seats are not filled. Make a good first impression by making eye contact, announcing the course name and number, and introducing yourself using whatever form of address is conventional on your campus (first names, Mr., Ms., Dr., Professor). Give the class a short bio (this could be on a slide with photos) including how your name is pronounced and spelled, your degrees and schools, rank and department, and research and teaching interests (explained briefly in nontechnical language for undergraduate classes).

Do a warm-up activity that shows interest in your students as people. For small classes, you might use a structured exercise in which they introduce themselves in relation to the course topic, for example, what they love about chemistry. For larger classes, consider partner or small-group introductions.

Gather information on the students by asking them to fill out index cards with their name (including the phonetic pronunciation if needed and a nickname if they prefer), how they would like to be contacted by you, their academic and job experience in the field related to the course, and any additional information such as favorite music, movies, TV shows, websites (Berk, 2008).

Visit their culture by using their music and movies in audiovisual materials, but don't move into their culture by name-dropping to seem "hip."

Spend some class time reviewing the syllabus with the students. Class time spent clearing up misunderstandings about the course structure will pay off in lower student and teacher stress across the semester. Students learn better with clear structures (BrckaLorenz, Ribera, Kinzie, & Cole, 2012).

Introduce the content of the course in a learning-centered activity, perhaps a mini-lecture followed by a small-group or pencil-and-paper activity, such as 10 true/false statements about the subject. Don't lecture during the whole class without a student learning activity, and don't dismiss the class early.

Continue to Create a Community of Learners

Learning atmosphere matters. Just like you, your students hit their peak performance sweet spot where challenge meets skill (Csikszentmihalyi, 2008). Part of being a good teacher is the ability to connect to students so that you create a comfortable, yet challenging atmosphere in your classes (Bain, 2004; Clement, 2010; McGlynn, 2001; Walvoord, 2008; Weimer, 2010). Engaged students learn better and experience their learning as more positive (Barkley, 2009).

Promote Active Learning

Students get more out of classes in which they can be active rather than passive learners. Here are suggestions for lively classes that help students learn:

- Don't lecture as your teachers might have. Instead, think "active and interactive learning" that produce learning quickly (Bean, 2011; Doyle, 2011; Hake, 1998; Hestenes, Wells, & Swackhammer, 1992; Weimer, 2002). Examples could include filling out a lab sheet, writing a summary of a short film, or discussing a topic in a small group.

- Design template modules (see the next section) for one or several classes on a topic including various learning activities such as didactic instruction, individual work, and group work. The modules can be filled in with new content for each course topic.

- Change the methods of intellectual stimulation every 10 minutes.

- Evaluate often—both the students and yourself. You can measure percent of understanding or confusion, boredom, how much students liked an activity, or any other variable that will be helpful for you to pace the class. Take the pulse of the class with quick class evaluations asking the students to raise their hands or use clickers, cell phones, or colored cardboard cards that can be raised in answer to class evaluation questions such as these:

- Did you learn something?

- Was this class worth your time today?

- How many feel they understood the subject better after class?

- How many still feel confused about the subject and want more class time spent on it next time?

- Make adjustments in teaching and grading methods that show you take their feedback seriously.

Many teachers, especially in the sciences, are concerned about sacrificing content class time for these kinds of learning activities, but students learn more if your course goals go beyond "covering content" to getting the students to do something with the content (Bahls, 2012; Walvoord & Anderson, 2010).

Use a Template for Good Flow and Clear Expectations

Develop a formula for the flow of a class that combines the best elements for teaching your subject matter. Here is an example of a template for a 50-minute class:

1. Introduce topic with student involvement (5–10 minutes)—examples: graded or ungraded quizzes on reading material, learning activity, short demonstration, presentation of a dilemma

2. Minilecture, audiovisual presentation, silent reading (5–10 minutes)

3. Student activity on content of minilecture (5–10 minutes)—examples: think-pair-share, calculations, short lab experiment, one-minute papers, online searches

4. Repeat steps 1–3 on another area of content if time permits. A 50-minute class might cover one or two teaching objectives with two to three subsidiary objectives, whereas a 75-minute class might have two or three objectives each with two or three subsidiary objectives.

5. Assess learning and class while summarizing (2–5 minutes)

Make Assessment Work for You

Assessment is an important part of your teaching role, but sometimes it feels as though you are working for assessment rather than assessment working for you. This section will help you take some of the stress out of the process. Assessments energize (the "E" of PACE) the students as they practice the skills they are learning and apply the material they are studying. Assessments also energize the teacher because they let you know how your performance is going and allow you to correct some techniques as you go.

Great Assignments and Easy Assessment

As you get more teaching experience, you will become better at designing great assignments that your students enjoy doing and that you enjoy grading. Some tips on how to complete your assessment responsibilities with a minimum of stress:

- Tie your assessment tools into your course goals and make that connection clear to the students so they don't feel they are being asked to do busy work. Fortunately, there are many resources that make this task easy for you (Banta et al., 2009; Suskie, 2009; Walvoord & Anderson, 2010).

- Aim to make assignments meaningful but not labor-intensive. Some possibilities:

  - Use in-class time for activities that promote learning while they act as assessments (Angelo & Cross, 1993). For example, assign short reaction papers to media, an exercise, or a discussion. These papers can be graded with grading partners and later recorded quickly by you or your teaching assistant (if you have the benefit of having one).

  - Consider mixing quick assignments like one minute in-class papers, graded pass/fail, with finely tuned larger assignments worth more points (Nilson, 2010).

  - Create assignments such as research or literature critiques by starting with a form or a tip sheet on how to do the critique. Then take some class time to demonstrate such a critique with the whole class participating with you.

  - Have the students work in small groups while you roam around offering consultations.

  - Require blog entries accomplishing several class goals, such as reading an assignment and then commenting on it.

  - Give shorter and more frequent tests, which are easier on the students and you. While multiple-choice exams are labor-intensive on the front end but easy to grade and record afterward, essay questions are easy to make up but hard to grade. Another advantage of using multiple-choice items is that you can measure their difficulty level through an item analysis, which will provide invaluable data allowing you to develop a test bank for future semesters. With experience, you can write items that test critical thinking as well as the memorization often associated with multiple-choice tests.

- Use grading rubrics set out in writing to the students ahead of time so that students don't have to play guessing games: "What does he really want?" (Stevens & Levi, 2004).

- Include collaborative learning activities. For example, instead of having every student work every problem in the chemistry book, demonstrate how to solve a type of problem and then have the students pair up with one partner to work on the first problem, then another partner to work on the second and so on. The threat of mild social embarrassment with peers for not knowing how to do the problems is a much more powerful motivator (Baumeister, 1982) for coming to class prepared than is turning in homework that only the teacher sees and grades. The advantage to the students is that they will actually learn how to work the problems and have a reality test on where they stand compared to other students' knowledge base without your having to post a grading curve. The advantage to you is that you have fewer papers to drag home and the satisfaction of seeing the students actually do the work on their own. If you wish, you can collect the papers to spot-check quality and to record attendance.

- Hold yourself to a grading or feedback schedule. Can you return papers by the class after they are turned in? Could you offer bonus points for early submission so that you can stagger your grading work-load? Specify in advance point penalties for late submissions.

Teach for Better Test Performance

Many students waste their study time in activities that don't yield results on their grade. I have never heard of a teacher grading students on how well they can reread a text during a test. Instead, most teachers test on the recall and application of course content. However, rereading the text is a common but unfruitful study method replicated by each generation of college students.

Students will do better on assessment activities if they have practiced those same activities while they are studying. Consider taking 10 minutes of class time to show them a study method that will be successful in your course. For example, a good study method in the sciences and social studies is SQ3R: *Study* a chapter looking at the headings and summary, formulate *Questions* about the headings, *Read* for the answers, *Recite* the answers so that you are practicing retrieval, *Review* the questions and the answers.

Find or develop a good study method for your subject matter. If you think that it is not your job to teach students study skills, consider which is worse, taking a bit of class time to teach how to study chemistry or feeling frustrated all semester that the students don't know how to study chemistry.

Teach for Better Writing

Regrettably, completion of a general education writing requirement doesn't give students competence in professional writing in your discipline (Robison & Walvoord, 1990). Hence, many departments require that students learn to write in their discipline. You might find yourself assigned to teach a writing intensive course in your discipline combining course content with writing techniques. There are excellent sources for how to teach writing and thinking through active learning in the classroom (Bean, 2011), but my goal here is to give you some quick tips for helping students write better without overloading yourself with papers to drag home.

1. Spend some class time coaching the students' paper preparation, from picking a topic, researching, mind mapping or webbing (Buzan & Buzan, 1996), to creating an outline.

2. For written assignments, help students by giving them a formula to get started. Here is the "CRAFT" formula I developed for my psychology classes (Robison, 1983). Students use the following guidelines to develop a draft worksheet to help them think through what they want to write.

    Criteria: What are the grading criteria? This is your grading rubric.

    Role: What role or perspective should the student writer take—science researcher, poet, advisor to parents?

    Audience: Who besides the teacher is an (imaginary) audience that the student is addressing—a journal editor, a blog audience, middle schoolers?

    Form/style: Is the assignment a lab report, a poem, a blog?

    Themes: What content do you want students to include—ideas from class discussions, readings, language lab lessons?

3. Have students submit preliminary sections to a partner or to an in-class small group to get coaching as they write. Circulate around the room grabbing teachable moments to help them increase their skills.

4. Require fewer papers, with revision and resubmission opportunities for each. Assign a preliminary grade to first drafts by filling in a grading rubric pasted at the end of the electronic paper, and write margin

comments suggesting improvements. Some comments will be more helpful than others (Bean, 2011). Give a preliminary grade to each paper, allowing students either to take the grade as the final grade for the assignment or to rewrite for a better grade. If they resubmit it, they type their changes in colored text and you read only the changes, adjust the grade, and add a final comment. The regrading time on the same assignment you have already graded is about five minutes per paper. The benefit to the students is that they get better grades and learn how to write and revise in the discipline. The benefit to you is that the time you spend giving feedback actually pays off as the students incorporate that feedback in their improved rewrites.

Apply Effective Work Habits

Your teaching role will become less stressful and more effective if you apply some of the following practices.

Pace Yourself Across the Semester

To keep your work and the rest of your life in balance, you need to plan. When you are constructing a syllabus, think selfishly about your need to work at a good pace across the semester by following these suggestions:

- Pace your assignments across the semester so that big assignments from your various courses are distributed across the semester instead of all landing in the last week. Front-loading assignments earlier in the semester is better for student motivation as well for your workload.

- Track all of your graded course assignments on one Tracking Sheet to see where their due dates intersect, and stagger them so that you never have two sets of assignments coming to you at the same time.

- Time the due dates around holidays and campus events so that you and your students have better work-life balance and do better work.

Other suggestions for self-pacing your teaching workload

- Decide on a quitting time each day and stick to your decision.

- Use the semester breaks well. Debrief from the previous semester, rest, and start to prepare for the next work. Divide 9 months of teaching work across 12 months.

- Decide on how much you will work at home, what types of projects to work on, and what projects are reserved for on-campus work only.

Pare Down Class Preparation Time

To prevent burnout and maintain balance in your life, keep your preparation time to no more than one hour of preparation for each hour of class. If you teach 12 hours a week and you prepare for 12 hours, that puts your teaching work week at 24 hours even before you add in grading and office hours. However, if you do a great job with class preparation the first time you teach a class, the second time will require only a few minutes reviewing notes, loading media, and gathering lab equipment. The time gained can be shifted over to your other role responsibilities, especially to your scholarly writing work. When I started teaching I averaged eight hours of prep time per one hour of class time. I wish someone had suggested the following protocol before I got to my third year of teaching headed for serious burnout.

1. Mind map all you know about the class topic. (On a mind map, discussed in Chapter 8 of this book, the topic is in the center of a piece of paper; spokes with major ideas radiate outward, while minor ideas radiate out from the spokes.)

2. Ask yourself the Big Questions related to this class. "If I'm a student in this class, what is the point of this material or the learning activities?"

3. Using the Big Questions, write class goals (objectives), learning activities, and in-class assessment tools.

4. Turn the mind map into a class outline of topics to be covered and learning activities with approximate timing laid out.

Study and Share Innovative Teaching Methods

You don't have to reinvent the wheel when it comes to excellent teaching. Faculty who study the impact of their teaching techniques on student learning (called the Study of Teaching and Learning or SoTL) publish their results in higher education journals such as the *Journal of Excellence in Teaching and Learning* or present at conferences such as *The Teaching Professor* and the *Lilly Conferences on Teaching Excellence*. After attending teaching conferences, try one or two techniques you have learned. Consider sharing your pedagogical innovations with colleagues at conferences or in journals (Hutchings et al., 2011; Weimer, 2006).

Advise Students Effectively

Here are tips for fulfilling and enjoying the advisory duties of your job:

- Be available within limits. Don't have an open door policy. Ask "someone in the know" what the norms are for faculty office hours on campus.

- When students show up for appointments, make the students your number one priority. Don't answer e-mail or the phone. Ask students for their agenda and then do your best to answer their concerns briefly so that you are available for other students. Today's graduate student is tomorrow's colleague and next decade's department chair.

- Consider streamlining advising time by meeting with students with similar advising needs in groups first, following up with individual appointments as needed.

  - Send out worksheets in advance of the group sessions. These might include graduation requirements, applications for internships, and other material relevant to the students' progress in the program.

  - When the group gathers, welcome participants and give a minilecture on the most important elements they need to consider in filling out their schedules for the next semester (year).

  - Allow time for questions and answers. Defer answering any idiosyncratic questions until the individual sessions.

  - Allow time for filling out sample schedules, applications, letters of recommendations, and so on.

- If you teach graduate students, pace mentoring to their needs. Some will arrive at your office, class, or lab already equipped with great writing and time management skills, whereas others will need more guidance. Some need a lot of structure, whereas others structure themselves. Some can think outside of the box; some can't even find the box. Have a written manual to guide grad students on how to get the most out of your guidance, including information such as the following:

  - Policies and suggestions related to the issues and problems that have occurred with other students. Many of grad students' faux pas with their professors happen more out of anxiety than because of maliciousness. Lower that anxiety by clarifying expectations about their working relationship with you.

  - Time lines for finishing theses, dissertations, articles, and presentations.

  - If you run a lab, lab procedures and safety measures.

  - Practicum and internship guidelines including decorum suggestions. Those opportunities might be the first time that your students have had a job in a professional setting.

  - Ethics in the field—maybe a reprint from your professional journal or maybe just a practical summary.

EXERCISE 18.1

Letter of Recommendation Template

Create a template for the letters; then individualize it for each student. Here is one to get you started until you develop your own.

Dear _____,

_____ [student's name] has asked me to write a letter of recommendation supporting his/her application to _____ [program, school, employer, and so forth].

I have known _____ [student's name] in the capacity of [check as many as apply].

Student—courses and grades:

_____

Advisee

Research assistant

Teaching assistant

Other _____

In the role of _____, [make your comments about the quality of the student's work]

_____

[Repeat for each capacity in which you know the student]

Writing skills

Research skills

Student assistant skills

[Perhaps add comments on other aspects of the student's performance, such as ethics, character, and relationships with faculty and other students.]

- Intellectual property laws and practices, including the practices of determining coauthorship in your field.

Use a Template for Letters of Recommendation

Most professors find writing letters of recommendation to be a dreaded, joyless responsibility to be avoided until procrastination becomes embarrassing. Be prepared for this request as your students move toward graduation. If you cannot in all honesty write a student a good letter because of either character grounds or class grades, encourage the student to find another recommender.

Exercise 18.1 will guide you to write a template for letters of recommendation. Such a template will make writing these letters less onerous and even a bit interesting.

Now for the best part of the template format: ask the students to fill in the template. After you receive their drafts electronically, quickly check the accuracy of their reported grades. Schedule 10-minute advising sessions to give the students feedback on whether their written perception of the work done with you matches your perception. This very interesting meeting will be an opportunity to confirm perceptions or correct any misperceptions of your work together. Soon after the meeting, while the conversation is fresh, revise the student's electronic copy, polish it, and ship it off to the school or place of employment.

The suggestions given in this chapter are not aimed at being a primer for all you need to know about teaching but rather a set of tips for teaching effectively, while lowering your stress and increasing your satisfaction with the role. Similarly, the next chapter will not cover everything you need to know to be a scholar in your field. Rather, the chapter is a set of tips for managing the scholarly role productively and happily.

Robison's Rule
Reach 'em to teach 'em.

Chapter 19

The Scholar

THE ROLE OF scholar is an important but ambivalent role for most professors. On the one hand, institutions often emphasize evidence of scholarship in the promotion and tenure process, sometimes even to the exclusion of evidence about a candidate's teaching and service roles. Furthermore, most faculty are highly trained scholars in their disciplines since most professors have attained a Ph.D. or equivalent degree. On the other hand, the scholar role is often the most stressful one, because it involves setting nonurgent, long-term goals that must be carried out through the completion of short-term action steps usually with no inherent deadlines. This process is challenging to most professors and when not done well leads to guilt, lowered self-esteem, and negative career implications.

Similar to the goals for the teaching chapter, this chapter is not aimed at teaching you how to do research; you have had ample training in those skills in graduate school, and there are resources for you to consult to amplify those skills (Rocco & Hatcher, 2011). Rather, this chapter aims to help you do your scholarly work more easily and peacefully through the development of key strategies that will increase your success as a scholar. For simplicity, even though research takes different forms in different disciplines, I will refer to all academic scholarship as "research," "writing," or "scholarship" as I offer suggestions for faculty readers who wish to complete scholarly projects with timeliness, creativity, and perhaps a bit of joy (Boice, 2000; Foss & Waters, 2007; Gray, 2010).

The Difficult Transition from Graduate Student to Scholar

The transition from graduate student to professor is a critical period in the life of a faculty member, because it involves learning to think like an independent scholar (Boice, 2000; Silvia, 2007). Successful independent scholars approach research differently than do unsuccessful scholars, who are often stuck in the "good student role," engaging in perfectionistic work habits that were highly reinforced in school—habits that impede their progress as successful independent scholars (Foss & Waters, 2007). Table 19.1 lays out the key

TABLE 19.1

Key Differences in the Successful Transition from Graduate Student

	Students and unsuccessful professor researchers	Successful professor researchers
Research literature	Research the literature thoroughly to find out what is done.	Know the literature or begin a project and backfill the literature later.
Motivation	Get assignments done and graduate. Get pubs to get promotion and tenure.	Explore interesting questions that build a body of work.
Collaborations and relationships	Please a mentor sometimes by extending mentor's research agenda. Please a committee as directed by mentor. Seek advice of committee as directed or approved by mentor. Review juried research or edits drafts that mentor will claim.	Work independently. Collaborate with colleagues and former mentors on equal footing with own ideas and interests. Develop relationships with "stars" in the fields. Mentor students. Review juried research on own. Befriend editors. Serve as editor.
Feelings about research	Intrigued but intimidated. Anxious and perfectionistic. Avoidant.	Curious, confident and risk taking. Eager. Persistent.
Output	Work in binges and bursts—low total output.	Work in small regular sessions—high total output.
Time management	Race to meet deadlines, crash afterward, get the flu.	Work at a constant reasonable pace on or ahead of deadlines. Get annoyed by procrastinating colleagues and become the envy of others for high productivity and good work-life balance.

differences among professors I have coached between those who have successfully made the transition from graduate student and those who haven't.

A successful scholar has two main tasks: creating a body of work and sustaining good work habits for a long and productive career.

Think "Body of Work," Not Publications

To avoid getting stuck in the "good grad student" identity, you need to make a paradigm shift from thinking about a series of short-term projects to thinking about a long-term research agenda that can be broken down into smaller projects shaping your work over many years. Similar to the application of PACE to the teaching role, there are specific steps to making a smooth transition to the scholar role.

Establish a Research Agenda

Fitting research and writing into your busy life as a professor gets easier when you imagine a body of work in which every piece you produce is part of a whole, like a mural of a town's history where every period of history merges into progressive scenes. A research agenda with intriguing questions can carry you for several or even many years into the future. It answers the question, "What is my purpose as a scholar?" Exercise 19.1 provides you with a path toward establishing a research agenda.

Discover Your Vein of Gold

In her excellent book *The Vein of Gold*, Julia Cameron (1996) describes the magic that happens when people go deeper into what they do well. For example, in his youth George Lucas had a crazy vision of another world and the characters in it. Decades later he has produced six *Star Wars* movies—intriguing entertainment and a good source of income for himself and others.

When you were imagining that award presentation in Exercise 19.1, did you find your vein of gold—the theme or themes that organize your lifetime body of work? If not:

- Think about problems to be solved instead of achievements.

- Think about potentially unique contributions to your discipline or the world, ideas you've wondered about, areas of research not yet fully explored.

Once you have established the power of a long-term agenda, divide it into half-decade segments, with accompanying benchmarks and milestones, such as number of articles published, in each segment. Use the backward planning skills from Part 2 of this book to break down each benchmark into smaller tasks until you have a series of projects and a checklist of 15- to 30-minute to-dos for each project.

Strengthen Your Strengths

Another way to think about developing a body of work is to focus on how the three strengths in your mission can lead you to your vein of gold. If one of them is "teach," what aspects of teaching can you study in a scholarly way? If one of your strengths is "empower," could you

EXERCISE 19.1

The Lifetime Achievement Award

This is an exercise of imagination, so you may wish to read through the directions and then close your eyes so that you can engage your imagination for a few minutes. After the exercise, jot down notes on your observations.

You are sitting off stage in a large auditorium where a professional group important to you has gathered. At 90 years young, you are about to receive an award for the body of work which you have developed over your lifetime. A younger beloved colleague, perhaps a former student, is reading your bio, covering your professional achievements in your field. As you listen, you are pleased at how your colleague has developed the threads and themes of that work almost as if all of your work was planned to come together this way. Listen to your colleague's award speech. . .

Now, capture your observations from the exercise.

study how empowerment relates to your discipline or to higher education? You might consider using the mission writing exercise found in Part 1 to create a mission statement specific to your research specifying three strengths, the one to three audiences for your research, and the key values that guide your work.

Writing Work Habits

Successful academic writers work differently from those who struggle to publish (Boice, 1990). In a nutshell, you will write better and more easily if you learn how to think like a writer.

Choose to Write

If you otherwise like your career as a professor but struggle with scholarship, try to see scholarship as part of the choice to continue doing well in that career. If you have gotten caught in the common faculty trap of resenting your administration's publication emphasis as a form of coercion, regain your sense of self-determination by choosing to develop scholarship as part of your tripartite job description. People who feel forced to do something are not as likely to draw on their intrinsic motivation and engagement as those who see themselves as determining their choices (Deci & Ryan, 1985, 2000; Lyubomirsky, King, & Diener, 2005; Spreitzer, Kizilos, & Nason, 1997).

Tie Your Writing into Your Pyramid of Power

Review your purpose, mission, and vision to see how those suggest some things you need to do to promulgate your message to your discipline or to your faculty colleagues. When your research is integral to the person you are, you will likely find a sense of flow as you work on it. Share your Pyramid of Power and your professional interests with a mentor, coach, or colleague for their observations about how you might integrate those factors into your body of work.

You might even imagine creating a Pyramid of Power for your scholarship role with its own specific purpose statement about your body of work, your mission of strength-based activities to fulfill that purpose, and your vision of possible outcomes and the specific goals that will make your scholarship satisfying and impactful.

Pick Interesting Projects

If you are a new assistant professor, don't feel obligated to publish articles based on your dissertation if you are no longer interested in that topic.

It would be better to put that project aside and give yourself permission to focus on something that represents where you are and where you are going. You may even find that new projects inspire you to work on your shelved projects. Sometimes writers even find that the old and new areas have a relationship.

You might choose to study a teaching technique that you have been developing and then to publish an article about it in one of the scholarship of teaching and learning (SoTL) journals.

Perhaps working with interesting colleagues can spark your interest to organize a panel or symposium proposal for your next discipline association meeting and then to spin off articles as a result of the synergy from that endeavor.

Most people find writing a challenging activity because it involves creating something out of nothing and managing a collection of random ideas into a well-organized, interesting, and innovative product. Writing is easier when you manage your energy by being jazzed about your topic instead of just grinding out sentences on a topic that fails to ignite a spark. You may have been given advice when picking a dissertation topic that is also relevant for professional book writing: pick the topic well because you will spend a lot of time and energy on it.

Write Fast, Bad Drafts, Then Revise Slowly

Serious writers prevent procrastination and emotional blocks to writing by not letting the perfect get in the way of the good. Successful writers who aim at quickly writing "bad" drafts feel free to compose knowing that they will revise later (Gray, 2010; Lamott, 1995).

There is no such thing as wasted writing, because writing clarifies thought. You write to find out what you think, while developing your argument and support as you go along. Sometimes you will discover the perfect theme sentence at the conclusion of a section, one that would never have appeared if you stared at a blank paper or screen commanding yourself to write that perfect theme sentence first.

Use free writing techniques to generate the ideas that flow from your outline (Elbow, 1998). Don't rewrite prematurely while you are generating a first draft. Instead, aim at *satisficing* in drafts. If you can't think of a word, put a blank line in the text where the word belongs. If you can't think of a reference, type: [reference ??]. Fill in the blanks during the next draft.

At the beginning of your career, aim to write short, concise articles. Save the masterpieces for mid- to late career when you know more about how your body of work fits into your discipline.

Plan Your Writing Time

You will never "find time" to write. Successful professionals set the time to write or to do anything else that matters and then build their time around those commitments. Sit down with your schedule, filling it in with your class meetings, class preparation, grading sessions, office hours, and standing meetings. You should still have about 10–12 hours across the week to work on your research and writing. If you don't, you are either overdoing class preparation time or overcommitting to service work.

Increase your scholarly success by making specific writing plans, including times, places, and tasks (Halvorson, 2011). Plan a writing session either on certain days of the week at certain times (Boice, 2000) or every day during designated times (Gray, 2010).

Plan a Project with Several Stages

Writers weave back and forth across the stages of a project, sometimes jumping forward two steps or completing the steps out of order. James Michener, author of many blockbuster historical novels set in such diverse places as Hawaii, Texas, Poland, and the Chesapeake Bay, lived in each geographic area while he wrote. He wrote each morning, studied library research documents and interviewed subjects in the afternoon, and then in the evening revised his earlier writing in light of the afternoon's information.

Here are the major stages of academic writing, but don't feel compelled to follow them in rigid order.

Prewriting

- Capture ideas that come at nonwriting times when you are not even thinking about writing, times that I call "bed, bath, and beyond," perhaps collecting them on sticky notes.
- Mind map and outline connections among the ideas.
- Have conceptual conversations with a mentor, coach, or colleague about themes and issues.
- Review data, conference materials, and notes from your reading.
- Journal about what discoveries you are making.
- Organize notes to discover relationships among ideas.

Free-Writing

- Identify your best writing times given your biorhythms and energy levels.
- Find a comfortable place to write and create your best conditions for writing including wearing your favorite jeans, writing with your best

pen, playing Mozart music, or engaging in a relaxation or meditation session before starting (Brown, 2011).

- Free-write quickly without lifting pen from paper or fingers from keyboard.

- Limit your writing session to 90 minutes and then take a break.

- Establish boundaries by turning off phones and e-mail alerts. Close your door and post a sign that sets a firm boundary: "Dr. Smith is in a writing session. Office hours start at 3 pm." Do not try to write during posted office hours. Establish boundaries for your home office as well, and do not write when small children are around unless you have another adult protecting your time and writing space.

- Check the research literature only after you have written key ideas or arguments.

Draft Writing

1. Write a bad first draft, throwing down sections in any order.

2. Use any writing medium you prefer. If you can write on a keyboard, eventually run a hard copy, reading to decide what really belongs. Reorder sections by computer or actually use scissors and tape to cut small sections apart, annotating each slip of paper with a code with page and paragraph number so that you can find where it is in the electronic draft (Foss & Waters, 2007). If you have a hard time cutting your precious words because they are part of your innermost being, archive discarded pieces into a "leftovers" file.

3. Connect the ideas, arguments, and conclusions into bigger chunks using transition expressions and sentences such as "another reason for that is . . . ," "the analysis shown in Table 1 . . . ," or "contrary to what Aristotle taught, Plato said . . ." (Graff & Birkenstein, 2010).

4. Marinate the section in time so that the flavors blend together while you work on a different section or a different project. After a few days, you can reread it as if you are a stranger to the piece because by then your memory will have faded for the exact wording you used. Now you are ready for the final stage: revision.

Rewriting and Revisioning

Don't waste time revising until the big ideas are captured. Then follow this process.

1. Re-outline the piece to see whether the larger ideas hang together.

2. Read for how each section flows into the next. Insert transition sentences as needed.

3. Make sure the paragraphs flow within each section and the sentences flow within each paragraph.

4. Read for the technical aspects of writing, such as spelling and punctuation. You might have an editorial assistant do that for you.

Write in Bites, Not Binges

Although many faculty think a book can be written only during a sabbatical writing binge, research on the writing habits of prolific academic writers reveals that they do most of their writing in small, daily doses instead of binges (Boice, 1989; Gray, 2010). Faculty are often averse to writing in small doses because many professors find it hard to get their heads into writing in the midst of other responsibilities. Once they try to break projects into small, manageable, timed steps, even skeptics are pleased with how much is accomplished through the cumulative progress of these small steps (Zerubavel, 1999).

To connect the big picture of your scholarly goals to the daily grind of writing in small bites, consider organizing your writing project in its own Dream Book, with its own miniature Pyramid of Power to lay out the purpose, mission, and vision of the project. This could be done in a three-ring notebook or in a computer file. Make the project mobile even when you are away from the office by including the following:

- Mind maps

- Research articles

- Tables of statistical analysis

- A pack of sticky notes to write other subgoals as they occur to you

- Separate sections for each part of the project with the bigger tasks broken down into 15-minute tasks; when you have waiting time, use your smartphone to complete calls or e-mail related to the project

- Printed or handwritten manuscript pages for editing

An author can move the tasks written on sticky notes from Dream Book to bathroom mirror, calendar, or computer screen and back again when the task has been completed. She can carry the equipment for tasks with her to use during a wait at the dentist's office or idle time at her daughter's soccer game.

Be Accountable

Every time you finish a writing session, note in your log (see Table 19.2) what you were working on and what you will want to do next. This ritual does two things: it quickly closes off that writing session so that you can get on to other things, and it saves start up time when you come back to the piece. You won't waste time asking, "Now where was I?"

Writing Log

In the production log in Table 19.2, list the date, the time spent writing in hours (and decimal fractions of hours), and pages produced or revised with an annotation about what type of writing activity you did that day ("O" for outlining, "W" for writing new text, "R" for revising, "A" for analyzing data, or whatever other activities are part of your scholarly work).

You might also use a Tracking Sheet from Part 2 of this book to lay out the big picture of all your writing projects and how they intersect with the time lines of your other duties and responsibilities. In the cells of the Tracking Sheet, annotate the week's tasks on each writing project, such as meeting with editors or a coauthor, searching the literature you want,

TABLE 19.2

Production Log

Date	Time log	Pages (or equivalent) and activity (O, W, R, A)	Notes and cracker crumbs

and so on. When working with coauthors, track the steps of the project on Tracking Sheets parked in a website cloud so that everyone involved can cross off their assigned tasks as they complete them.

Writing can be a depressing, isolating activity. All good writers live with self-doubt. A common joke goes: "Writing is easy; you sit by yourself staring at the blank screen until beads of blood appear on your forehead." Your writing will bring you better results and more satisfaction during the process if you imagine yourself as a part of a large virtual community involved with your writing.

Writing is ultimately social because you are writing for real people in your audience—for example, other scientists, artists, or historians. Picturing real people reading your piece will help you write for their needs. For this book, I actually wrote profiles of my typical readers and imagined them reading what you are now reading.

As part of your scholar role, it is helpful to include accountability to other people, who might include a mentor, coach, colleague, writing group, or spouse. In the early stages of a piece, it is invaluable to have a conceptual conversation with someone similar to your ideal reader's profile, who can ask you tough but friendly questions such as "How do you plan to show that the Civil War was more a fight over states' rights than a fight over slavery?" Prior to publication, you are also writing for acquisitions editors, developmental editors, and copy editors who will give you feedback on your project.

The threat of mild social embarrassment or the avoidance of it can motivate you (Baumeister, 1982) to reach your benchmarks so that you can celebrate your progress with your accountability people. People who work on their goals with accountability, and the threat of a self-imposed penalty for failure to complete the goal, actually complete their goals 80% of the time, which compares with a completion rate of 35% for people who don't use such accountability (Ayres, 2010). See suggestions for the various forms of accountability relationships in Part 2 of this book, including relationships with colleagues, partners, or groups who get together in one room for "study hall," in which they all write in silence for an hour.

Before a semifinished product goes to those "official" people, get feedback early and often from "friendly colleagues," as Tara Gray (2010) calls them. Friendly colleagues care about you and your work, want you to do well, and will give you serious yet supportive critiques that are pegged to the level of the draft. Such people could include colleagues in your writing group or fellow researchers in your field.

This is another of the many benefits of developing good networks with colleagues (see Part 3 of this book). Having the courage to send imperfect preliminary drafts to supportive colleagues gives you the courage to send final drafts to journal editors and funding agencies. "Final" does not mean perfect; it means excellent and on time.

When you ask for feedback, give your reader a worksheet asking for the specific feedback you need from that reader, such as answers to the following questions:

- Did I support my argument with sufficient evidence?

- Are my conclusions warranted from the data I collected?

- What am I missing in the introduction?

The Publishing Process

Turn your finished product in when it is on time and, hopefully, excellent.

- Write for the specifications of the publication to which you would like to submit.

- Expect rejections, but rejoice if you get a "rewrite and resubmit" response.

- Rewrite incorporating the reviewers' comments as you rewrite. If you really don't understand a reviewer's comments, ask the editor for an interpretation.

- Build relationships that build your writing. Develop relationships with editors by reviewing manuscripts—a few, not many. At conferences, peruse the book displays. Don't assume the person behind the display is a salesperson; that person is very likely an acquisitions editor eager to meet aspiring authors who want to publish.

Learn to Rewrite

All good writing is rewriting. If you aim for bad first drafts, you can shape up your writing later in the process. Take a course, read a publication guide in your field, or get a writing coach. Lessons learned will generalize to writing that you do in the future, when you will no longer need as much guidance.

Like every other skill a peak performer aims to master, writing improves in the doing—as long as you get helpful instruction and feedback and engage in extensive deliberate practice.

Robison's Rule
Writing is never finished and never perfect.

Chapter 20
The Servant Leader

THE MERE MENTION of the word *leadership* can strike terror in the heart of a faculty member. I can hear readers saying, "No, don't make me cross to the dark side—the administration!" One of the ironies of life as a professor is that faculty complain about having service responsibilities at the same time as they complain about not having a say in administrative decisions about curriculum, teaching loads, and other policies relevant to the execution of their duties. These professors seem to miss the connection between shared governance and the opportunity for service.

When I use the term *leadership* to describe faculty service, I am not suggesting that you pursue a career in higher education administration but rather that you think of leadership as modern leadership scholars do: the exercise of positive influence for the greater good from any position in an organization (Kouzes & Posner, 2012).

Exercise 20.1 (Manning, 2013) explores the experience of leadership as one of service and positive influence.

For the exercise, you may have chosen a person in a leadership position, such as a dean or a department chair. Perhaps you chose your person of influence from another area of your life—your grandmother, your baseball coach, or your spouse. Although leadership can take place through an elected or appointed leadership position with a title and official role description, leadership can also be exercised through any role in which you influence others to act for the greater good (Wergin, 2006).

Holding the view that leadership is exercised only in positions of power can cause colleges to ignore the many talents of faculty. In a recent British study, full professors believed that faculty leadership knowledge and skills were underutilized in their universities, yet there are many ways that faculty lead without having positions of leadership (Macfarlane, 2011).

Modern scholars view leadership as socially constructed, collective, and distributed across an organization (for example, Kezar, Carducci, & Contreras-McGavin, 2006; Kezar, Gallant, & Lester, 2011; Kezar & Lester,

EXERCISE 20.1

Leader as Positive Influence

Think of someone whose positive interaction with you motivated you to do more than you originally expected to do, raised your level of awareness about important matters, increased your maturity level, and led you to transcend your own self-interest for the good of the group.

1. Describe the characteristics and behavior of this person that are particularly relevant to her or his impact on you. What did she or he do that really made a difference?

2. Describe your characteristics or behavior in the interaction. What needed to be true of you to allow the other to influence you?

2011; Raelin, 2003). Using those characteristics suggests many ways that faculty can exercise "grassroots leadership":

- Vision-sharing

- Awareness-raising

- Networking

- Mobilizing people

- Garnering resources

Many faculty tell me they hate to "play politics" on their campuses. An alternative perspective is that exercising faculty leadership skills connects you to administrators, peers, and students in ways that can smooth out the tough work of the academy and increase your work satisfaction. Adopting a philosophy of leadership as service and influence can take you from feeling frustrated to feeling empowered as you tackle issues that matter to you.

Influence can be not just top-down but also reverse hierarchical and sideways. As a faculty member, you influence your chair, dean, students, and fellow faculty. People of influence are those who do the following:

- Take initiative for a common purpose (Sorenson & Hackman, 2002).

- Accomplish the tasks of setting direction, building commitment and creating alignment (Martin, 2006).

- Foster others' growth by challenging them to high standards (Collins, 2001).

In thinking of yourself as a person of influence, who or what would you like to influence and to what action would you like to influence them?

Leverage Your Service for the Greatest Benefit

Professors who experiment with and strengthen their leadership skills in service positions gain experience and wisdom relevant to all of their roles (Kouzes & Posner, 2003). Once faculty think of service positions as positions of influence, they are more likely to take on leadership positions such as offering to chair a committee after serving on it for one year or to rotate into a department chair position for three years.

- Find out what service opportunities are valued by your institution: department, college, community, professional association.

- Use the discernment exercise in Part 2 of this book to match the service opportunities that matter to your institution to your Pyramid of Power so that these opportunities continue to enrich your sense of meaning and life satisfaction (Seligman, 2011).

- Consider creating a Pyramid of Power for your service role with its own purpose, mission, vision, and goals to guide your decision-making about how your service fits in with the rest of your professional goals.

- Avoid unhealthy goals for being of service, such as self-aggrandizement, resistance to necessary change, or service merely to complete a job requirement.

Check which of these benefits are ones you value:

- Professors who make good choices about networking and community building get the support they need for their teaching and research and open opportunities for their students (Boice, 2000).

- Professors who share their role responsibilities with colleagues and students decrease their workloads (Robertson, 2003) while earning the respect of fellow academics, thus raising their social capital, a valuable resource for career advancement (Baker, 2000).

- Professors who commit to the common good of their institutions, their disciplines, or higher education create renewable resources, especially relationships. When professors connect with others who share common goals they prevent the "tragedy of the commons," which occurs when resources are depleted by unnecessary competition and a scarcity mentality (Harden, 1968).

- Professors who impact their institutions leave a legacy.

You also provide leadership outside your college in your profession, both informally through the relationships you establish and maintain and formally when you serve associations on boards or through elected offices. While there are many excellent books on how to be a good positional leader in the academy (see especially Buller, 2012; Chu, 2012; Cipriano, 2011; Higgerson, 1996; Kouzes & Posner, 2003; Wheeler et al., 2008), the section that follows gives a short summary of skills that will help you in all the roles in which you influence others. You might not even have thought of these familiar skills as leadership skills. Increasing awareness of how you use and can practice them every day will increase your effectiveness.

Get the Most from Your Service Positions

In addition to the questions in Part 2 of this book about discerning opportunities, use the following questions to become clear about the costs and benefits of service positions.

1. What does the job require? What will be the biggest challenges? What skills or knowledge are required? What will happen if you don't take the position? Be sure you understand the expectations of the job description and those of the people to whom you will be accountable.

2. What will this opportunity do for you and what kind of influence do you want to have in the position? Does it give you more money, released time for research, campus recognition, tenure portfolio support, or experience for the next rung on your career ladder? Only you can say whether the benefits can offset the cost of this position.

3. Discern whether the timing is right for you to accept this opportunity.

- What other things will you not do if you take this on? What will it take you away from? For example, if you become department chair before getting tenure, will the position distract or enhance your application?

- What is going on in your personal life (single, new baby, caring for infirmed parents) that might distract from or enhance your ability to meet the position's responsibilities? And how will the position affect your personal life?

4. Ask for sufficient support such as administrative help, space, equipment, and staff at the front end, when you have the most leverage to get it.

5. Discuss with your supervisor how you want announcements to be made about your taking the position so that you make a good first impression in your new role and instill confidence in your ability. The announcements should refer to your accomplishments as a leader so that the constituents affected will perceive you as both qualified and "one of us." We want our leaders to be in our tribe yet able to lead the tribe competently.

6. What is your exit plan? How long will you stay in the role? What will be the signs you will look for that will signal you to move on to a more demanding leadership position or to return to what you were doing before you were so rudely interrupted by this position? Who will succeed you? Who will make that decision? Will the person volunteer or be elected, appointed, or sought by a search committee? What are your responsibilities to select, train, or empower your successor?

7. Think of your contribution as a "both/and" proposition, such as how to leverage the role for the greater good of the institution, department, and yourself. What legacy do you want to leave? Where is your influence likely to be the greatest? Do you want to use the experience of this position

to transition to a new career niche, for example, that of a dean, director, or other position? Can you contribute your service in ways that can benefit your career after you have transitioned out of the job? For example, perhaps negotiating space for your department in the new science building will result in more lab space for your graduate students.

Chairing a Department

Chairs don't think of themselves as bosses or personnel managers, but the quality of their relationships with faculty is a key factor in faculty retention and engagement. Chairs have a most important responsibility, that of creating an interpersonal work environment that combats isolation, a key factor frequently given by faculty leaving an institution (Cipriano, 2011; Wheeler et al., 2008). Because of the high value faculty place on autonomy, chairs often joke about the role of chair as one of "herding cats." Yet engaging employees in mutually beneficial activities deepens their commitment, which benefits the institution (Spreitzer et al., 1997).

Faculty become department chairs in many different ways, but almost always without preparation or prior leadership experience. As one dean commented to me during a campus visit, "The problem with this place is that it is run by amateurs, myself included." Service in chair positions would be improved if institutions provided basic leadership training opportunities, such as a one-day leadership workshop or even a process of allowing the successor of a department chair who is leaving to shadow the chair during the semester before the successor begins the job. Whenever I have been asked to do leadership development workshops for department chairs on campuses, the attendees are very grateful for the opportunity for structured skill building.

If you wish to become an academic leader, there are many resources for you to look to for more instruction. I especially recommend the resources in Part 3 of this book for social intelligence skills, as well as some of the department leadership books that emphasize applying such skills to academic leadership—for example, how to handle conflict (Higgerson, 1996) and how to "create a positive interpersonal work environment" (Wheeler et al., 2008). The discussion in this book highlights some tips for academic leaders to minimize their stress while maximizing their effectiveness.

Establish an Atmosphere of Mutual Respect and Trust

1.   Before taking on the job, get the support you need, and be clear about your responsibilities and resources. If possible, shadow the previous chair

to learn what tasks are required in the job and when they are sequenced, such as when to prepare the budget or work on next year's schedule. This preparation will cut down considerably on feelings of being overwhelmed by the tasks during your first year.

2. Take time to get to know your faculty. Don't make any big changes until you have been in the job a while. Take time to interview everybody, asking, "What can I do to support you in your goals?" Don't promise anything yet, but use your best listening skills, and take notes. Those notes will be invaluable later when you have opportunities to advocate for your faculty.

3. Build good work relationships by accepting others as they are. Accepting others allows them to feel comfortable enough to listen to you and negotiate goals.

4. Maintain open and honest communication, especially on unpopular issues. Remain fair and open-minded to others' perspectives, and appreciate their contributed ideas whether you agree with those viewpoints or not. You don't have to be good friends with your faculty to get along with them, but remind those with whom you are good friends that in your work role you are aiming at fairness not favoritism.

5. Don't have an open door policy; instead have a few open door hours per week so that you are available but also have protected time to get your thinking work done. Establish similar boundaries with e-mail as suggested earlier in Chapter 18 by compartmentalizing your incoming e-mail and your e-mail time.

6. Avoid gossip, defined as spreading news, especially bad news, for its own sake. When others begin to gossip or complain, encourage better communication by saying something like "Sounds like you have an issue with Tom that you need to discuss with him instead of with us." Take on the role of mediator only if absolutely necessary and only if you have training in mediation.

7. When presiding over meetings, establish ground rules for airing a conflict in meetings, such as no swearing, insults, or raised voices. Suggest that the parties involved "buy the floor" to speak by summarizing what the previous speaker has said. Insist that the steps for conflict management be followed.

When conflicts arise, recognize how your input may have contributed (intentionally or unintentionally) to the confusion. Use the conflict management skills in Part 3 of this book, and consider offering a conciliatory gesture such as owning responsibility for your part in a misunderstanding or apologizing when appropriate.

8. Slow down your communication. Your first response is not always your best, so next time someone says something annoying, pause before responding.

9. Aim at being a buffer for the reactions of others rather than reacting yourself. (See Part 4 of this book for keeping yourself resilient.)

10. Think of yourself as a liaison, getting clear on the expectations from both groups so that you can advocate for your faculty and translate administrative policies.

11. Spend time listening to your faculty's vision about what would make the department better, such as improved teaching resources and better research space, then connect the dots into a department vision. Get buy-in from the majority of your faculty before you share that vision with the appropriate people—dean, provost, director of teaching and learning—who can help you achieve it.

12. When you have helped the department achieve a goal, share the credit with those that helped you. Sharing credit is like lighting someone else's candle in the darkness—it doesn't diminish your light but increases the light in the room.

13. Familiarize yourself with practical group dynamics so that you can lead meetings more effectively.

- *Groupthink:* A group can come up with a solution that no one truly believes in. Such groupthink represents a negative element of social conformity. It tends to occur in pressured situations when someone offers a solution and no one disagrees, and the silence is interpreted as a conclusion that everyone else agrees, which leads to no one speaking an opposing opinion. To avoid taking an action no one wants, give everyone some thinking time before or during a meeting and poll everybody anonymously to assess the support for a suggestion.

- *Extrovert/introvert differences in groups:* Extroverts like to develop thoughts through discussion, while introverts prefer processing information internally. To allow everyone's voice to be heard, give worksheets and an agenda ahead of meetings so that introverts have thinking time. Then during the meeting, solicit the contributions by using some version of a think-pair-share format, with everyone doing a task alone, then with a partner or group, and then sharing back with the larger group.

- *Stages of group development:* Groups go through stages in how the members act with one another. These have been described by Tuckman (1965) as "forming, norming, storming, and performing." At first people are overly polite. Then the group begins to set norms for how to act, followed by times of great conflict, which if weathered successfully, develop the group into a high-performance team.

- *Necessary skills:* To do a good job as a chair and lower your stress, develop skills in negotiation, delegation, and conflict management. The demands of the chair's job to manage people, space, and money with limited resources increase the likelihood of conflict. In a survey of 800 department chairs, confrontation was listed as the second most stressful event after work overload (Gmelch & Burns, 1993). To increase your skills, read, attend workshops at higher education conferences, and seek wise counsel from other chairs or deans on your campus and beyond.

Be Clear About Decision Making

The options for decision making fall on a continuum from leader-directed decisions with no group ownership of the decision to group-based decisions with maximum ownership by the whole group. Be clear about which decision-making method you are using and why. Although there is some research to support the notion that leaders have preferences for how they make decisions along this kind of continuum, the more familiar leaders are with all the methods, the less likely they will get stuck in a favorite. For a similar model to my own, see the one designed by Vroom and Yetton (1973).

←——————————————————————————————→

| Leader | Task force | Committee | Majority | Consensus of Entire Group |

The decision options range from small decisions that leaders can make alone (at the left end of the continuum) to decisions made by the entire group (at the right end). There are relative advantages and disadvantages with each method. The left end of the continuum represents decisions that do not need buy-in from the larger constituency—for example, a room change for a department meeting—while the right end of the continuum represents decisions that require a buy-in from the greatest number of people—for example, a curriculum change in the requirements for the major.

In between those extremes are decisions that are appropriately made by a small task force with the responsibility of making recommendations, those coming from a committee that handles part of a group's workload, and those requiring a majority vote, which might be appropriate for many of a group's policy decisions.

The time expenditure also varies from the left to the right side of the continuum. Leader-only decisions can usually be made quickly because they involve only one person, whereas more time is needed when a whole group engages in a consensus decision.

Different decision methods play off one another. When less buy-in is needed, using the left end of the continuum will save time. When more buy-in is required, use the right end, because the exchange of the time used leads to better group support.

The Satisfaction of Service

Executed with lowered stress and increased effectiveness, academic service can be a satisfying part of your career path if you get a chance to fill the right opportunity at the right time. With careful attention to how service fits your life management system, you can develop skills that transfer to your other roles and make a contribution of positive influence and service to your institution.

Robison's Rule
Your school needs you. See your service as an
opportunity to enlarge your influence.

Chapter 21

Life Roles

> You are the only person with whom you spend the rest of your life.
>
> —Mark Twain

WHEN LIFE IS going well at home and at work, it is easier to prevent stress spillover from one domain to the other. Each role that you occupy acts as a buffer in case one of your roles is temporarily not going well. This chapter addresses how to put more balance into your roles outside of work.

Your Role as Householder

Make your abode, humble though it may be, a haven for relaxation and socialization with intimates. Decorate according to your taste, have comfortable spaces and furniture, and surround yourself with meaningful and aesthetically pleasing objects. Whether you live in a house, apartment, log cabin, or RV, you will need to take care of similar tasks to support and maintain easy living. Get help on tasks that you do not do well so that you can concentrate on those that you do well and are indispensable for, such as parenting your children or making value-based financial decisions. Hire good reliable people, and be clear about their tasks and the standards for each task.

Systems for Your Home

Getting a few systems in place at home will increase ease at home and free you to be more productive at work. Use the template approach to organize regularly occurring household tasks. Have your systems work hard so you don't have to.

- Shop weekly rather than running to the store frequently. Print grocery lists with frequently purchased items arranged in order of the aisles of your favorite grocery store, and post them on the bulletin board or fridge. Train all housemates who can read to circle items that are running out. Add materials needed to make main dishes you have planned, and the list is ready when the designated shopper is ready to shop.

- If you do any cleaning yourself, have cleaning supplies handy and a cleaning schedule that fits your lifestyle. Use the Focused 15 exercise from Part 2 of this book to complete a few 15-minute cleaning tasks a day so that you don't have to dedicate the weekend to the house. Involve the whole household. Even two-year-olds can participate in a 10-minute toy pickup at night.

- Use larger blocks of weekend time for bigger household projects, such as painting or planting.

- Establish minimum standards for "clean enough," and simplify those routines. Do more thorough cleaning when guests are coming. Get on the same page with the other adults in the house about who does what, when, and how.

- Make bill paying, filing, and record keeping routine tasks that you can do during your favorite TV show or while listening to music. A once-a-week schedule will keep those tasks from getting onerous.

- To prevent the "arsenic hour" right before dinner when blood sugar drops and no one knows what's for dinner, do more cooking on the weekends, making double batches and freezing the second batch for later in the week. Make slow-cooker meals. Spend a few minutes after dinner planning the next night's dinner, getting ingredients ready for the slow cooker, or defrosting one of those second batches that you made on the weekend. Even better, plan a two-week menu rotating leftovers with freshly made dishes.

Cut Down on Stress

You can make life less hectic by planning ahead.

- Lay out clothes the night before.

- Make lunches the night before.

- Routinize travel packing with a "formula," such as one jacket, two pairs of slacks, and four shirts for a three-day conference. Pack a plastic box with these items: cosmetic bag with your lotions and potions, travel alarm, extra phone charger, passport, book light, and other standard traveling items. When it is time to pack, move the contents of the box into a suitcase, and add clothes using a template packing list specific to occasion and season—for example, "beach," "fall mountain hiking," "winter professional conference."

- Eliminate "hurry sickness" by setting early mental deadlines for getting to places early and getting tasks done ahead of due dates.

- Color-coordinate your closet. Plan your outfits for a week at a time, and hang those pieces near the front of the closet. Rehang the pieces that don't need cleaning or laundering back in their proper places. Do your laundry at a low-energy time of the day or week. Drop off and pick up dry cleaning on the way to other errands.

- Group related errands by location to save time and gasoline.

Finances and Abundance

Faculty often have a "monk mentality" in which they think of themselves as poor. Of course, real monks don't have to worry about money unless they are the leaders of the monastery. Here are some tips for living with an attitude of gratitude and a sense of abundance no matter what your salary. Getting your finances in order will help you feel that you have the financial resources for your needs.

- Live beneath your means. The easiest time to do this is to keep living on what you were making before you got your last raise and bank the difference.

- Pay yourself first. Set aside your savings into a pre-tax fund such as a 401K or a 403B.

- If you belong to a spiritual community, consider tithing. If you are not part of a religious group, contribute to favorite causes.

- Interview several financial planners and hire one that you trust.

- Diversify your investments and invest for the long term. Don't panic or change strategies during the downturns.

- If you have children, give them an allowance just for being a kid in the house and then pay them separately for chores over their regular duties assigned to them as members of the household. As they mature, teach them how to save and invest.

- Live abundantly.
  - Have a rainy day fund—6–12 months living expenses "just in case."
  - Have a sunny day fund—a fund that is extra savings over your long-term investments and that you earmark for special purchases and experiences that bring you joy: artwork for your home office, a vacation, or salsa lessons.

Friendship and Family Roles

Social connection is the biggest long-term contributor to happiness (Seligman, 2011). Not all faculty have mates and children, but all need social support to live happy and productive lives. This section offers some general tips for work and social friendships followed by specific tips for those faculty with family roles. Here are some tips for all adult relationships.

- Be a good friend. Cultivate the social intelligence skills presented in Part 3 of this book so that others will find you to be a good candidate for their friendship. Keep confidences. Don't gossip. Aim to resolve or at least manage conflict in relationship-friendly ways.

- Reflect on your own relationship history, from the best to the worst, to give you clues to what experiences you want to replicate or avoid.

- Pace self-disclosure to the intimacy of the friendship. There may be events in your life that you do not want to share until a relationship proves trustworthy and solid.

- If you become friends with someone at work, downplay your relationship in the work setting so that neither of you is in a position of being questioned about favoritism when it comes to such matters as tenure, promotions, or teaching assignments. Recuse yourself when professional decisions come up regarding your friends.

- If you find yourself no longer having things in common with a friend, avoid dramatic breakups by spending less time together until the friendship fades away to a comfortable level.

- Find easy, repeatable ways to sustain your circle of the family members that you like but don't see regularly. Reunions are expensive; family blogs and social media messages are not.

- Limit contact with toxic people, even if you are related to them. They drain you and divert your energy from spending time with quality people who love and respect you. Pick your holiday activities carefully according to your values instead of out of obligation.

- Family of origin relationships vary from intimate to highly contentious. Develop a vision for how you want to relate to each relative and communicate with all no matter how close or distant they are to you with clarity, kindness, and compassion.

- If partnered, get clear on who "manages" the in-laws. Keep open communication with your mate on issues in the families. Avoid secrets;

they take a lot of energy to maintain and undermine the trust in the primary relationship.

Your Partner Role

Sharing your life with someone can be the most satisfying relationship of all—when it goes well. Marriage statistically has a protective value that favors longevity and wellness. Research suggests this effect probably occurs because marriage stabilizes a person's risk-taking behaviors in health and safety and prevents loneliness, a leading predictor of early death (Seligman, 2011; Waite & Gallagher, 2001). While the research on the benefits of marriage has not yet been extended to other intimate relationships, it is likely that most marriage-like relationships experience the same benefits. Here are some tips:

- Partner well. Pick an emotionally healthy partner with whom you have lots in common.

- Create a sense of joint purpose by replicating the Pyramid of Power and Dream Book activities of Part 2 with each other after you have completed the exercises individually. Develop a long-term and short-term vision of your coupleship. Review and change your vision through the stages of life.

- Be a "good-finder" with your mate. Find the best in each other and appreciate the privilege of being in each other's lives. Research shows that positivity in marriage is maintained by having a healthy dose of holding positive illusions (Murray, Holmes, & Griffin, 1996) and adoring each other on a global level even though partners have an accurate knowledge of each others' specific attributes (Neff & Karney, 2005). It is still important to give positive feedback so that partners feel appreciated. Remember that couples require five positives for every negative to feel that things are going well (Gottman, 1999).

- Be clear about your division of labor. Regularly review and revise your expectations about who does what and how, in cleaning, cooking, and parenting.

- Make joint decisions about money, but have some separate money as well, so you never feel like you are "begging" for an allowance or lunch money.

- Sustain your primary relationship with time and attention. You can maintain a high-quality relationship with an average of 20 minutes a day during the week, with more catch-up time on the weekend, if you do the right things with your 20 minutes. This is especially true for commuter relationships, common among academics who cannot find jobs in the same town.

- Reflect at the end of the day on how your day went. Review goals and calendars for the coming days. Exchange affection. Even if busy, you can find time for a 15-second kiss, a long kiss by busy couples' standards and much more satisfying than those usual routine hello and goodbye pecks.

- Develop mutual support through a monthly partner sit-down, in which you set goals, review goals, and celebrate successes. Keep your relationship fun and fresh by setting goals that matter in the areas where your values match. Such goals might include travel, activities with the children, and fun things you do as a couple. The sit-down ritual cuts down or eliminates nagging, especially if you write decisions reached in a marital log that can be reviewed later. Imagine a life free of "Yes, I told you" and "No, you didn't."

- Create inexpensive, undemanding rituals and traditions that you two can do on a regular basis to keep the good feelings alive.

- Get really good at conflict management skills so that you can work out the little and big conflicts that will come your way. Use the suggestions from Part 3 of this book. John Gottman found that only one-third of marital conflicts can be resolved; the remaining two-thirds can be successfully managed by using your skills on small parts of the conflict. For example, a morning person will not convert a night owl partner, but the two of them can establish some courtesy rules about the noise and lights from media. If the conflict seems too difficult for the two of you to figure out, consider a few consultation sessions with a couples' counselor. You don't have to get major "head shrinking" to move in the right direction.

- Dual professional couples have some special challenges in addition to those affecting all couples including: competition versus cooperation, determining residence and when to stay or move, living long-distance as "married but not cohabitating," the tenure clock and the biological clock, and uneven career development and satisfaction. Use the tools in this book to support each other, especially focusing on developing a shared vision and using good communication skills. Treat your mate as your best colleague, because he or she is.

Your Role as Parent

Raising children is like writing a book. Few people enjoy the process, but most are glad they did it after it is over. Both children and books take a lot of work and sacrifice but enlarge your world. Both child-rearing and book-writing are not for those who need instant gratification for their efforts. However, if you do a good job with your book, good reviews happen within months of publication. If you do a good job with your kids, you might get thanked after 18–25 years. Even excellent parents get many more bad reviews along the way—for example, when the teacher tells you your kid is working below potential or when your child tells you, as our daughter did, that you are the meanest parents in the county. There is truth to the maxim that grandchildren are sweet revenge. Ours tell their mother that she is the meanest mom in their neighborhood. She figures she must be doing something right. Here are a few tips for maintaining your sanity while helping your children grow into people you want to be friends with.

- Have kids for the right reasons—because you want to experience bringing a life into and/or bringing a child up in this world rather than because you "should," because your parents want grandchildren, or because you want children to fulfill your unfulfilled needs for love and achievement.

- Timing is important. Early career faculty are frustrated that the tenure clock and women's biological clocks are ticking loudly at the same time. There is movement toward more family-friendly policies, such as time off the tenure clock so that parents can enjoy family time without a heavy scholarly production schedule. If these changes are not yet in place at your institution, you and others might also start conversations about policy changes on campus. Meanwhile, plan to get support from your parenting team, including your mate, other family if they live nearby, and well-chosen paid helpers.

- Make it your business to learn enough about child development to have realistic expectations about age-related behaviors and milestones. Ask the child development or family science faculty to recommend reputable popular books or websites about parenting. My current favorite is the brain-based parenting book *The Whole-Brain Child*, by Siegel and Bryson (2012).

- Raise your children with a "syllabus" in mind, including the skills and information they need to become happy and productive adults. Topics might include health education, good social graces, financial management, religious education, and sex education. Raising your children this way will save them from being like one of our daughter's roommates, who pulled an all-nighter trying to master laundry skills from her mom the night before the car headed off to freshman week. This approach will also prevent you from being one of those dreaded helicopter parents who hover over their college-age children because they did not plan ahead on how to adequately launch their young adults.

- Maintain good boundaries between your life goals and those of your children. Don't get caught up into fulfilling your ego needs through your children's accomplishments. Instead, help your children find and develop their own talents.

- Teach your children to "nag" themselves about the directives you wish them to live by. This is a skill that comes in handy in adulthood so that reminders about safety, health, and social graces are in their heads, not just in yours.

- Give your children age-appropriate responsibilities within the context of the family community so that they see themselves as part of a larger community. Yes, it does take more time and patience to teach and supervise the skills rather than to do the chore yourself, but many benefits accrue when you do take the time. As their skills develop, you get labor from well-trained helpers while they prepare for adult living.

- Spend quality time with the children every day. Cook dinner with them, supervise homework, and tuck them into bed with some reading at night. When they feel included and secure, they might leave you alone when you have to work at home. Don't count on it, but they might.

- Start having family meetings early. Even two-year-olds can offer suggestions about what they want to do on a family day trip. The adults should always have a pre-meeting in which they decide the parameters of the options. Then they can give the kids a sense of participation on age appropriate decisions. Family meetings are also the place to discuss household problems but don't turn all meetings into nag sessions. They should also be called to plan fun adventures.

- Have family rituals that everybody looks forward to. Maybe these are connected to seasonal events such as the first summer trip to the beach, to accomplishments such as going out for ice cream if grades are B or better, or to religious holidays like coloring Easter eggs or lighting the menorah.

- If you are parenting with a mate, be sure to continue planning fun couple time separate from family time. Although some research shows that parents find child care less satisfying than most other activities, including housework (Kahneman, Krueger, Schkade, Schwartz, & Stone, 2004), other research shows that satisfaction with parenting is higher for couples with good relationships (Rogers & Waite, 1998).

*** Robison's Rule***
You only get one life to live—at least as far as we know—
so make it a good one.

Epilogue

AUTHORS HAVE MANY hopes when they choose to write a book. My two hopes are that readers will do productive great work while they live happy and balanced lives and that readers will become positive influences for more balanced institutional cultures. I will leave you with a few concluding thoughts about both of these hopes.

This book is chock-full of tools and techniques to help you become happier and more productive. Don't tyrannize yourself with a new "should" about having to adopt all of these techniques. Instead, pick the ones that seem like reasonable next steps to your becoming and remaining a peak performing professor. Use existing cues and rewards to add new practices into what you are already doing so that your learning curve will be less steep and your workload less time consuming. When you need more help, reread and try other practices that address your concerns and consult with appropriate financial, psychological, and medical professionals to individualize some of the recommendations of this book.

In the years that I have been encouraging professors to take a gradual approach to continuous improvement, other professional sustainability approaches have been developed that have gained international popularity. These include the Pomodoro technique developed by Francesco Cirillo, who used a timer in the shape of a *pomodora* (tomato) to time 25-minute work sessions followed by a break (Nöteberg, 2009) and the Kaizen approach, a Japanese method aimed at making small continuous improvements that make the work flow easier and more productive (Imai, 1986 ; Maurer, 2013).

Here is a summary of the steps to follow to implement a peak performance model of work-life balance:

1. Identify the key elements of success in any skill or endeavor.

2. Find exemplars of each element who can model it either in writing, on video, or in person.

3. Insert the new elements inside your already over-learned habits using the same cues and rewards that you already use.

4. Engage in deliberate practice of the element.

5. Use assessment and feedback to see if the correct skills are building.

6. Repeat with each element and then begin to practice integration until the whole skill becomes automatic. In other words, standardize to sustain.

The kind of change recommended in this book will require time and energy on the front end that will pay off on the back end in time saved, goals achieved, and satisfaction enjoyed. Faculty in my workshops often ask questions about how to stay motivated year after year for the long haul of a lifetime career in higher education. The following are practices that peak performing professors use to maintain their motivation:

• Spend as much of each day as possible doing activities directly related to your vision. Consult your Pyramid of Power as needed.

• Every time someone asks you to do something, use discernment questions to evaluate the task against your priorities.

• Review your life management system (Pyramid of Power and Dream Book) at least once a quarter. Review and revise your Tracking Sheet once a week, but check it once a day, either at the beginning or end of the day, to keep on track. Archive completed tasks. Revise the tasks in next week's cells accordingly. Examine items that are carried over from one day to another or from one week to another for relevance or to put the spotlight on a problem to be solved.

• Reassure yourself that once you get your life planning system in place, you won't be working too hard at your life management system to enjoy life. The planning steps from Part 3 of this book take about one hour a week but gain you five hours of useable discretionary time. Research has shown that self-control is needed to establish habits but is less needed once the habits are established (De Ridder, Lensvelt-Mulders, Finkenauer, Stok, & Baumeister, 2012). I have encouraged you to get your systems in place and let them work for you—"set 'em and forget 'em"—so you are free for creativity and fun.

• Limit the number of days in which you exceed eight hours of work, because overwork results in lowered productivity. Make sure you are really working when you are working, not "fixin' to work," getting motivated to work, or worrying about work. PACE yourself and your work by Powering, Aligning, Connecting, and Energizing your priorities, tasks, people, and energy with one another.

- Do first things first (Covey, Merrill, & Merrill, 1994). Load the most important tasks to the front end of the month, week and day. Hard tasks seem easier in the morning because a rested will is a stronger will (Baumeister & Tierney, 2011).

- Keep notes on where you were on each of the projects that your tasks relate to so that you eliminate start-up time.

- Make mountains into molehills by subdividing your relevant goals into small enough to-dos that take only 15–30 minutes, so that a few can be done in each day. Plan the details of each task, such as when and where you will do them and what you will do if tempted by interruptions and distractions (Gollwitzer & Oettingen, 2011; Halvorson, 2011).

- Take advantage of the power of positive rituals by having cues for repeatable tasks (Loehr & Schwartz, 2004).

- Keep your goals in any system that you can access and will realistically use throughout the day: day planner, personal digital assistant, smart-phone, or computer. Write your goals into the cells of your Tracking Sheet or, if you must, transcribe them into a daily to-do list (Daily Tracking Sheet or a VAST list). Eventually, most peak performing professors discard the daily to-do lists in favor of weekly Tracking Sheets.

- If you feel unmotivated about an activity, check out whether it is aligned with your vision. If it isn't, delegate, negotiate, or eliminate the task. Consider approaching your boss or bosses to renegotiate your job description to things you are motivated to do.

- If you still feel unmotivated about the activity itself but find it supports your overall life plan, especially maintaining a good relationship with your supervisors, juxtapose doing it with doing something you are motivated to do. Work on the unpleasant but necessary task first for a half hour, and then work on the other, more desirable task for 15 minutes. Keep alternating until the unpleasant one is completed. Be sure to leave clues about where you were in each task so that you can effectively toggle switch back and forth.

- If you are not motivated by much of anything you are working on, review your life management system to rediscover purpose and passion. Every few months keep a 24-hour time log for a week as a reality check to see whether you are aligning your time, tasks, and priorities and to see how long it takes to do your frequently occurring tasks. Only as a last resort, consider changing jobs or careers.

- Enlist the social support you need, including people you can be accountable to for the completion of small subgoals. These could be close friends or family, people at the gym in your spinning class, or professional helpers such as financial planners, editors, fitness trainers, coaches, and therapists. Find easy, reliable, repeatable ways to support and keep in touch with your intimate and social circles.

- Use the wellness and well-being practices habits in Part 4 of this book to increase and maintain your energy. (Of course, if you are concerned about energy, have a physical to rule out conditions that affect energy such as thyroid, diabetes, and depression.) Once you decide which wellness and well-being practices best support you, "set 'em and forget 'em" by making pre-commitments as to when, where, how, and with whom you will carry out these practices.

- Follow the completion of tasks with breaks and rewards and the completion of major projects with celebrations matched to whether the accomplishments are small, medium, or large.

- Make all of this life stuff a game in the same way that professional game designers use the best of self-control and goal attainment to design effective games: setting clear and attainable goals, giving instantaneous feedback, and offering enough encouragement for people to keep practicing and improving (McGonigal, 2011). The players of these games have fun while they are achieving the goals of the game. That is a worthy goal for your life as well.

- Work and live from your most authentic self: be intentional, focused, flexible, reflective, healthy, imperfect, connected, and playful.

Although this book was primarily written to empower professors to take control of their life management, the book is also aimed at sparking a conversation about institutions of higher education supporting their most precious resource, their faculty. I am hoping that readers who have found the book helpful will recommend it to their friends and select it as a study guide for faculty groups and learning communities who want to discuss and implement some of its strategies. I am hoping that other scholar-practitioners continue the conversation begun here concerning the responsibility that institutions need to take for their faculty's engagement and productivity. I am also hoping this book inspires academic leaders, such as directors of faculty development centers or centers for teaching and learning, deans and vice provosts of faculty, to prioritize initiatives toward supporting faculty in their quest for productive work and work-life balance. Many schools have already initiated institutional practices toward that end. Some of the successful initiatives are ones I have seen as I travel to campuses:

- Family-friendly policies such as time off the tenure clock for family leave, "concierge" services for faculty covering travel, referrals to child care and elder care programs, prepared dinner pickup, and dry cleaning drop-off and pickup (Philipsen & Bostic, 2010).

- Wellness programs with economic incentives such as health insurance discounts.

- Cohort "classes" of tenure applicants to review criteria and successful applications and to support one another during the arduous process of portfolio and application preparation. Cohort classes of immediate posttenure faculty to offer help on discerning "what next?"—especially in selecting appropriate service opportunities.

- Faculty development and Center for Teaching and Learning programs on the specific skills in the roles of faculty, particularly teaching skills (Hutchings et al., 2011).

- Hiring, assessment, rank, and tenure tied to the intersection of institutional mission and professors' missions. When institutions value an aspect of faculty work such as assessment, faculty become and remain engaged in that aspect (Evans, 2012; Walvoord, 2010). Both willfulness and wayfulness are important motivators. When people understand *why*, they feel connected to the bigger picture; understanding why motivates people and enhances self-control. When people understand *what* to do, they are less impulsive and less vulnerable to temptation and can plan actions by breaking down difficult goals into manageable steps (Vallacher & Wegner, 1989).

- Leadership development for all faculty, not just those ambitious about careers in higher education administration (Bolman & Galos, 2011).

- Department chair training, mentoring, and shadowing programs. In addition to the oft-mentioned curriculum development, course scheduling, and budget preparation skills developed by such programs where they do exist, I would like to see skills in social intelligence added, including listening and conflict management, so that chairs can be sensitive to their role as linchpins of faculty alignment with meaningful and challenging work, a precursor condition to peak performance (Austin, 2010; Wheeler, 2012).

- Peer groups for goal completion, continued education, writing, and teaching development and evaluation.

When a token group grows in numbers from less than 15% of a larger group to a critical mass (20–40%), their influence begins to create change in the larger group (Kanter, 1984). My hope is that when a number of professors on a campus PACE themselves with peak performance practices, they will be a force for positive institutional change. Not that teaching loads will lessen, research pressure will lighten, or salaries will increase—what will happen instead is that the positive synergy created by professors who perform at their peak while maintaining wellness, well-being, and kindness will influence and change their campus culture. When a subset of such professors serve in leadership positions, they can help their institutions look at policies related to supporting professors.

Mine is not the only voice calling for a quiet revolution that prioritizes faculty needs for meaningful work and supportive institutional practices. The other thread of the conversation is about institutional change toward a more faculty-supportive culture. Palmer and Zajonc (2011) and Lee, Bach, and Muthiah (2012, p. 74) speak of the connection between faculty development and improvement in higher education. Lee, Bach, and Muthiah (2012) make a plea to take faculty development seriously with a "postindustrial paradigm of academic renewal" that goes beyond productivity as defined as people doing more and which "trusts that people who live out their authentic life purpose will revitalize institutions for the common good" (p. 74). Coming to the conversation with an institutional vision, these authors call for institutional practices that support faculty "heart" and "soul," or faculty authenticity, what I would define as the professors' capacity to work at their peak doing the right job, with the right skills, the right people, and the right kind of support. The positive synergy of professors working from authenticity in institutions that support those endeavors will allow the professors to provide the best education, scholarship, and service, a benefit that will spread its influence throughout the institution and beyond. I've done this work so that you can carry this conversation forward.

Robison's Rule
*Long-term work-life balance is often attained at the expense
of short-term imbalance.*

References

Ambrose, S. A., Bridges, M. W., Lovett, M. C., DiPietro, M., & Norman, M. K. (2010). *How learning works: Seven research-based principles for smart teaching*. San Francisco, CA: Jossey-Bass.

Amen, D. G. (2002). *Healing ADD: The breakthrough program that allows you to see and heal the 6 types of ADD*. New York, NY: A Berkley Book.

Amen, D. G. (2006). *Making a good brain great: The Amen clinic program for achieving and sustaining optimal mental performance*. New York, NY: Three Rivers Press.

Angelo, T. A., & Cross, K. P. (1993). *Classroom assessment techniques: A handbook for college teachers* (2nd ed.). San Francisco, CA: Jossey-Bass.

Arden, J. B. (2009). *Rewire your brain: Think your way to a better life*. New York, NY: Wiley.

Astin, A. W., Astin, H. S., & Lindholm, J. A. (2011). *Cultivating the spirit: How college can enhance student's inner lives*. San Francisco, CA: Jossey-Bass.

Austin, A. (2010). Supporting faculty members across their careers. In K. J. Gillespie & D. L. Robertson (Eds.), *A guide to faculty development* (2nd ed., pp. 363–378). San Francisco, CA: Jossey-Bass.

Ayres, I. (2010). *Carrots and sticks: Unlock the power of incentives to get things done*. New York, NY: Bantam.

Baber, A., & Waymon, L. (2007). *Make your contacts count* (2nd ed.). New York, NY: AMACOM.

Bach, D. J., & Robison, S. (2011, October). *East meets west: Ancient wisdom, new science, engaged faculty*. Workshop conducted at the Professional and Organizational Development of Higher Education Annual Conference, Atlanta, GA.

Bahls, P. (2012). *Student writing in the quantitative disciplines: A guide for college faculty*. San Francisco, CA: Jossey-Bass.

Bain, K. (2004). *What the best college teachers do*. Boston, MA: Harvard University Press.

Baker, W. (2000). *Achieving success through social capital*. San Francisco, CA: Jossey-Bass.

Banta, T. W., Jones, E. A., & Black, K. E. (2009). *Designing effective assessment: Principles and profiles of good practice*. San Francisco, CA: Jossey-Bass.

Barkley, E. F. (2009). *Student engagement techniques: A handbook for college faculty*. San Francisco, CA: Jossey-Bass.

Barry, N. H. (2012). The gentle art of mentoring in higher education: Facilitating success in the academic world. *To Improve the Academy, 31*, 103–114.

Barsade, S. (2002). The ripple effect: Emotional contagion and its influence on group behavior. *Administrative Science Quarterly, 47*(4), 644–675.

Bartholomew, K., & Horowitz, L. M. (1991). Attachment styles among young adults: A test of a four category model. *Journal of Personality and Social Psychology, 61*, 226–244.

Baumeister, R. F. (1982). *Public self and private self*. New York, NY: Springer-Verlag.

Baumeister, R. F. (1991). *Meanings of life*. New York, NY: The Guilford Press.

Baumeister, R. F., Bratslavsky, E., Finkenauer, C., & Vohs, K. D. (2001). Bad is stronger than good. *Educational Publishing Foundation, 5*, 323–370.

Baumeister, R., & Tierney, J. (2011). *Willpower: Rediscovering the greatest human strength*. New York, NY: Penguin Press.

Bean, J. C. (2011). *Engaging ideas: The professor's guide to integrating writing, critical thinking, and active learning in the classroom* (2nd ed.). San Francisco, CA: Jossey-Bass.

Benson, H., & Proctor, W. (2003). *The breakout principle*. New York: Scribner.

Berk, R. A. (2008). Music and music technology in college teaching: Classical to hip hop across the curriculum. *International Journal of Technology in Teaching and Learning, 4*, 45–67.

Bliss, E. C. (1978). *Getting things done*. New York, NY: Bantam Books.

Block, P. (1993; 1996). *Stewardship: Choosing service over self interest*. San Francisco, CA: Berrett-Koehler.

Boice, R. (1989). Procrastination, business, and bingeing. *Behavior Research Therapy, 27*, 605–611.

Boice, R. (1990). *Professors as writers: A self-help guide to productive writing*. Stillwater, OK: Forums.

Boice, R. (2000). *Advice for new faculty members: Nihil nimus*. Boston, MA: Allyn & Bacon.

Boice, R. (2011, June). *Exemplary new professors: A summary of 22 years of study*. Plenary presented at Lilly East Conference on College and University Teaching, Washington, D.C.

Bolles, R. (2013). *What color is your parachute? A practical manual for job-hunters and career-changers*. Berkeley, CA: Ten Speed Press.

Bolman, L. G., & Galos, J. V. (2011). *Reframing academic leadership*. San Francisco, Jossey-Bass.

Bolton, R. (1979). *People skills*. New York, NY: Simon and Schuster.

Boone, A. R. (1938, January). The making of *Snow White and the Seven Dwarfs*. *Popular Science Monthly*, 50–52, 131–132.

Bonwell, C., & Eison, J. (1991). *Active learning: Creating excitement in the classroom*. ASHE ERIC Higher Education (Report No. 1). Washington, DC: The George Washington University, School of Education and Human Development.

Boyatzis, R., & McKee, A. (2005). *Resonant leadership: Renewing yourself and connecting with others through mindfulness, hope, and compassion*. Boston, MA: Harvard Business School Publishing.

Bray, N. J., & Del Favero, M. (2004). Sociological explanations for faculty and student classroom incivilities. *New Directions for Teaching and Learning, 99*, 9–19.

BrckaLorenz, A., Ribera, T., Kinzie, J., & Cole, E. R. (2012). Examining effective faculty practice: Teaching clarity and student engagement. T*o Improve the Academy, 31*, 149–160.

Brown, B. (2010) *The gifts of imperfection*. Center City, MN: Hazelton.

Brown, B. (2012). *Daring greatly: How the courage to be vulnerable transforms the way we love, parent, and lead*. New York, NY: Gotham Books.

Brown, D. (2011, August). *Enhancement of peak performance in sports, the workplace, and the performing arts*. Workshop conducted at the meeting of the Harvard Medical Summer School, Cape Cod, MA.

Buckingham, M., & Clifton, D. O. (2001). *Now discover your strengths*. New York, NY: The Free Press.

Buehler, R., Griffin, D., & Ross, M. (1994). Exploring the "planning fallacy": Why people underestimate their task completion time. *Journal of Personality and Social Psychology, 67*, 366–381.

Buettner, D. (2010). *The blue zones: Lessons for living longer from the people who've lived the longest*. Washington, DC: National Geographic.

Buller, J. L. (2012). *The essential department chair: A comprehensive desk reference* (2nd ed.). San Francisco, CA: Jossey-Bass.

Burns, D. (1999). *Feeling good: The new mood therapy*. New York, NY: Avon.

Burns, J. M. (2010). *Leadership*. New York, NY: Harper Perennial Political Classics.

Buzan, T., & Buzan, B. (1996). T*he mind map book. How to use radiant thinking to maximize your brain's untapped potential*. New York, NY: Plume.

Cameron, J. (1996). *The vein of gold: A journey to your creative heart.* New York, NY: Jeremy P. Tarcher/Penguin.

Campbell, J. (with Moyers, B.) (1991). *Power of myth.* New York, NY: Anchor Books.

Chabris, C., & Simons, D. J. (2010). *The invisible gorilla: And other ways our intuitions deceive us.* New York, NY: Crown Archetype.

Chancellor, J., & Lyubomirsky, S. (2011). Happiness and thrift when (spending) less is hedonically (more). *Journal of Consumer Psychology, 21,* 131–138.

Chronicle of Higher Education (2009, August 28). Faculty and staff views: Sources of stress described in the past two years. *Chronicle of Higher Education, 2009–2010 Almanac Edition, 56 (1),* 27–28.

Chu, D. (2012). *The department chair primer: What chairs need to know and do to make a difference?* (2nd ed.). San Francisco, CA: Jossey-Bass.

Cipriano, R. E. (2011). *Facilitating a collegial department in higher education: Strategies for success.* San Francisco, CA: Jossey-Bass.

Clement, M. C. (2010). *First time in the college classroom.* Lanham, MD: Rowman & Littlefield Education.

Cloud, H. (2006). *Integrity: The courage to meet the demands of reality.* New York, NY: HarperCollins.

Collins, J. (2001). *Good to great: Why some companies make the leap and others don't.* New York, NY: HarperCollins.

Collins, J., & Porras, J. (2002). *Built to last: Successful habits of visionary companies.* New York, NY: HarperBusiness Essentials.

Colten, H. R., & Altevogt, B. M. (Eds.). (2006). *Sleep disorders and sleep deprivation: An unmet public health problem.* Washington, DC: The National Academies Press.

Colvin, G. (2008). *Talent is overrated: What really separates world-class performers from everybody else.* New York, NY: Penguin Group.

Covey, S. R. (2004). *Seven habits of highly effective people.* New York, NY: Free Press.

Covey, S. R., Merrill, A. R., & Merrill, R. R. (1994). *First things first.* London, United Kingdom: Simon & Schuster.

Crescioni, A. W., Ehrlinger, J., Alquist, J. L., Conlon, K. E., Baumeister, R. F., Schatschneider, C., & Dutton, G. R. (2011). High trait self-control predicts positive health behaviors and success in weight loss. *Journal of Health Psychology, 16,* 750–759.

Csikszentmihalyi, M. (2008). *Flow: The psychology of optimal experience.* New York, NY: Harper Perennial.

Dalai Lama & Cutler, H. C. (2004). *The art of happiness at work.* New York, NY: Riverhead Trade.

Dallman, M. F., Pecoraro, N. C., & La Fleur, S. E. (2005). Chronic stress and comfort foods: Self-medication and abdominal obesity. *Brain, Behavior, and Immunity, 19*, 275–280.

Davidson, R., & Begley, S. (2012). *The emotional life of your brain: How its unique patterns affect the way you think, feel, and live—and how you can change them.* New York, NY: Hudson Street Press.

Davidson, R. J., Kabat-Zinn, J., Schumacher, J., Rosenkranz, M., Muller, D., Santorelli, S. F., Urbanowski, F., Harrington, A., Bonus, K., & Sheridan, J. F. (2003). Alterations in brain and immune function produced by mindfulness meditation. *Psychosomatic Medicine, 65*, 564–570.

De Ridder, D.T.D., Lensvelt-Mulders, G., Finkenauer, C., Stok, F. M., & Baumeister, R. F. (2012). Taking stock of self-control: A meta-analysis of how trait self-control relates to a wide range of behaviors. *Personality and Social Psychology Review, 16*, 76–99.

Deci, E. L., & Ryan, R. M. (1985). *Intrinsic motivation and self-determination in human behavior.* New York: Plenum.

Deci, E., & Ryan, R. (2000). Self-determination theory and the facilitation of intrinsic motivation, social development, and well-being. *American Psychologist, 55*, 68–78.

Diamond, R. M. (2008). *Designing and assessing courses and curricula: A practical guide* (3rd ed.). San Francisco, CA: Jossey-Bass.

Di Pellegrino, G., Fadiga, L., Fogassi, L., Gallese, V., & Rizzolatti, G. (1992). Understanding motor events: A neurophysiological study. *Experimental Brain Research, 91*, 176–180.

Diener, E., & Rahtz, D. (Eds.). (1999). *Advances in quality of life theory and research* (Vol. 4). Norwell, MA: Kluwer Academic Publishers.

Diener, E., Suh, E. M., Lucas, R. E., & Smith, H. L. (1999). Subjective well-being: Three decades of progress. *Psychological Bulletin, 125*, 276–302.

Doyle, T. (2011). *Learner centered teaching: Putting the research on learning into practice.* Sterling, VA: Stylus Publishing.

DuBrin, A. J. (2001). *Human relations: Interpersonal, job-oriented skills* (7th ed.). Upper Saddle River, NJ: Prentice-Hall.

Duckworth, A. L., Grant, H., Loew, B., Oettingen, G., & Gollwitzer, P. M. (2011). Self-regulation strategies improve self-discipline in adolescents: Benefits of mental contrasting and implementation intentions. *Educational Psychology: An International Journal of Experimental Educational Psychology, 31*, 17–26.

Duckworth, A. L., Peterson, C., Matthews, M. D., & Kelly, D. R. (2007). Grit: Perseverance and passion for long-term goals. *Personality Processes and Individual Differences, 92*, 1087–1101.

Duhigg, C. (2012). *The power of habit: Why we do what we do in life and business*. New York, NY: Random House.

Dux, P., Tombu, M., Harrison, S., Rogers, B., Tong, F., & Marois, R. (2009). Training improves multitasking performance by increasing the speed of information processing in human prefrontal cortex. *Neuron, 63*, 127–138.

Dweck, C. S. (2008). *Mindset: The new psychology of success*. New York, NY: Ballantine Books.

Dweck, C. S. (2012). Mindsets and human nature: Promoting change in the Middle East, the schoolyard, the racial divide, and willpower. *American Psychologist, 67*, 614–622.

Easterbrook, G. (2004). *Progress paradox: How life gets better while people feel worse*. New York, NY: Random House Trade Paperbacks.

Easterlin, R. A., McVey, L. A., Switek, M., Sawangfa, O., & Zweig, J. S. (2010). The happiness–income paradox revisited. *Proceedings of the National Academy of Sciences of the United States of America, 107*, 22463–22468.

Ekman, P. (2007). *Emotions revealed: Recognizing faces and feelings to improve communication and emotional life* (2nd ed.). New York, NY: Holt.

Elbow, P. (1998). *Writing without teachers*. Oxford, United Kingdom: Oxford University Press.

Emmons, R. A., & King, L. A. (1988). Conflict among personal strivings: Immediate and long-term implications for psychological and physical well-being. *Journal of Personality and Social Psychology, 54*, 1040–48.

Epstein, R. A. (2011). Cognitive neuroscience: Scene layout from vision and touch. *Current Biology, 21*, 437–438.

Ericsson, K. A. (Ed.). (2009). *Development of professional expertise: Toward measurement of expert performance and design of optimal learning environments*. New York, NY: Cambridge University Press.

Ericsson, K. A., & Smith, J. (1991). Expert and exceptional performance: Evidence on maximal adaptations on task constraints. *Annual Review of Psychology of Psychology, 47*, 273–305.

Evans, E. L. (2012). Faculty engagement in program-level outcomes assessment: A learning process. *To Improve the Academy, 31*, 37–52.

Fairweather, J. S. (2002). The mythologies of faculty productivity: Implications for institutional policy and decision making. *The Journal of Higher Education, 73*, 26–49.

Fink, D. L. (2013). *Creating significant learning experiences: An integrated approach to designing college courses* (Updated ed.). San Francisco, CA: Jossey-Bass.

Fiske, S. T., & Taylor, S. E. (1984). *Social cognition*. Reading, MA: Addison-Wesley.

Flower, L., & Hayes, J. R. (1980). The cognition of discovery: Defining a rhetorical problem. *College Composition and Communication, 31,* 21–32.

Forni, P. M. (2003). *Choosing civility: The twenty-five rules of considerate conduct.* New York, NY: St. Martin's Griffin.

Foss, S., & Waters, W. (2007). *Destination dissertation: A traveler's guide to a done dissertation.* Lanham, MD: Rowman & Littlefield Publishers.

Frederick, S., & Loewenstein, G. (1999). Hedonic adaptation. In D. Kahneman, E. Diener, & N. Schwarz (Eds.), *Scientific perspectives on enjoyment, suffering, and well-being* (pp. 302–329). New York: NY: Russell Sage Foundations.

Fredrickson, B. L. (2001). The role of positive emotions in positive psychology: The broaden-and-build theory of positive emotions. *American Psychologist, 56,* 218–226.

Fredrickson, B. L. (2009). *Positivity: Top-notch research reveals the 3 to 1 ratio that will change your life.* New York, NY: Three Rivers Press.

Fredrickson, B. L., & Losada, M. (2005). Positive affect and the complex dynamics of human flourishing. *American Psychologist, 60,* 678–686.

Fritz, R. (1989). *The path of least resistance: Learning to become the creative force in your own life.* New York, NY: Ballantine Books.

Gallup Foundation (2009). *Strengths Finder.* New York, NY: Gallup Press.

Gappa, J. M., Austin, A. E., & Trice, A. G. (2007). *Rethinking faculty work.* San Francisco, CA: Jossey-Bass.

Garfield, C., & Bennett, H. (1984). *Peak performance: Mental training techniques of the world's greatest athletes.* New York, NY: Warner Bros.

Gesell, I. (1997). *Playing along: 37 group learning activities borrowed from improvisational theater.* Duluth, MN: Whole Person Associates.

Gmelch, W. H., & Burns, J. S. (1993). The cost of academic leadership: Department chair stress. *Innovative Higher Education. 17,* 259–270.

Gmelch, W. H., Lovrich, N. P., & Wilke, P. K. (1984). Stress in academe: A national perspective. *Research in Higher Education, 20,* 477–490.

Goldsmith, M. (2009). *Mojo: How to get it, how to keep it, how to get it back if you lose it.* New York, NY: Hyperion.

Goleman, D. (2005). *Emotional intelligence: Why it can matter more than IQ* (10th ed.). New York, NY: Bantam.

Goleman, D. (2006). *Social intelligence: The new science of human relationships.* New York, NY: Bantam Books.

Gollwitzer, P. M., & Brandstätter, V. (1997). Implementation intentions and effective goal pursuit. *Journal of Personality and Social Psychology, 73,* 186–199.

Gollwitzer, P. M., Fujita, K., & Oettingen, G. (2004). Planning and the implementation of goals. In R. F. Baumeister & K. D. Vohs (Eds.), *Handbook of self-regulation: Research, theory, and applications* (pp. 211–228). New York, NY: Guilford Press.

Gollwitzer, P. M., & Oettingen, G. (2011). Planning promotes goal striving. In K. D. Vohs & R. F. Baumeister (Eds.), *Handbook of self-regulation*: *Research, theory, and applications* (2nd ed.). New York, NY: Guilford.

Gortner, E. M., Rude, S. S., & Pennebaker, J. W. (2006). Benefits of expressive writing in lowering rumination and depressive symptoms. *Behavior Therapy, 37,* 292–303.

Gottman, J. M. (1994). *What predicts divorce: The relationship between marital processes and marital outcomes.* New York, NY: Lawrence Erlbaum.

Gottman, J. M. (1999). *The marriage clinic: A scientifically based marital therapy.* New York, NY: W.W. Norton.

Graff, G., & Birkenstein, C. (2010). *They say, I say: The moves that matter in academic writing.* New York, NY: W. W. Norton.

Granovetter, M. S. (1973). The strength of weak ties. *American Journal of Sociology, 78,* 1360–1380.

Granovetter, M. S. (1973). The strength of weak ties. *American Journal of Sociology, 78,* 1360–1380.

Grant, A. M. (2013). *Give and take: A revolutionary approach to success.* New York, NY: Viking.

Gray, T. (2010). *Publish and flourish.* Las Cruces: New Mexico State University Teaching Academy.

Gross Davis, B. (2009). *Tools for teaching* (2nd ed.). San Francisco, CA: Jossey-Bass.

Gruber, J., Mauss, I. B., & Tamir, M. (2011) A dark side of happiness? How, when, and why happiness is not always good. *Perspectives on Psychological Science, 6,* 222–233.

Grunert O'Brien, J., Millis, B. J., & Cohen, M. W. (2008). *The course syllabus: A learning-centered approach* (2nd ed.). San Francisco, CA: Jossey-Bass.

Haidt, J. (2012). *The righteous mind: Why good people are divided by politics and religion.* New York, NY: Pantheon Books.

Hake, R. R. (1998). Interactive-engagement versus traditional methods: A six-thousand-student survey of mechanics test data for introductory physics courses. *American Journal of Physics, 66,* 64–74.

Hallowell, E. M., & Ratey, J. J. (2011). *Driven to distraction: Recognizing and coping with attention deficit disorder* (rev. ed.). New York, NY: Anchor Books.

Halvorson, H. G. (2011). *Succeed: How we can reach our goals.* New York, NY: Hudson Street Press.

Hamilton, D. R. (2011). *The contagious power of thinking.* London, England: Hay House.

Hanh, T. N. (2007). *Living Buddha, living Christ* (10th ed.) New York, NY: Penguin Group.

Hanson, R., & Mendius, R. (2009). *Buddha's brain: The practical neuroscience of happiness, love, and wisdom*. Oakland, CA: Harbinger.

Harden, G. (1968). The tragedy of the commons. *Science, 162*, 1243–1248.

Harter, J. K., Schmidt, F. L., & Keyes, C.L.M. (2002). Well-being in the workplace and its relationships to business outcomes: A review of the Gallup studies. In C. L. Keyes & J. Haidt (Eds.), *Flourishing: The positive person and the good life* (pp. 205–224). Washington, DC: American Psychological Association.

Hatfield, E., Cacioppo, J. T., & Rapson, R. L. (1994). *Emotional contagion*. Cambridge, United Kingdom: Cambridge University Press.

Hawking, S., & Mlodinow, L. (2010). *The grand design*. New York, NY: Bantam Books.

Hays, K. F., & Brown, C. H. (2004). *You're on: Consulting for peak performance*. Washington, DC: American Psychological Association.

Herzberg, F. I. (1987). One more time: How do you motivate employees? *Harvard Business Review, 65*, 109–120.

Herzberg, F. I., Mausner, B., & Snyderman, B. B. (1959). *The motivation to work*. New York, NY: John Wiley.

Herzberg, F. I., Mausner, B., & Snyderman, B. B. (1993). *The motivation to work*. Piscataway, NJ: Transaction Publishers.

Hestenes, D., Wells, M., & Swackhammer, G. (1992). Force concept inventory. *The Physics Teacher, 30*, 141–151.

Higgerson, M. L. (1996). *Communication skills for department chairs*. Bolton, MA: Anker.

Hutchings, P., Huber, M. T., & Ciccone, A. (2011). *The scholarship of teaching and learning reconsidered: Institutional integration and impact*. San Francisco, CA: Jossey-Bass.

Hyman, M. (2012). *The blood sugar solution: The ultrahealthy program for losing weight, preventing disease, and feeling great now!* New York, NY: Little, Brown and Company.

Imai, M. (1986). *Kaizen: The key to Japan's competitive success*. New York: Random House.

Iyengar, S. (2010). *The art of choosing*. New York, NY: Twelve.

Jett, Q. R., & George, J. M. (2003). Work interrupted: A closer look at the role of interruptions in organizational life. *Academy of Management Review, 28*, 494–507.

Jones, L. B. (1998). *The path: Creating your mission statement for work and for life*. New York, NY: Hyperion.

Kabat-Zinn, J. (2005). *Full catastrophe living: Using the wisdom of your body and mind to face stress, pain, and illness*. New York, NY: Bantam Dell.

Kabat-Zinn, J. (2011). *Mindfulness for beginners: Reclaiming the present moment—and your life*. Boulder, CO: Sounds True.

Kahneman, D., Krueger, A. B., Schkade, D. A., Schwartz, N., & Stone, A. A. (2004). A survey method for characterizing daily life experience: The day reconstruction method. *Science, 306,* 1776–1780.

Kahneman, D., & Tversky, A. (1979). Intuitive prediction: Biases and corrective procedures. *TIMS Studies in Management Science, 12,* 313–327.

Kanter, R. M. (1984). *The change masters*. New York, NY: Simon and Schuster.

Kenrick, D. T., Griskevicius, V., Neuberg, S. L., & Schaller, M. (2010). Renovating the pyramid of needs: Contemporary extensions built upon ancient foundations. *Perspectives on Psychological Science, 5,* 292–314.

Kezar, A., Carducci, R., & Contreras-McGavin, M. (2006). *Rethinking the "L" word in higher education: The revolution on research in leadership*. San Francisco, CA: Jossey-Bass.

Kezar, A., Gallant, T. B., & Lester, J. (2011). Everyday people making a difference on college campuses: The tempered grassroots leadership tactics of faculty and staff. *Studies in Higher Education, 36,* 129–151.

Kezar, A., & Lester, J. (2011). *Enhancing capacity for leadership: An examination of grassroots leaders in higher education*. Palo Alto, CA: Stanford University Press.

Kiecolt-Glaser J. K., & Newton, T. L. (2001). Marriage and health: His and hers. *Psychological Bulletin, 127,* 472–503.

Kirschenbaum, D. S., Humphrey, L. L., & Malett, S. D. (1981). Specificity of planning in adult self-control: An applied investigation. *Journal of Personality and Social Psychology. 40,* 941–950.

Klauser, H. A. (2001). *Write it down, make it happen: Knowing what you want and getting it*. New York, NY: Fireside.

Koo, M., & Fishbach, A. (2008). Dynamics of self-regulation: How (un)accomplished goal actions affect motivation. *Journal of Personality and Social Psychology, 94,* 183–195.

Kouzes, J. M., & Posner, B. Z. (2003). *The academic administrator's guide to exemplary leadership*. San Francisco, CA: Jossey-Bass.

Kouzes, J. M., & Posner, B. Z. (2012). *The leadership challenge: How to make extraordinary things happen in organizations* (5th ed.). San Francisco, CA: Jossey-Bass.

Lakein, A. (1973). *How to get control of your time and your life*. New York, NY: David McKay.

Lamott, A. (1995). *Bird by bird: Some instructions on writing and life*. New York, NY: Anchor.

Lardon, M., & Leadbetter, D. (2008). *Finding your zone: Ten core lessons for achieving peak performance in sports and life*. New York, NY: Perigee Trade.

Latham, G. P., Locke, E. A., & Fassina, N. E. (2002). The high performance cycle: Standing the test of time. In S. Sonnetag (Ed.) *Psychological management of individual performance A handbook in the psychology of management in organizations* (pp. 201–228). Chichester, England: Wiley.

Latham, G. P., & Locke, E. A. (2007). New developments in and directions for goal-setting research. *European Psychologist, 12,* 290–300.

Lauderdale D. S., Knutson, K. L., Yan, L. L., Liu, K., & Rathouz, P. J. (2008). Self-reported and measured sleep duration: How similar are they? *Epidemiology, 19,* 838–845.

Ledford, G. E., Jr. (1999). Happiness and productivity revisited. *Journal of Organizational Behavior, 20,* 25–30.

Lee, S. V., Bach, D. J., & Muthiah, R. N. (2012). An exploration of the spiritual roots of the midcareer faculty experience. *To Improve the Academy: Resources for Faculty, Instructional, and Organizational Development, 20,* 69–83.

Leider, R. J. (1997). *The power of purpose: Creating meaning in your life and work.* San Francisco, CA: Berrett-Koehler.

Leonard, G. (1992). *Mastery: The keys to success and long-term fulfillment.* New York, NY: Plume.

Levinson, R. W., & Gottman, J. M. (1983). Marital interaction: Physiological linkage and affective exchange. *Journal of Personality and Social Psychology, 45,* 587–597.

Linley, A. (2008). *Average to A+: Realising strengths in yourself and others.* Coventry, United Kingdom: CAPP Press.

Linley, A., Willars, J., & Biswas-Diener, R. (2010). *The strengths book: Be confident, be successful, and enjoy better relationships by realising the best of you.* Coventry, United Kingdom: CAPP Press.

Locke, E. A., & Latham, G. P. (1990). *A theory of goal setting and task performance.* Englewood Cliffs, NJ: Prentice Hall.

Locke, E. A., & Latham, G. P. (2002). Building a practically useful theory of goal setting and task motivation: A 35-year odyssey. *American Psychologist, 57,* 705-717.

Locke, E. A., & Latham, G. P. (2006). New directions in goal-setting theory. *Current Directions in Psychological Science, 15,* 265–268.

Loehr, J. E. (1991). *Mental toughness training for sports: Achieving athletic excellence.* New York, NY: Plume.

Loehr, J. E. (1997). *Stress for success: Jim Loehr's program for transforming stress into energy at work.* New York, NY: Three Rivers Press.

Loehr, J. E., & Evert, C. (1995). *The new toughness training for sports: Mental emotional physical conditioning from one of the world's premier sports psychologists.* New York, NY: Plume.

Loehr, J., & Schwartz, T. (2004). *The power of full engagement: Managing energy, not time, is the key to high performance and personal renewal.* New York, NY: Free Press.

Lutz, A., Brefczynski-Lewis, J., Johnstone, T., Davidson, R. J. (2008). Regulation of the neural circuitry of emotion by compassion meditation: Effects of meditative expertise. *PLOS ONE, 3,* 1–10.

Lyubomirsky, S. (2008). *The how of happiness: A new approach to getting the life you want.* New York, NY: The Penguin Press.

Lyubomirsky, S. (2011). Hedonic adaptation to positive and negative experiences. In S. Folkman (Ed.), *Oxford handbook of stress, health, and coping* (pp. 200–224). New York: Oxford University Press.

Lyubomirsky, S., & Boehm, J. K. (2010). Human motives, happiness, and the puzzle of parenthood. *Perspectives on Psychological Science, 5,* 327–334.

Lyubomirsky, S., King, L. A., & Diener, E. (2005). The benefits of frequent positive affect. *Psychological Bulletin, 131,* 803–855.

Lyubomirsky, S., Sheldon, K. M., & Schkade, D. (2005). Pursuing happiness: The architecture of sustainable change. *Review of General Psychology, 9,* 111–131.

Lyubomirsky, S., & Tkach, C. (2003). The consequences of dysphoric rumination. In C. Papageorgiou & A. Wells (Eds.), *Rumination: Nature, theory, and treatment of negative thinking in depression* (pp. 21–41). Chichester, United Kingdom: John Wiley & Sons.

Macfarlane, B. (2011). Professors as intellectual leaders: Formation, identity and role. *Studies in Higher Education, 36,* 57–73.

Mah, C. D., Mah, K. E., Kezirian, E. J., & Dement, W. C. (2012). The effects of sleep extension on athletic performance of collegiate basketball players. *Sleep, 34,* 943–950.

Manning, T. T. (2013). Leader as positive influence: A self-reflection exercise. Used with permission from T. T. Manning.

Marks, S. R., & MacDermid, S. M. (1996). Multiple roles and the self: A theory of role balance. *Journal of Marriage and the Family, 58,* 417–432.

Maurer, R. (2013). The spirit of Kaizen: Creating lasting excellence one small step at a time. New York, NY: McGraw-Hill.

Martin, A. (2006). *Everyday leadership.* Colorado Springs, CO: Center for Creative Leadership.

Maslow, A. H. (1954). *Motivation and personality.* New York, NY: Harper & Row.

McCaul, K. D., Hinsz, V. B., & McCaul, H. S. (1987). The effects of commitment to performance goals on effort. *Journal of Applied Social Psychology, 17,* 437–452.

McClelland, D. C. (1988). *Human motivation.* Cambridge, United Kingdom: Cambridge University Press.

McGlynn, A. P. (2001). *Successful beginnings for college teaching.* Madison, WI: Atwood Publishing.

McGonigal, J. (2011). *Reality is broken: Why games make us better and how they can change the world.* New York, NY: Penguin Press.

McKeachie, W., & Svinicki, M. (2013). *McKeachie's teaching tips: Strategies, research, and theory for college and university teachers.* Belmont, CA: Wadsworth Publishing.

McKnight, K. S., & Scruggs, M. (2008). *The second city guide to improv in the classroom.* San Francisco, CA: Jossey-Bass.

Medina, J. (2008). *Brain rules. Twelve principles for surviving and thriving at work, home, and school.* Seattle, WA: Pear Press.

Mednick, S. C., Nakayama, K., Cantero, J. L., Atienza, M., Levin, A. A., Pathak, N., & Stickgold, R. (2002). The restorative benefit of naps on perceptual deterioration. *Nature Neuroscience, 5,* 677–681.

Middaugh, M. F. (2011). *Understanding faculty productivity: Standards and benchmarks for colleges and universities.* San Francisco, CA: Jossey-Bass.

Miller, G. A. (1956). The magical number seven, plus or minus two: Some limits on our capacity for processing information. *Psychological Review, 63,* 81–97.

Miller, G. A. (2003). The cognitive revolution: a historical perspective. *Trends in Cognitive Sciences, 7,* 141–144.

Muraven, M., & Baumeister, R. F. (2000). Self-regulation and depletion of limited resources: Does self-control resemble a muscle? *Psychological Bulletin, 126,* 247–259.

Murray, S. L., Holmes, J. G., & Griffin, D. W. (1996). The benefits of positive illusions: Idealization and the construction of satisfaction in close relationships. *Journal of Personality and Social Psychology, 70,* 79–98.

Neff, L. A., & Karney, B. R. (2005). To know you is to love you: The implications of global adoration and specific accuracy for marital relationships. *Journal of Personality and Social Psychology, 88,* 480–497.

Nilson, L. B. (2010). *Teaching at its best: A research-based resource for college instructors* (3rd ed.). San Francisco, CA: Jossey-Bass.

Nolen-Hoeksema, S., Wisco, B. E., & Lyubomirsky, S. (2008). Rethinking rumination. *Perspectives on Psychological Science, 3,* 400–424.

Nöteberg, S. (2009). *Pomodoro technique illustrated: The easy way to do more in less time.* Raleigh, NC: Pragmatic Programmers.

Oaten, M., & Cheng, K. (2006). Longitudinal gains in self regulation from regular physical exercise. *British Journal of Health Psychology 11,* 717–733.

Oishi, S., Diener, E., & Lucas, R. E. (2007). The optimum level of well-being: Can people be too happy? *Perspectives on Psychological Science, 2*, 346–360.

Oz, M. C., & Roizen, M. F. (2008). *You: The owner's manual—An insider's guide to the body that will make you healthier and younger* (updated and expanded ed.). New York, NY: HarperCollins.

Palmer, P. (2000). *Let your life speak: Listening for the voice of vocation.* San Francisco, CA: Jossey-Bass.

Palmer, P., & Zajonc, A. (2011). *The heart of higher education: A call to renewal: Transforming the academy through collegial conversations.* San Francisco, CA: Jossey-Bass.

Pannapacker, W. (2012, October 19). It's your duty to be miserable! *The Chronicle of Higher Education, 59*(8), A32.

Park, N., & Peterson, C. (2009). Character strengths: Research and practice. *Journal of College and Character, 10*(4).

Parks, K. M., & Steelman, L. A. (2008), Organizational wellness programs: A meta-analysis. *Journal of Occupational Health Psychology, 13*, 58–68.

Peterson, C., & Park, N. (2006). Character strengths in organizations. *Journal of Organizational Behavior, 27*, 1149–1154.

Peterson, C., & Seligman, M. (2004). *Character strengths and virtues: A handbook and classification.* New York, NY: Oxford University Press.

Philipsen, M. I., & Bostic, T. B. (2010). *Helping faculty find work-life balance: The path toward family-friendly institutions.* San Francisco, CA: Jossey-Bass.

Pillemer, K. (2011). *Lessons for living: Tried and true advice from the wisest Americans.* New York, NY: Hudson Street Press.

Pink, D. H. (2002). *Free agent nation: The future of working for yourself.* New York, NY: Warner Business Books.

Pollan, M., & Kaiman, M. (2011). *Food rules: An eater's manual.* New York, NY: Penguin.

Prather, A, A., Puterman, E., Lin, J., O'Donovan, A., Krauss, J., Tomiyama, A. J., Epel, E. S., & Blackburn, E. H. (2011). Shorter leukocyte telomere length in midlife women with poor sleep quality. *Journal of Aging Research, 2011*. Retrieved from http://www.hindawi.com/journals/jar/2011/721390/.

Prior, V., & Glaser, D. (2006). *Understanding attachment and attachment disorders: Theory, evidence and practice child and adolescent mental health series.* London, United Kingdom: Jessica Kingsley Publishers.

Raelin, J. A. (2003). *Creating leaderful organizations: How to bring out leadership in everyone.* San Francisco, CA: Berrett-Koehler.

Raffone. A., & Srinivasan, N. (2010). The exploration of meditation is the neuroscience of attention and consciousness. *Cognitive Processing, 11*, 1–7.

Rath, T. (2007). *Strengths Finder 2.0*. New York, NY: Gallup Press.

Richlin, L. (2006). *Blueprint for learning*. Sterling, VA: Stylus Publishing.

Robertson, D. R. (2003). *Making time, making change: Avoiding overload in college teaching*. Stillwater, OK: New Forums Press.

Robertson, J. C. (1997). *Peak-performance living: Easy, drug-free ways to alter your own brain chemistry and achieve optimal health*. San Francisco, CA: Harper.

Robertson, I., & Cooper, C. (2011). *Well-being: Productivity and happiness at work*. New York, NY: Palgrave Macmillan.

Robinson, E. (2005, February). Why crunch time doesn't work: Six lessons [Article]. Retrieved from http://www.igda.org/why-crunch-modes-doesnt-work-six-lessons.

Robinson, J. P., & Godbey, G. (1997). *Time for life: The surprising ways Americans use their time*. University Park, PA: Pennsylvania State University Press.

Robison, S. M. (1983, August). *CRAFTing the psychology assignment: Techniques to improve students' writing*. Paper presented at the annual convention of the American Psychological Association, Anaheim, CA.

Robison, S. (2007, November). *Living purposely in a distracting world: A blueprint for work-life balance for busy professionals*. Workshop presented as the annual conference of Lilly National, Miami University of Ohio, Oxford, OH.

Robison, S. (2010). Time, stress, and burnout: What to do if you feel overwhelmed. In B. E. Walvoord & V. J. Anderson, *Effective grading* (pp. 90–97). San Francisco, CA: Jossey-Bass.

Robison, S. M., & Walvoord, B. (1990). Using social science to help yourself and others: Robison's human sexuality class. In B. E. Walvoord & L. P. McCarthy, *Thinking and writing in college* (pp. 144–176). Urbana, IL: National Council of Teachers of English.

Rocco, T. S., & Hatcher, T. (2011). *The handbook of scholarly writing and publishing*. San Francisco, CA: Jossey-Bass.

Rock, D. (2009). *Your brain at work: Strategies for overcoming distraction, regaining focus, and working smarter all day long*. New York, NY: HarperCollins.

Rogers, S. J., & Waite, L. K. (1998). Satisfaction with parenting: The role of marital happiness, family structure, and parents' gender. *Journal of Marriage and Family, 60*(2), 293-308

Rubin, G. (2009). *The happiness project: Or why I spent a year trying to sing in the morning, clean my closets, fight right, read Aristotle, and generally have more fun*. New York, NY: HarperCollins.

Ryan, R. M., & Deci, E. L. (2000). Self-determination theory and the facilitation of intrinsic motivation, social development, and well-being. *American Psychologist, 55*, 68–78.

Schaper, D. (2007). *Living well while doing good*. New York, NY: Seabury Books.

Schwartz, B. (2004). *Paradox of choice: Why less is more*. New York, NY: HarperCollins.

Schwartz, T. (2010). *The way we're working isn't working: The four forgotten needs that energize great performance*. New York, NY: Simon and Schuster.

Schwebel, D. (2009). Impaired faculty: Helping academics who are suffering from serious mental illness. *Academic Leadership: The Online Journal, 7*(2).

Seligman, M.E.P. (2002). *Authentic happiness*. New York, NY: Free Press.

Seligman, M.E.P. (2006). *Learned optimism: How to change your mind and your life*. New York, NY: Pocket Books.

Seligman, M.E.P. (2011). *Flourish: A visionary new understanding of happiness and well-being*. New York, NY: Free Press.

Shaver, P., & Hazan, C. (1987). Romantic love conceptualized as an attachment process. *Journal of Personality and Social Psychology, 52*, 511–524.

Sheldon, K. M., Cummins, R. K., & Kamble, S. (2010). Life balance and well-being: Testing a novel conceptual and measurement approach. *Journal of Personality, 78*, 1093–1134.

Sheldon, K. M., & Lyubomirsky, S. (2007). Is it possible to become happier? (And if so, how?). *Social and Personality Psychology Compass, 1*, 1–17.

Sheldon, K. M., & Lyubomirsky, S. (2012). The challenge of staying happier: Testing the hedonic adaptation prevention model. *Personality and Social Psychology Bulletin, 38*, 670–680.

Sher, B. (with Gottleib, A.) (2003). *Wishcraft: How to get what you really want*. New York, NY: Ballantine Books.

Siegel, D. J. (2007). *The mindful brain: Reflection and attunement in the cultivation of well-being*. New York, NY: Norton.

Siegel, D. J. (2010). Mindsight: The new science of personal transformation. New York, NY: Random House.

Siegel, D. J., & Bryson, T. P. (2012). *The whole-brain child: 12 revolutionary strategies to nurture your child's developing mind, survive everyday parenting struggles, and help your family thrive*. New York, NY: Bantam Books.

Silvia, P. (2007). *How to write a lot*. Washington, DC: American Psychological Association.

Sinek, S. (2009). *Start with why: How great leaders inspire everyone to take action*. New York, NY: Portfolio.

Sorenson, G., & Hackman, R. G. (2002). Invisible leadership: Acting on behalf of a common purpose. In C. Cherry & L. R. Matusak (Eds.), *Building leadership bridges 2002* (pp. 7–24). College Park, MD: International Leadership Association.

Spreitzer, G. M., Kizilos, M. A., & Nason, S. W. (1997). A dimensional analysis of the relationship between psychological empowerment and effectiveness, satisfaction, and strain. *Journal of Management, 23,* 679–704.

Stanier, M. B. (2010). *Do more great work: Stop the busywork. Start the work that matters.* New York, NY: Workman.

Steel, P. (2007). The nature of procrastination: A meta-analytic and theoretical review of quintessential self-regulatory failure. *Psychological Bulletin, 133,* 67.

Stevens, D. D., & Levi, A. J. (2004). *Introduction to rubrics: An assessment tool to save grading time, convey effective feedback and promote student learning.* Sterling, VA: Stylus Publishing.

Stevenson, B., & Wolfers, J. (2013) Subjective well-being and income: Is there any evidence of satiation? *American Economic Review,* Papers and Proceedings, May.

Suskie, L. (2009). *Assessing student learning: A common sense guide* (2nd ed.). San Francisco, CA: Jossey-Bass.

Tay, L., & Diener, E. (2011). Needs and subjective well-being around the world. *Journal of Personality and Social Psychology, 10,* 354–365.

Taylor, S. E. (2002). *The tending instinct: How nurturing is essential to who we are and how we live.* New York: Holt.

Taylor, S. E. (2008). Fostering a supportive environment at work. *The Psychologist-Manager Journal, 11,* 265–283.

Taylor, S. E., Klein, L. C., Lewis, B. P., Gruenewald, T. L., Gurung, R.A.R., & Updegraff, J. A. (2000). Biobehavioral responses to stress in females: Tend-and-befriend, not fight-or-flight. *Psychological Review, 107,* 411–429.

Tieger, P. D., & Barron-Tieger, B. (1992). *Do what you are—discover the perfect career for you through the secrets of personality type.* Boston, MA: Little, Brown and Company.

Tieger, P. D., & Barron-Tieger, B. (1993, Winter). Personality typing: A first step to a satisfying career. *Journal of Career Planning and Placement, 53,* 50–56.

Travers, J., & Milgram, S. (1969). *An experimental study of the small world problem.* Sociometry, 32, 425–443.

Troupe, Y., & Liberman, N. (2003). Temporal construal. *Psychological Review, 110,* 403–421.

Tuckman, B. (1965). Developmental sequence in small groups. *Psychological Bulletin, 63,* 384–399.

Twale, J. D., & De Luca, B. M. (2008). *Faculty incivility: The rise of the academic bully culture and what to do about it.* San Francisco, CA: Jossey-Bass.

UC Irvine, Center for Occupational & Environmental Health (2005, March 9–11). Fourth Conference on Work Environment and Cardio Disease, Newport Beach, CA. Available at www.coeh.uci.edu/ICOH/.

Vallacher, R., & Wegner, D. (1989). Levels of personal agency: Individual variation in action identification. *Journal of Personality and Social Psychology, 57,* 660–671.

Vroom, V. H., & Jago, A. G. (1988). *The new leadership: Managing participation in organizations.* Englewood Cliffs, NJ: Prentice-Hall.

Vroom, V. H., & Yetton, P. W. (1973). *Leadership and decision making.* Pittsburgh, PA: University of Pittsburgh Press.

Waite, L., & Gallagher, M. (2001). *The case for marriage.* New York, NY: Doubleday.

Walvoord, B. E. (2008). *Teaching and learning in college introductory religion courses.* New York, NY: Wiley-Blackwell.

Walvoord. B. E. (2010). *Assessment clear and simple: A practical guide for institutions, departments, and general education* (2nd ed.). San Francisco, CA: Jossey-Bass.

Walvoord, B., & Anderson, V. (2010). *Effective grading: A tool for learning and assessment in college* (2nd ed.). San Francisco, CA: Jossey-Bass.

Warren, R. (2012). *The purpose driven life: What on earth am I here for?* Grand Rapids, MI: Zondervan.

Watson, E. E., Terry, K. P., & Doolittle, P. E. (2012). Please read while texting and driving. *To Improve the Academy, 31,* 295–309.

Weimer, M. (2002). *Learner-centered teaching: Five key changes to practice.* San Francisco, CA: Jossey-Bass.

Weimer, M. (2010). *Inspired college teaching: A career-long resource for professional growth.* Hoboken, NJ: John Wiley & Sons.

Weimer, W. (2006). *Enhancing scholarly work on teaching and learning: Professional literature that makes a difference.* San Francisco, CA: Jossey-Bass.

Wergin, J. F. (2006). *Leadership in place: How academic professionals can find their leadership voice.* Bolton, MA: Ancher.

Wheatley, M. J. (1994). *Leadership and the new science: Learning about organization from an orderly universe.* San Francisco, CA: Berrett-Koehler.

Wheatley, M. J. (2009). *Turning to one another: Simple conversations to restore hope to the future.* San Francisco, CA: Berrett-Koehler.

Wheeler, D. W. (2012). *Servant leadership for higher education: Principles and practices.* San Francisco, CA: Jossey-Bass.

Wheeler, D. W., Seagren, A. T., Becker, L. W., Kinley, E. R., Mlinek, D. D., Robson, K. J. (2008). *The academic chair's handbook* (2nd ed.). San Francisco, CA: Jossey-Bass.

Whyte, J. (2012). *AARP new American diet: Lose weight, live longer.* Hoboken, NJ: John Wiley & Sons.

Wood, A. M., Linley, P. A., Maltby, J., Kashdan, T. B., & Hurling, R. (2011). Using personal and psychological strengths leads to increases in well-being over time. A longitudinal study and the development of the strengths use questionnaire. *Personality and Individual Differences, 50,* 15–19.

Wright, T. A., & Cropanzano, R. (2000). Psychological well-being and job satisfaction as predictors of job performance. *Journal of Occupational Health Psychology, 5,* 84–94.

Wright, T. A., & Cropanzano, R. (2004). The role of psychological well-being in job performance: A fresh look at an age-old quest. *Organizational Dynamics, 33,* 338–351.

Young, J. A., & Pain, M. D. (1999). The zone: Evidence of a universal phenomenon for athletes across sports. *Athletic Insight: The Online Journal of Sports Psychology, 1,* 21–30. Retrieved from http://www.athleticinsight.com/Vol1Iss3/Empirical_Zone.htm.

Zapf, D. (2002). Emotion work and psychological well-being: A review of the literature and some conceptual considerations. *Human Resource Management Review, 12,* 237–268.

Zauberman, G., & Lynch, J. G. (2005). Resource slack and propensity to discount delayed investments of time versus money. *Journal of Experimental Psychology: General, 134,* 23–37.

Zerubavel, E. (1999). *The clockwork muse: A practical guide to writing theses, dissertations, and books.* Cambridge, MA: Harvard University Press.

Zimbardo, P. G. (1990). *Shyness: What is it, what to do about it.* New York, NY: Perseus Books.

Zimbardo, P., & Boyd, J. (2009). *The time paradox: The new psychology of time that will change your life.* New York, NY: Free Press.

Zull, J. E. (2002). *The art of changing the brain: Enriching the practice of teaching by exploring the biology of learning.* Sterling, VA: Stylus Publishing.

Zunin, L., & Zunin, N. (1994). *Contact: The first four minutes.* New York, NY: Ballantine Books.

Appendix

Comparing Generation I and Generation II Systems

	Gen I—Time Management	Gen II—Life Management
Assumptions	1. You can get everything done by using the right time management techniques. 2. You can manage time. 3. Time is what is measured by clocks and calendars.	1. No one can get it all done because creative people can think up more "it" than they will have time for in a lifetime. You need to get the right things done. 2. You can't manage time, because time is a construct that helps us make sense of our physical world of seasons and the movement of celestial bodies (Hawking & Mlodinow, 2010). All that you can manage are tasks. 3. Time is a perception measured by how you feel about what you have done, are doing, and will do in your life.
Basis	Techniques will help you to manage time better and become more efficient in completing more tasks quickly.	A sense of meaning and purpose will help you define what tasks are to be done to be productive and happy and contribute to your world.
Methodology	Hundreds of seemingly helpful techniques that don't seem to help because they presume you already know your priorities.	A life management system that does help because it offers you a decision-making system for setting your priorities. Then, the techniques from Gen I systems will be helpful.
Audiences	Middle-management business-people who work at desks and attend meetings.	Intellectual professionals such as physicians, lawyers, scientists, and professors who divide their work days across multiple environments such as clinics, courtrooms, labs, libraries, and classrooms as well as offices.
Relationship of time management and happiness	An empty task list at the end of a day is a measure of happiness.	Your relationship to time is highly predictive of your happiness. You need to feel at peace about the past, excited about the future, yet anchored in the present (Zimbardo & Boyd, 2009).
Perspective	*Chronos* or clock time—the time of doing.	*Kairos* or expansive time—the time of being that forms the center of doing.

Index